THE PASSIONS OF THE POET

Edited by Forward Press Editors

First published in Great Britain in 2010 by:
Forward Press
Remus House
Coltsfoot Drive
Peterborough
PE2 9JX
Telephone: 01733 890099
Website: www.forwardpress.co.uk

All Rights Reserved
Book Design by Spencer Hart & Tim Christian
© Copyright Contributors 2010
SB ISBN 978-1-84418-535-1

FOREWORD

In 2009, Poetry Rivals was launched. It was one of the biggest and most prestigious competitions ever held by Forward Press. Due to the popularity and success of this talent contest like no other, we have taken Poetry Rivals into 2010, where it has proven to be even bigger and better than last year.

Poets of all ages and from all corners of the globe were invited to write a poem that showed true creative talent - a poem that would stand out from the rest.

We are proud to present the resulting anthology, an inspiring collection of verse carefully selected by our team of editors. Reflecting the vibrancy of the modern poetic world, it is brimming with imagination and diversity.

As well as encouraging creative expression, Poetry Rivals has also given writers a vital opportunity to showcase their work to the public, thus providing it with the wider audience it so richly deserves.

Ted Medler ... 1	Royston E Herbert ... 53
Steven Jackson ... 2	Gladys Burgess ... 54
Martin Norman ... 11	Shirley Atkinson ... 56
David Gasking ... 12	Kenneth Jackson ... 57
Sally Elizabeth Taylor ... 15	Rob Barratt ... 58
Lucy Green ... 16	Anne Furley ... 59
Lynn Martindale ... 17	Rachel Connor ... 60
Sharon Lambley ... 18	Beryl Mapperley ... 61
Philip Mee ... 20	Lynn Noone ... 62
Rachel Keers ... 21	Melissa Brabanski ... 63
Rob Wheeldon ... 22	Mark Tough ... 64
Nsikak Ukpong ... 24	Coralee Harrison ... 65
Jessie Shields ... 25	Ron Constant ... 66
Adele Simone Pierce ... 25	Claire Rogers ... 67
Patricia Stone ... 26	Catrin Thomas ... 68
Theresa Hartley-Mace ... 28	Katey Russell ... 70
Maria Sheikh ... 29	Carol Paxton ... 71
Valerie Hall ... 29	Herdis Churchill ... 72
Margaret Day ... 30	Olive Willingale ... 73
Sullivan The Poet ... 32	David Anderson ... 74
Lavinia Bousfield ... 34	Jacqueline McLaughlin ... 75
Tyrone Dalby ... 36	Emma Thacker ... 76
Pauline Anderson ... 38	Anna Greaves ... 77
John Beals ... 39	Dean Cooper Elston ... 78
Trayce Hamilton ... 39	Nichola Keel ... 79
T G Bloodworth ... 39	H J Clark ... 80
Carrieann Hammond ... 40	Stephen Timothy ... 81
Sophie Mason ... 42	Tony Douglass ... 82
Sylvia Olliver ... 44	Sandy Phillips ... 83
Peter J Morey ... 46	Kriss Simone ... 84
G F Pash ... 46	Robert Keith Bowhill ... 85
Alvin Culzac ... 46	Barbara Lambie ... 86
Edna Sparkes ... 47	Susie Field ... 88
Eddie Byrne ... 48	Farah Ali ... 89
Elizabeth M Procter ... 50	Graham Peter Metson ... 90
Leah Vernon ... 52	Sarah Penrice ... 91
David Adamson ... 52	Alexandra Martin ... 92
Arthur May ... 53	John Hickman ... 93

Name	Page
Eric Savage	94
Grant Meaby	95
W H Stevens	96
Elaine Harris	97
Sarah Sidibeh	98
Fergus McAteer	99
Lisa Livingstone	100
Fran Hunnisett	101
Peter Ridgway	102
Barry Dillon	103
Stephen Guy Craggs	104
Doris E Pullen	105
Frank Sutton	106
Lisa Pease	107
Margaret Hickman	108
Robert Collins	109
Joan Fowler	110
Don Woods	111
John D'Arcy	112
Peggy Howe	113
Morag Grierson	114
Doris Townsend	115
George Edward Bage	116
Martin Selwood	117
Ann Voaden	118
Joan May Wills	119
Mark Anthony Love	120
Kathleen McBurney	121
Paramita Chakraborty	122
Julie Preston	123
Louis Cecile	124
Penelope Kirby	125
Wendie Hayes	126
Lisa Mills	127
Edwin David Bowen	128
Sonia Richards	129
Bryn Strudwick	130
Brian Morton	131
Roy Mottram-Smale	132
Liz Davies	133
Joyce Hefti-Whitney	134
Fredrick West	135
Abhilasha Tyagi	136
Tessa Paul	137
Paul R Denton	138
Brian Fisher	139
Rosa Johnson	140
Gail Charles	141
David Blakemore	142
Laila Lacey	143
Trevor Leah	144
Colleen Biggins	145
Paull Hammond-Davies	146
Alma Sewell	147
Sammy Wells	148
Evelyn Eagle	149
Josephine Foreman	150
Barbara Dunning	151
Stephen Shimmans	152
T Stuart	153
Derek Haskett-Jones	154
Pam Lutwyche	155
Geoffrey Speechly	156
Sheila Bruce	157
D M Griffiths	158
Diana Robertson	159
Peggy Morrill	160
Iris Crew	161
David Ord	162
Dorreen Young	163
Adele Rawle	164
Arthur	165
David Watkins	166
Sue Gerrard	167
Philip J Loudon	168
Omer Ahmad	169
Gwendoline Douglas	170
Gillian Humphries	171
Dave Slater	172
Ciara Duggan	173
Laura Cheshire	174
Glynnis Morgan	175
Roy Hobbs	176
Dea Costelloe	177
Martin Harris Parry	178
Mariana Zavati Gardner	179
Jennifer Hooper	180
Janet Hewitt	181
Stephanie Foster	182
Len Peach	183
Nell Thompson	184
Jim Wilson	185
Jo Allen	186
Georgie Ramsey	187
Jason Pointing	188
Thelma Jean Cossham Everett	189
Sudakshina Mukherjee	190
Joséphine Kant	191
Shirley Clayden	191
Julia Pegg	192
Brian Grace	193
Winifred Curran	194

Name	Page
Usmaa Umer	194
Robert Brooks	195
Greta Robinson	195
John Murdoch	196
Mark Boardman	197
D Carr	198
Colin Burnell	199
Julie Paton	200
Shane Jordan	201
Alison Williams	202
Richard Mahoney	202
Ronald Rodger Caseby	203
Thomas Baxter	203
Sandra Leach	204
Maria Howson	204
Anne Szczepanski	205
Elizabeth Bevans	205
Keith Tissington	206
Jennifer Parker	206
Anne Leeson	207
Jeanette Gaffney	208
David J C Wheeler	209
Corrina O'Beirne	210
Sylvia Westley	211
Florence Barnard	212
Robert William Lockett	213
Don Friar	214
Jimmy Broomfield	215
Sarah Davies	216
Richard Ford	217
Barbara Maskens	218
Hacene Rahmani	218
Diana Mudd	219
Janet Mansi	219
Kate Robinson	220
Glenys M Bowell	220
Philip Eames	221
Geoffrey Louch	221
Phyllis Wright	222
V M Archer	223
Pat MacKenzie	224
Joy Staley	225
Shirley Katherine Monaco	226
Alan Orpe	227
S Beatrice Ally	228
Cyril Maunders	229
Andrew Pardoe	230
Norma Spillett	231
Ray Dite	232
Stuart Wright	233
Gordon Bannister	234
Joan Beer	235
Maureen Brudenell Masters	236
Shirley Cowper	237
Les D Pearce	238
Jonathan Simms	239
Terrence St John	240
Anne Smith	241
Steve Selwood	242
Jack Blades	243
Robert Quin	244
Mab Jones	245
Nita Garlinge	246
Sageer Khan	247
Peter Payne	248
Helen Langstone	249
James Williams	250
Janette M Coverdale	251
Marie Coyles	252
Alan R Coughlin	253
Hannah Cowan	254
Adele Hodgkiss	255
Steven Kenny	256
Cezanne Jardine	257
Lee Blunt	258
KJ Lee-Evans	259
Joan Herniman	260
Carol Bradford	260
Sharron Hollingsworth	261
Frank Tonner	261
Debra Ayis	262
Lee McLaughlin	262
Rev Shirley Ludlow	263
Carl Kemper	263
H G Griffiths	264
Ana-Marie McKeever	264
Chrissy Baynes	265
St Catherine Henville	265
Glenys B Moses	266
Supriya Choudary	267
James Curwen	268
Vernon Ballisat	268
Irene Grant	269
Susan Westphal	269
Yagnaseni Bhattacharya	270
Celia Smith	270
John Waby	271
David Bakal	271
Hugh Rose	272
Genio Halvdan Kittil Engen	272
Jennifer Bell	273
Anton Nicholas	273

Name	Page
John Mangan	274
Sonja Mills	274
D Hallford	275
Kimberly Davidson	275
Sandra Moran	276
Peter Butterworth	276
Chris Meredith	277
Rachel Sutcliffe	277
Maureen Thornton	278
Diana Kwiatkowski Rubin	278
David Jones	279
Pam Russell	279
Doreen Gardner	280
Barry Ryan	281
Reginald Gent	282
Mary Williams	283
Carly Burns	284
Susannah Woodland	284
Barry Scott Crisp	285
Peter Cullen	285
Trevor Vincent	286
Thelma Barton	286
Hazel Yates	287
Maggie Kitson	287
Stella Bush-Payne	288
Niall McManus	288
Snikpohd	289
Terence Iceton	289
Pauline Kavanagh	290
Ann Beard	291
Joan L Carter	292
Jonathan Bryant	293
Nicola Scott	294
Norma Anne MacArthur	295
Naomi Smallwood	296
Cyril Joyce	296
Christine White	297
Charles Keeble	297
Joyce Willis	298
Tracey Celestin	298
Eileen Gallagher	299
Anthony Michael Doubler	299
Thomas E Dixon	300
Lorraine England	300
Zoe Jacobs	301
Terry Knight	301
Rachel Willmington	302
Keith Newing	302
Audrey Williams	303
Shirley Jaggard	303
Jane Cooter	304
Mary Porter	304
Tawfeeq Elahi Samad	305
Philip Anthony Amphlett	305
Colette Breeze	306
Josie Earnshaw	306
Freda Symonds	307
Donald Tye	307
Joann Littlehales	308
Meriel Malone	308
Peter J Sutton	309
Mavis Johnson	309
Keith Powell	310
Anne Hetherton	310
E Riggott	311
Diana H Adams	311
James Baxter	312
Russ Pratt	312
Iris Ina Glatz	313
Gerard Kenny	313
John Stewart	314
Jane Finlayson	314
Liz Dicken	315
Ann Warner	315
Michael Cotton	316
Robert Neill	316
Darran Ganter	317
Roy Gunter	317
Andrew Cain	318
Ingrid Rankin	318
David Hamey	319
Carlene Dandy	319
Ian Davey	320
Imogen Brand	320
Tony Dougan	321
Angela Matheson Cutrale	321
Garry Bedford	322
S Jean Brenner	322
Jainisha Patel	323
Daniel Crowley	323
Dorothy Durrant	324
Christine Renee Parker	324
Anthony Webster	325
Nicholas G Charnley	325
Ann Dempsey	326
Gill Mainwaring	326
Ann Margaret Holden (Rowell)	327
Natalie Williams	327
Mary Rose	328
Audrey Allen	328
Catherine Hislop	329
Rod Pilkington	329

Rosemary Whatling 330
Nesta Nicholson 330
Andrea Ratter 331
Nola Small 331
Jean Paisley 332
Elizabeth Jenks 332
Doris Mary Miller 333
Mavis Downey 333
Adrian Horton 334
Margaret Dilloway 334
Hazel Wilson 335
Paul Thompson 335
Christopher Thomas 336
Nigel Lloyd Maltby 336
Pat Adams 337
Aidan Martin 337
Mary Cole 338
Sandie Miles 338
Mick Nash 339
Barbara Pearce 339
David Marland 340
Beryl Smyter 340
Hazel Hudson 341
Lilian Fulker 341
Decima Watkins 342
Christine Flowers 342
Joanna Maria John 343
Jessica Powell 343
Diane Full 344
Judy Hopkin 344
Jacqueline Ives-Ward 345
Leah Rouse 345
Daphne Cornell 346
Neelam Shah 346
John Walker 347
Elizabeth Scharer 347
Maurice Colclough 348
Hetty Launchbury 348
Jayne Manning 349
Samantha Williams 349
Lynne Walden 350
Dorothy Beaumont 350
P B Norris 351
Dulcie Beatrice Gillman 351
J G Ryder 352
Eluned Ellis 352
Alex Cyril 353
Alan Pow 353
Elaine Day 354
Barbara Buckley 354
Ellen Spiring 355

Hayley Huttlestone 355
Guy Fletcher 356
Neil Ommanney Roper 356

LONELINESS

The loneliness sounded like chattering monkeys,
jabbering macaws, huge raindrops falling from
the high jungle canopy. I wasn't alone,
but my vigil was lonely.

My three companions were suffering the same . . .
for we had lain in ambush these last six days.
Inserted by helicopter into Long Pa Sia
followed by a three-day silent routine approach; eating cold,
carrying our litter, not smoking, not washing . . .
nothing to give our position or direction of travel away.

Six days we had watched, just enough across the border
to make it embarrassing had we been caught.
Separated . . . silent . . . sleeping
two-on and two-off at four-hourly intervals.

Surrounded by a hundred hues of greens and browns . . .
except for the blue-white mildew rotting
our clothing and equipment.
The loneliness was like a crowd . . . without the people.
It was with us like an alien presence. We were the aliens.

On the morning of the seventh day they came . . .
a patrol of nine fellow human beings.
They had no reason to believe that we were near . . .
watching . . . waiting.
Slowly they entered our killing zone.

'Boss' pressed the clacker which sent
all but three of them to oblivion.
Before the echo of the Claymore mine had rumbled
off into the hills
the others were killed, quickly, professionally . . .
each by a single, well-aimed bullet.

Within seconds the loneliness returned.
The monkeys went back to doing what monkeys do,
the macaws remained silent a moment longer.
The re-group was signalled.
We each made our own way to the RV-point
leaving the area as we found it . . .
littered with loneliness.

Ted Medler

THE AWFUL PEOPLE OF DEAD-END DRIVE

Welcome all to Dead-End Drive.
It really is a sorry dive.
I'm sure you got here by mistake,
So turn right back! It's not too late!
Or venture on, you braver few,
And cast your eyes o'er this awful view.
A cul-de-sac of ghastly folk.
A rotten egg with putrid yolk.

At Number 1, he'll make you ill,
Life's lovelorn loser, Stinky McGill.

Stinky McGill was a lonely man.
He'd been alone for quite a span.
For there's much in a name, you must agree,
As the girls would pass and always see
McGill with crossed, yet smiling, eyes
Underneath a swarm of flies.
He'd wink and give a loving sigh,
The girls would run and often cry.
So, Stink McGill could only dream
For a sweeter scent, but it would seem
No perfume made would ever work
On the pits of this sweaty berk.
If you sat beside Stinky McGill,
I wouldn't blame you if you lost the will
To go on breathing, or hold your breath
And count the seconds to a welcome death.
But how to describe this poor young boy?
To ponder on it is no joy.
We'll start from the feet and go up from there,
Until we reach his greasy hair.
The flies, you know, would circle long,
Because our boy could really pong.
Stinky's sandals were the perfect shoe,
Open-toed, an unsightly view
Of his ten digits and dirty nails,
Wafting like a skunk's entrails.

And when, at last, he'd don his socks,
Between his parents' gasps and shocks,
The holes were neither vent nor aid
To the fouler stench his body made.
Even in winter he'd only wear
His bean-stained vest without a care.
His armpits, they were ever free
For all to smell and all to see.
But Stinky's breath was the party piece,
A mix of egg and chip-fat grease.
How, you ask, could a girl then miss
The chance of a romantic kiss
With Stink McGill, fortune's fool,
His puckered mouth alive with drool?
The only girl who'd ever swoon
Is probably living on the moon!

And now the Grumps of Dead-End Drive
Who live together at Number 5.

Mr Grump was a lazy brute,
He had holes in every single suit.
And Mrs Grump would curse and moan
To her poor friends on the telephone,
'He's a useless fool,' she would declare,
'He refuses to trim his nasal hair!'
Good for nothing, old Mr Grump,
A hairy, spotty, human lump.
'What can you do, but eat and sleep?'
Mrs Grump was prone to cry and weep.
'Burp and smell the whole day through,
I wish I'd never married you!'
But Mr Grump had a gift unknown,
Yet his trumpet he had never blown,
For in his sleep, when deep enough,
On comfy beds, or even rough,
He could snore aloud like no other,
While Mrs Grump would run for cover,
And kick him, shouting, 'It's the sofa, lad!
No man could ever snore as bad
As you, foul beast, your ghastly breath
Is worse than any grisly death.

The neighbours bang, they hear you too.
Please stop snoring, or we're through!'
But Mr Grump was long and gone,
His snores were like a rotten song.
Loud as bellows and foghorn wails,
The air he breathed, as strong as gales.
The pickled eggs and cheesy crisps
Rippled through his snoring lisps.
Poor Mrs Grump could only beg,
Or desperately reach for her trusty peg
And clasp it firmly on her nose,
A woman full of tired woes.
She placed a cork within each ear
And gave old Grump a loving sneer.
'Sweet dreams, you horror of a man.
Of you, I'm really not a fan!'
But Mr Grump could never hear,
His dreams were full of fanatic cheer.
He'd scored again in the Snorers' Cup
And gone about ten-nil up!
Collected gold for the smelliest belch,
Coupled with a bottom squelch!
Mrs Grump, at toss and turn,
Would never, ever start to learn
That Mr Grump was more than zero.
A sleeping, snoring, belching hero!

At Number 7 is Enid Chubb,
A cook who makes disgusting grub!
Mr Chubb was a brilliant cook,
Baking cakes by the baking book.
World-renowned, exalted high,
He didn't even have to try.
The only problem was his daughter,
He should have put her out to slaughter.
As Enid Chubb was a savoury baker,
For adding sugar, you couldn't make her.
Jam tarts made with tomato paste,
Always spat out in great haste.

Lovely muffins, crammed with chips.
Of chocolate? No, but potato bits!
Her taste buds, see, had never grown.
The bitter ones had over-blown,
And sweetness was a thing she lacked.
It really was a sorry fact.
For moods are matched with the food we eat,
And time spent with Enid was no treat.
Like burnt toast mixed with lemon curd,
Enid was the foulest bird.
She'd growl and snap when beating eggs
To soufflé, mixed with cabbage dregs!
Her rolling pin was like a tree,
Thick and gnarled for all to see.
She'd wield it high about her head,
But it couldn't dent her homemade bread!
The news is that she's branching out.
To Enid Chubb there is no doubt,
That her bakery will be the best,
And put her cooking to the test.
It's Dead-End Drive's only shop,
She hopes it doesn't get the chop.
There are cakes and tea for all to try,
You might go in and wonder why
Anyone would ever buy
A meat and gravy, apple pie!

Knock at Nora's. It's Number 2.
I bet it's the last thing you ever do!

Nora Fouler is ninety-nine
And you can often hear her whine
That her bones ache in the winter cold,
She'll curse the world, for being old.
They made her retire at forty-three,
She had to because of her dodgy knee.
You see, she was the first of all
The women to play in men's football.
A goalkeeper extraordinaire,
A feline diver, full of flair.

With hands like shovels catching all,
And gripping on to every ball.
Her arms were long like fighting snakes,
None had seen her get the shakes.
Springing high, then swooping low,
Cor blimey! She could really go!
Old Fingers Fouler, as she was known,
Was seated on the keeper's throne.
In '66 she played in goal
For England, she would fill the hole.
But as we know, at forty-three
She was let down by her dodgy knee.
So Nora moved to Dead-End Drive
In the summer of '75.
A bitter goalie, hating sport
Of every kind and every sort!
If you ask the kids, 'Who's Fingers Fouler?'
Watch their faces grow much paler.
They'll stammer, 'D'you mean Nora, Sir?
The ball-popper with the facial fur?'
For Nora now has a newer name,
A fearful calling just the same.
As her garden is a hellish plot,
The danger there is just as hot,
For if any mis-kicked ball should drop
Onto her grass, she'll proceed to pop
And madly grin at the whistling sound,
Of the balls becoming less than round
And dying flat upon her hand.
Her gappy smile wide and grand.
The cackling laugh, ringing out and true,
Another victim for this awful shrew.
We all know when another's burst,
We heard the last. We heard the first.
The happy cheer from Nora Fouler,
Ball-popper and manic, geriatric howler!

Look! The house with the broken gate.
Boris Bunglesworth lives at Number 8.

Boris 'Four-Eyes' Bunglesworth had only one dream
To drive in a magnificent flying machine.
He was just a boy in World War One
And heard all tales of the fearful 'Hun'.
He had waited in earnest for World War Two,
Yet only marvelled at those who flew,
For not only was Bunglesworth practically blind,
He also had no power of mind.
'You can clean our planes,' the sergeant said,
'But if I let you fly, we'd all be dead.
Some were born for flying, son,
But you are not a lucky one.
Here's a brush. Get to it, lad!
Scrub your best. Don't make me mad!'
And so it passed. The enemy abolished
By British planes which Boris polished.
He'd played his part and done a job,
He'd even earned a fair few bob.
But naught could quench his thirst to fly.
He'd scrubbed the planes. He had to try!
If memory serves, it was late at night
And Boris kept far from sight.
The other soldiers, in the mess,
Had no idea and couldn't guess
That Boris had wings to fly
Up into the midnight sky.
He jumped aboard a waiting plane,
The man was really less than sane.
The lights, all lit, were the same to him.
He turned the key with added vim.
'Red means go!' he said out loud,
He'd soon be drifting as a cloud.
He hit the button: 'Ejector Seat',
Still dreaming of his flying feat.
And fly he did, though without the plane.
Oh what a sorry human stain.
He soared, head-first, into the sky,
The soldiers heard old Boris cry,
'I'm flying, lads! At last it's true!
I knew one day that I'd show you!'

He flew head-long into the sarge,
With a head and body, shoulder barge,
But shell-shocked Boris could not miss
The waiting blow from Sarge's fist.
So Bunglesworth left the forces fast,
In a full and fresh-set body cast.
We see him now in Dead-End Drive.
It's true he made it out alive.
Those years ago, from World War Two,
The only time that Boris flew.
So be aware, if you're by his gate
At Dead-End Drive, it's Number 8.
Look through his window and you will see,
Bunglesworth sat on the settee,
With his flying cap and goggles bound,
Listen close and hear the sound
Of aeroplane noises from his lip,
On a homemade landing strip!

At Number 3 the walls are thin,
As Betty Bugle makes a din!

Betty Bugle was born to be
A singer of fine rhapsody.
Her lungs were large and swimmer-strong,
Fit for singing any song.
She toured the world as a child star,
The critics said, 'She's going far!
She sang on ships. She cruised the Med.
She sang in the shower. She sang in bed.
She sang when eating, it is true!
Sang when sneezing, or with the flu!
Betty did ten shows a week,
She really was a singing freak!
The days were long. The stress, it grew.
The way to cope, as Betty knew,
Was smoking sixty cigs a day.
She'd smoke them all, come what may.
She smoked in the shower. She smoked in bed.
The smoke poured out from her singing head.
She smoked when eating, it is true!

POETRY RIVALS' COLLECTION 2010 - THE PASSIONS OF THE POET

Smoked when sneezing, or with flu!
But as her fingers grew more yellow,
It was clear she could not bellow.
Her lungs were rotten, she had no choice
But to sing in a bass and gravel voice.
Her public cried and audiences waned,
But still it wasn't the fags she blamed.
'Those sorry losers! What do they know?'
She'd curse through every puff and blow.
Her life-long fans, who once adored,
Were set to push her overboard.
Once, when she sang upon the ship,
The captain helped the wheel to slip.
He turned it quick, for he was brave,
And waited for the biggest wave.
The people booed her final song
And in a second she was gone!
Washed away in the beat of a heart
The captain made the engines start.
'Full power!' he screamed, shouting so,
He pleaded for the ship to go.
So Betty was found, washed-up ashore,
Without a penny. She was poor.
And Dead-End Drive was the perfect place
For her to hide her shameful face.
Like all the noises in the street,
None are pretty, none are sweet.
Her sandpaper coughs and smoky fumes
Are wound up in her spluttered tunes.
She sings and smokes, that's all she knows,
Her high notes are now only lows.
You'll find her house. It's easy to spot
Cigarette smoke from the chimney pot,
And cardboard windows because, you see,
She cracks the glass too easily!

At Number 4, hear him roar!
Rex the Rottweiler guards his door.

Rex the Rottweiler, for fifteen years
Has had every postman weeping tears.

He was born a pup in Dead-End Drive,
And will live there till the day he dies.
He guards his house each day and night.
He barks from the morning with all his might.
He growls by day at the shadows of the sun
And howls at the moon when the day is done.
Rex always bites off what he chews,
Be it postmen's hats or postmen's shoes.
Ol' Rex is known to walk himself,
He has to keep up his dogged health.
He wants to be fit to give good chase,
And beat all cats in this rat race!
For Rex thinks he's the beauty mark,
When he strolls around the park
Found at the bottom of Dead-End Drive,
Where a world of madness seems to thrive.
For a street of chaos would be lacking,
Without this mongrel's constant yapping!

But even the sun shines on Dead-End Drive.
At times it buzzes like a hive.
They're a sorry lot, from the outside in,
But they have each other, and that's the thing.
We see them all together again,
For they have street parties now and then.
There's Enid Chubb, who caters well,
And Stinky McGill, who brings his smell,
Trying hard to catch Betty Bugle's eye,
If I were him I wouldn't try.
It's tough to see her through the smoke.
It makes old Bunglesworth start to choke.
He thinks his plane is going down,
In his flying hat and dressing gown.
The Grumps are laughing. They've made up.
They're patting Rex, the Dead-End pup.
And even Nora has joined the group,
Without her teeth, she's slurping soup
And telling all of playing in goal,
Then asking for another bowl!

For the vile folk in this noisy street,
Are mad enough to want to eat
The sickly food of Enid Chubb.
The horrid, mangy, boiled grub.
But, like in life, they've found a place.
A way of living at a pace
Which suits them well, and they survive
In chaos, together, in Dead-End Drive!

Steven Jackson

THE AWAKENING!

Gently sniffing in quiet stirrings
Where a robin sings a last outcry of soothing solace, before dusk's embrace,
My young Labrador catches the gaze of an elderly lady,
Bringing to life what could have been a silent passing,
Sharing her joy at seeing him,
She rekindles sadness at losing her close companion,
With heartfelt warmth and intimacy,
'I still talk to him as if he's with me,'
And 'Now I cannot have another since my fall.'
Her zimmer frame supporting her determined and painstaking footsteps in the snow,
Wishing to catch just a sense of 'past love',
Looking to stroke Lionel, as he wavers behind me,
I quickly say, 'A rescue dog,'
Yet in her frozen pain, she draws beyond herself,
'Well done for helping him,'
Before she moves peacefully into the cold winter twilight!

Martin Norman

THE OUTBACK SHUFFLE
(Inspired by an original musical theme entitled 'Australia' by Jamie Gasking, composed at the age of 10-11 years, shortly before his death in an accident in July 2003)

Oh, yesterday I met this character
Who described himself as an ambassador
For this great destination really far out
A truly bonza country without a doubt

Australia
Australia
Right up on top
Down under
Australia
Australia
Out of this world
Another hemisphere

When I stared into his eye he didn't look away
But stated with conviction, transport yourself that way
Coz Oz is a place that knows where it's at
So polish up your boomerang 'n' stick corks on your hat

Hey, g'day mate!
Come on!
Let's do the outback shuffle
Forget the Sunday suit
No worries, no kerfuffle
Fair dinkum, it's a beaut
Hey, cobber!
Too right!
Just do that outback shuffle
Cor, strewth, it's not so tough
A bitta huff 'n' puff'll
Soon set you right enough

In Australia
Australia
Out of this world
Another hemisphere

If you're on the hunt for some novel winner
There's always surfing in for Christmas dinner
If Holly and the Ivy just pass you by
Bib 'n' tucker on the beach might be worth a try

In Australia
Australia
Right up on top
Down under
Australia
Australia
Out of this world
Another hemisphere

Remember that we of Antipodes
Started right out from scratch and I don't mean fleas
So you can have crowds who dance and holler out
Or take an aboriginal walkabout

Though I should warn you
as well
There are these few precautions
That you should keep in mind
Observe the local etiquette
And you will get on fine
Okay then
Here goes . . .

Never pick a fight with a wombat
When he's playing his didgeridoo
Okay, that fellah's not built for combat
But he's got mates who can see to you
And the last thing that you want to stir up
Is a row with a kookaburra
Or a kick from a kangaroo

Strewth, mate
That's true!
And this is important too . . .

Don't get bushed in the Bush
Or come to grief on the Reef
Don't put airs on the Rock
Or get fleeced by the sheep
Steer well clear of all such things
Oh, and here's another point
If you value your health and well-being
Don't ask the flying doctor
Where he's hiding his wings
Don't forget to make room for the woomeras
And clap the wallabies who wannabe
Never mix up platypi with apple pie
Or the possum with anything unwholesome
Don't tell echidna that he is spineless
Or suggest the emu's short on brains
Stick to calypso with koalas
And don't pinch their eucalyptus

Remember all that
And you can't go wrong

In Australia
Australia
Out of this world
Another hemisphere

And the great thing is this: Tammy, Vicky or Sal
Can do just as well as Tom, Dick or Hal
No bars to climbing up our greasy pole of luck
If you smell like a dingo or've gotta nose like a duck

In Australia
Australia
Right up on top
Down under
Australia
Australia
Out of this world
Another hemisphere

And if it happens you're Matilda, or Sheila or Bruce
We won't keep you waiting in the barbie queues
No, we'll drag you up front declaring, Good on yer, 'n' such
And we'll pile your plate high, insisting nothing is too much

Coz we say . . .
Hey! G'day, mate!
Come on!
Let's do the outback shuffle
Forget the Sunday suit
No worries, no kerfuffle
Fair dinkum, it's a beaut
Hey, cobber!
Too right!
Just do that outback shuffle
Cor, strewth, it's not so tough
A bitta huff 'n' puff'll
Soon set you right enough

In Australia
Australia
Right up on top
Down under
Australia
Australia
Out of this world
Another hemisphere

David Gasking

HUG

A hug is a wonderful, wondrous thing,
God must be so clever.
I think I love this simple way
Of how we fit together.

Sally Elizabeth Taylor

UNTITLED
(In celebration of Alfred Lord Tennyson - Poet Laureate)

Somersby - that well-beloved place
Where first gazed upon the sky
He who marbled moon and cloud
Lincolnshire born - Lincolnshire proud.

Before Alfred could read - once, during a storm
Out in the garden he declared, arms outstretched
'I hear a voice speaking in the wind far, far away'
Inspiration he would not forget.
He thrilled to Christmas bells of four hamlets
Thru' the mist answering each other hill to hill
A mingling, tingling of his father's parish
Awakened a wish in the poet, honing his skill.

On stepping stones to higher things
That great blow of destiny hovering
Tennyson immortalised a friendship 'In Memoriam'
Worthy of honours bestowed by the sovereign.
Onwards he charged - half a league onwards
Yet how airy the tread at Maud's garden gate
There is no happy-ever-aftering down by the river
Tirra-Lirra and a mirror sealed a fair lady's fate.

As I linger and loiter along by The Brook
With willow weed and mallow
A fairy foreland still remains
Twinkling in the shadows.
Where violets bloom and the woodbine blows
Therein lies a treasure trove
With immemorial elms and innumerable bees
Alfred Lord Tennyson
Lincolnshire proud - Lincolnshire pleased.

Lucy Green

MY BROTHER, MY HERO

You are an inspiration to everyone you meet
You smile, you whistle
Never complaining
Relentless pain, but worse the indignity
My Brother, my Hero

Your adult life had just begun
Fate came and intervened
So close to death, our prayers were heard
You survived, your torment just begun
My Brother, my Hero

With courage and determination you learn to live again
Your passion for cars
We were so proud
The wasted legs, just an inconvenience
My Brother, my Hero

Our lives progressed, no true love for you
You cradled my first born
He adores you in return
A bond which has never been broken
My Brother, my Hero

Faithful friends come to visit, we laugh and reminisce
We talk of our children, of idyllic holidays
Unselfishly you listen, having nothing to offer
My Brother, my Hero

My heart cries its silent tears
As I leave you each morning
Your twisted body, useless and dying
In Heaven, together we will walk one day
My Brother, my Hero.

Lynn Martindale

DO YOU KNOW?

Do you know
How much
I love you?
Can you feel it
In your heart?
My pulse quickens
When you
Start to talk
My eyes shine
My soul
Is happy
That you
Are mine
You are
A magnet
Attached to
My core
You don't
Always show
Your feelings
It's confusing
At times
You tell me
I am stunning
And we
Shouldn't part
The one thing
I desire
Is for you
To say
To me
'I love you
My darling
Will you
Marry me?'
Do you know
How long
I've waited
For love
To come
My way?
It seems
Like an eternity
Don't let it

Slip away
We don't need
To lose track
Of who we are
Now the door
Is open
We can carry on
And explore
We do things
Together
That are funny
And nice
Like the time
We went away
And I was
Shown paradise
Do you know
I am satisfied
Just to be
The person
That you love
Wouldn't
You agree?
We come from
Different backgrounds
Opposites attract
We balance
The scales
Now
That's not bad
My darling
I would
Like to say
To you
Never forget
The love
We shared
Never turn
Your back
On me
I am
Full of
Passions
A woman
Without woe
Only now

Can you see
The goddess
In me
That everyone
Knows
And loves.

Sharon Lambley

A BENEDICTION FOR THE BENTHAMITES

Summer days are dying
Haunted swallows flying south
Through the night's ephemeral light.
Fowl and fox wear the mist
Alert to the poacher's snapping fist.
And the ganoid trout turns about escaping to the open sea.
The cenotaphs of trees stand monument to a million leaves
Shed upon a battlefield,
Where the silent earthworm breeds and feeds.
Abandoned, a rust-encrusted plough lies meat for the metal eaters now.
And 'neath the earth stiff as whiskers; victims of its scalpel blades
Lie the meadow tenants in their frozen graves.
A crowman at attention hangs
In crucifixion midst this ice-bound prism land.
A sentry at the entrance guarding Mother Earth's chill tomb.
She who waits the paschal warmth of spring to thaw her fertile womb.
A time of shepherds calling across the bleak unyielding moor
Of druids and magicians, of bolts drawn tight on Heaven's door.
Of tarradiddle fortunes hidden in a winter's map of stars
As poets rhyme the tick of time in spit and sawdust bars.
Beads bleed red from tortured boughs
The bloody holm oak's haemorrhage.
Twinkling poison parasites tease old maids on Christmas night
With puckered lips they stand and kiss 'neath those pearly fingertips.

In the bombazine cowled crypt of night
Where Jack the Tailor cuts his shroud;
'Neath Hesperus process the crowds.
Bearing flames of sanctuary light
In mourning for the summer
Benediction for the Benthamites.

Philip Mee

SEASONS

Spring is now showing,
From the sky to the ground.
The sparkling waters flowing,
As the love has been found.
Can I wait knowing
That the love is for me?
Or am I being silly
Cos my heart is forever glowing?

Autumn is drawing near,
The colour begins to fade.
From the distance comes the fear
And everything lies in the shade.
The words I've wanted to hear,
Come ever so distant and quiet
And everything becomes so clean,
As your truth becomes quite clear.

Winter is so very cold,
As the sheet covers the ground.
The bitterness sweeps all around
And the whiteness grows so old.
Your love has left my side,
Your lies have shown through,
The light that came from you,
I just can't believe you lied!

Summer has begun once more,
The colours bursting through and through,
All things gone are back anew,
As the summer sun shines at my door.
Again, I have found true love,
That I never thought I would,
Together forever just like we should,
A true blessing sent from God above.

Rachel Keers

RELATIVITY RAP

Some of them fools think they are real clever
But check Einstein, he wrote the line
Relativity he found divine
Mass and energy is the same thing
E=mc squared is da bling

E equals energy
M equals mass
And the mc sparks the time to pass
The square root of two holds the whole thing together
And the workings of this process are both elegant and clever

The equation describes the speed of light's accretion
And properties of mass to energy conversion
From the well of gravity springs space/time
The structure of which creates the world line

A curved prism light gave Newton insight
That the structure and laws of thermodynamics
Is the structural wave form which lights the planets
The sun is a changeable force with a moving boundary
Which gives heat and light to you and me
Spectral light emissions are part of the effect
That curves space/time to a constant effect

With energy the world resounds
There is always motion where light is found
E and mc squared gets it together
And creates all kinds of cosmic weather
Photons and electrons perform the trick
That lets the clockwork universe tick
It is not clockwork, Newton's bucket is wrong
But try making that into a song

I understood Newtonian physics at school
For every action an opposite, I was no fool
Well dense energy equals mass
They didn't teach me that in class
Compressed energy is released in a dance
A physical activity not left to chance
All the sums must balance out
And that's what stars are all about

Nuclear fusion will cause no confusion
If you get over the simple delusion
That everything is in a fixed state
That's not how particles interrelate

A black hole, it has no mass
Progress and motion towards its devotion
No light escapes this non-Euclidian potion
Into what dimension does the energy emerge?
The whole damn thing is truly absurd

Now please don't see this as a retraction
Let me illustrate this action
One, two, three, all states emerge, mass and light and energy
Extend from a singularity.
Unleashed potential all around
And that was how the light was found

The Lambda principle lets there be light
Who's to say it's not cosmologically right?
The balanced creation of energy
That creates everything mysteriously
Electrons and photons like to dance
And will interact given half the chance

With its strange polarity
That exists on every scale
The perfect geometry of this tale
The golden ratio that makes every thing go
It's the strangest thing that we all know

To all of us it's quite clear, the Earth's a sphere
You cannot see the curve of the Earth for its mighty girth
The curve of the line resting on the equator
Is the truth of the now in the past and the later?

Now it all seems quite neat, these marvels of science
The globe travelling in relative motion and geodesic compliance
But the point of an arrow that curves on a dime
This is the essence of circular time
Gravity curves nature to a constant degree
And even time is a singularity

Come on now, and don't be morons
Just innovate your interneurons
The Wheeler-De Witt equation freezes time
But is quantum gravity the key to undoing this mystery?
The Tachyon may be faster than the speed of light
And into history it sets flight
I hope this rhyme found the time
To show you that physics is so sublime.

Rob Wheeldon

PRICELESS

Like a priceless work of art
You have become a priceless work crested in my soul
Day in, day out, I can't imagine that a thought of you
Has become a line painted from Mona Lisa.

How priceless is your worth
That an image of you is faultless
Now you have become a part of me
That I can't live without.

I have searched the galleries of hearts
I have seen many countless works of art
But none can be compared to you
My priceless work of art.

How priceless is your beauty
That none could paint your true image
You are priceless as you are
A precious work of art made for me.

Nsikak Ukpong

SYNONYMOUS

Beacons warn of my dangerous plight,
A ship grounded on a forbidden night,
Contact embodied, is so remote,
Synonymous words of desire,
Tears fuelling the cruel mire,
The enigma of our being,
Forget you! No secret tryst
Dreaming of emancipated bliss,
Forbidden fruit, my garden of Eden,
Destiny, fate will have its way,
Dreaming of you every day,
My soul is retching to forget,
Lovers' words, and your eyes
My head has said goodbye!

Jessie Shields

MYSTERIOUS SOMEBODY

We could have a conversation but nothing, no connection, no spark.
In the same room, you were mysterious, gorgeous, intimidating and dark,
Wanting something so bad, turned sour, cold and uninviting.
To tell you how I feel, many times I wanted; many times I nearly gave it you in writing,
Your words, your voice, your presence, you took many things including my heart.
Everything you are, were and can be, I see myself, and you were such an art,
When you weren't there, I would be lost inside,
But still kept face, my emotion I had to hide,
I just wanted to know you. Near or far,
In a universe full of people, you were my mysterious star,
One day I will see you again, when that day comes,
You will never know, you will never be stunned,
We could have a conversation but nothing, no connection, no spark.
In the same room you will be mysterious, gorgeous, intimidating and dark.

Adele Simone Pierce

MY JOURNEY THROUGH LIFE

I was a baby in my pram
Unaware of life's problems
Like money or a traffic jam
As long as I was fed
Clothed and kept warm
Unaware of the rain and snow
Unaware of the storm

I started to look around
At the world in which I was born
People rushing here and there
Some big, some small, some with no hair
Some of the time it is light
Then it is dark
When it is dark, they say it is night
When it is light, they say it is day
At night I sleep
In the day I play

When I could walk
When I could talk
Some words I could not understand
When I walked, Mum held my hand
I sat in a high chair
I was fed with a spoon
I would have liked to do it myself
But Mum said it was too soon

At school I learned nursery rhymes
We played games at playtime
Tried to catch each other
But at 4pm I was glad to return home to Mother
I played netball and rounders
I also did PE
I did lots of writing, reading too
I went on school trips
Found lots to do

Then I felt grown up, but I knew I was not
Still a child I was told, sorry, I had forgot
Tests and exams gave me stress
But life was full of happiness
Make-up and fashion I kept my eye on the boys
It seemed so long since I'd played with toys
I did not know what the future held for me
I did my best then waited to see

Then I left school
Went out to work
Went out dancing
Picked up every perk
I went to the cinema
On holiday with friends
I had a great time
I hoped it would never end

Then I became an adult
It was time to settle down
Shopping for a wedding
I had to get to town
Weddings cost money
As I was finding out
Money was a problem
But that's what it was all about

Married life began
The honeymoon was over and done
Responsibilities were now my worry
Everything had to be thought about
Without hurry
I wanted to have children of my own
To love and care for, like my mother cared for me
But I had to realise
This would be more responsibility

My children are now fully grown
I have put them through school
I have done my best
Now it's time to take a rest

I remember the things that I did
A long time ago, when I was a kid
Then I look back and see
They did things similar to me
Who are we to grumble
If now and again we take a tumble?

Life is a mixture of ups and downs
Sadness, laughter, even frowns
Like a book read from the beginning
Until it ends
Somewhere in the middle
We make friends
Life is a cycle
Each generation does the same
Each has their claim to fame.

Patricia Stone

SEA OF DREAMS

As I peer towards the horizon of the sea,
I visualise an ocean filled with hope for me!
Carrying me to a land beyond uncertainty
And a universe with no fear,
Beyond there is beautiful, relaxing music
And this is all I can hear!
I absorb the comfort of my dream
Of wishes to come true,
I feel the warmth of the sunbeam,
As it shines down upon me
And when the ocean splashes gently up at me,
I'll know there is some magic coming from the sea,
Giving me some hope, even in my dreams,
Then everything will be
Just as I had hoped and dreamed
And all so magically!

Theresa Hartley-Mace

SOUL MATE

He is the introvert moon waiting to be caressed
He is a maladroit chef with colossal hands
He is a blistered, piquant mincemeat curry
He is a Mercedes with a clandestine number plate
He is Concorde on a mysterious voyage
He is a Rolex watch, indispensable and untainted
He is a penny black stamp, invaluable yet juvenile
He is champagne plus caviar on a Sunday twilight
He is the Eiffel Tower emigrating from France
He is an aggressive archer aiming at his target
He is an angry tank full of ammunition
He is an encumbered machine gun waiting to draw blood
He is a clown with an enclosed manifest circus
He is a thorn with adoring red, rosy cheeks
He is my best friend, my counsellor and my lover
He is my soul mate.

Maria Sheikh

THE HEART OF SPRING

The heart of spring is calling to me, now.
The long winter is through; the heart of spring
Is making me glad, and telling me how
Good life really is; wisteria in
Profusion, clings to my stout wall . . . Oh wow!
Lilacs of purple and cream, waft their scent . . .
Oh my! What a heady perfume steals my
Senses; the heart of spring was truly meant
To gladden a mortal's soul; cherry pie
Sweetness, apple tree joy, the trill of bird
And the thrill of knowing the reason why?
Endless winter was a feeling absurd!
Full-blown kingcups are nodding by a stream
The heart of spring brings images supreme.

Valerie Hall

MAG'S BAGS

I like bags,
All sorts of bags,
Where they come from I don't care,
They can come from anywhere,
Whatever their use, I don't mind at all,
I have them hung on my bedroom wall,
I have bags for potatoes and bags for candles,
Bumbags, handbags and bags with no handles,
Old bags, new bags and bags for suits,
Money bags, make-up bags and bags for mucky boots,
String bags, plastic bags, paper bags and nylon bags,
School bags, sandwich bags and even some doggy bags,
Glitzy little evening bags and matching leather travel bags,
Canvas bags, camera bags and bright pink computer bags,
But my favourite bag I've ever had
Is the little green one that belonged to my dad.
He gave it to me when I was quite small
And told me to keep it until I was all
Grown up and ready to look into its space
And remember the fun times and picture his face,
For my old dad was my very best friend.
All through the summer we would spend
Time on the riverbank fishing for bream,
Then off to the park for vanilla ice cream,
We collected conkers from the woods near our house
And helped Mrs Green when her cat caught a mouse.
He showed me his medals he'd got during the war
And when asked how he won them, he wouldn't say more,
He taught me to play the spoons and banjo
And we sang songs together and put on a show,
We went searching for treasure on Mablethorpe sands,
Went on the big dipper, screamed and held hands,
Ate candyfloss that blew in the wind everywhere
And we both ended up with sticky pink hair,
But we didn't mind, we just laughed at our plight
And ate three more, we were both sick that night!
When the weather was bad we'd stay indoors,
But that didn't prevent us having adventures galore,
An old bed sheet was our tent on the moor,
We ate beans on toast as we sat on the floor,
A torch and a book kept us happy all night,
Ghost stories he'd tell and give me a fright,
We pretended I was a shopkeeper whose
Shop sold nothing other than shoes,

'I'd like a pair of shoes, size five in blue.'
'We only have red in a size two.'
But Dad said, 'They'll do.'
And we made pancakes for tea
And ate them with glee,
And in the winter when it was cold,
He made us porridge in an extremely old
Saucepan, bigger than me,
And we'd wash it down with a big mug of tea.
And Dad had a secret store
Of chocolate he hid behind his wardrobe door,
And in the middle of the night,
We'd sneak it out and have a bite,
But Mum found the wrappers on the floor,
And under the bed and said,
'No more!'
And we looked at each other and gave a sly wink,
There was more hidden under the bathroom sink.
And when I was small, to my dad I would say,
'Can we go to the park again today?'
I'd sit on the long steel horse and shout, 'Faster!'
And he'd push me so high I would scream with laughter.
My bags for potatoes, my bags for candles,
My bumbags, my handbags, and those with no handles,
My old bags, my new bags, bags for my suits,
My money bags, make-up bags and bags for my mucky boots,
My string bags, my plastic bags, my paper bags and nylon bags,
My school bags, my sandwich bags and even my doggy bags,
My glitzy little evening bags and matching leather travel bags,
My canvas bags, my camera bags
And my bright pink computer bags,
All hang together on my wall,
But my favourite bag of all
Is the little green one I've always had,
Cos it belonged to my dad.

Margaret Day

A CUP O' NAILS . . .

Where are they now
Those men;
Men whose wax crayon images
filled the empty colouring book of my childhood?
Whose olive drab corduroy and
canvas escarpments rose endlessly
from their tarred and hobnailed leather foothills;
Up and up and away to dizzying felt-capped summits
soaring high above my child's upturned face.
Their peaks, lost, in a grey-blue billowing cumulus of
scented and fragrant pipe smoke.
Sweat and work-stained shoulders vague,
undefined.
Swimming and shapeless in the swirling cirrus
of a sudden woodbine squall.
The roaring gale of their shouts and laughter,
gusting and echoing
high amongst their florid and razor-veined precipices.
Are they really no more?

Where are their voices?
Gravel-gargled tones, worn gruff.
Men's voices.
Born of tar and ember and smoking, spitting steel
in the black, bronchial and fuming bellies
of gestating warships.
'Two pines of black and tan' voices.
Voices that would have smothered the very words
'Skinny latte' at birth!
Vocal fingerprints, tobacco-smoked and stained;
Their ridges and grooves scarred, worn rough
and rubbed raw from hawking and bellowing
above the caulker's hammer;
The tom-tom tattoo of the riveters'
hissing, bucking, air guns.
Rasping basso profundo pipes that could demand
'A cup o' nails 'n' some 'ot water.'
And turn not a single head.
Have they all been silenced?

Where are the hard men?
Those men with the great torn and callused paws
and gentle eyes that stooped to tousle
my over-long child's hair.
That cuffed my ear, gentle as a breeze,

with affectionate banana bunch fingers?
The same hands that ran, gloveless and unafraid,
the singing steel hawsers; Tight as bowstrings;
As they rode the frost and sleet-slicked steel aloft.
Great grey and rust sails, tacking and shivering,
to and fro, fro and to in the wild,
ice-sequinned winter winds.
Iron working men;
Men made of
the same unforgiving ore
they worked and enslaved and bent to their will.
With their weather-worn and nut brown
tobacco pouch faces
and knotted, corded and veined walnut forearms.
Are they all gone?

Where is that child?
Grown now: To grey and sire and grandsire;
Precipice and snow-covered peak now to his own gentle
and expectant upturned and tousle-haired faces.
The men, the iron men of his childhood;
No more now than waning pastel memories
in a faded and dog-eared child's colouring book.
Where will these new and tender shoots find theirs:
Their men of steel, their towering summits; Their 'heroes'?
The bright poster paint images with which
to fill the empty pages of their scrap books?
They will find them as I found mine:
The dishonest, the weak and the whey-faced,
the craven and the feckless tainted my child's world.
But there rested not a one in my colouring book,
and there will be none in theirs.
Trust the children . . . They will find their heroes.
Amongst all the cowardice, deceit, avarice and treachery;
There will *always* be heroes . . .

Sullivan The Poet

A CHILD WITH AUTISM
(I dedicate this poem to Caroline and Gary who are blessed with endless patience)

To be a companion for his brother
Much wanted was this little boy
Looking at the child with love
Their hearts were full of joy

When he didn't do the things
Like other girls and boys
His parents noticed he never played
With his brother or his toys

The doctor said, 'Don't worry,
His development is just slow'
When there was no improvement
Seeking more help they did go

He makes a noise but never talks
Locked in a world of his own
And walks around upon his toes
In a place full of love, his home

Holding his head on one side
And slapping his little hands
His parents feeling the distress
For no one understands

I don't know what makes sense anymore
When I look upon this child so fair
I've prayed for understanding
Sometimes I feel full of despair

A visitor came and told his mother
'He might have autism my dear,'
She listened carefully to what was said
And her heart was filled with fear

Their plans they had were shattered
The hopes and dreams for their son
The child they loved had autism
Now new plans for him have begun

Bravely they will fight for his future
And get all the care he needs
Determined they searched the Internet
To make sure their child succeeds

'No one knows my feelings,'
My daughter said to me,
'I have to lock them deep inside
Or despondent I would be

I'll go to the ends of the Earth
For the answers that I seek
With no one to show me the way
And the pitfalls, I fear are deep

I have to hold my family together
For them I must be strong
Through the sleepless nights we suffer
Which go on and on and on . . . ?'

I wonder is this God's purpose?
Sent to this man and his wife
Giving them their gentle love and care
To guide their child through life

He has severe autism
Which is bafflement to me
This much wanted, precious child
And his loving and caring family

I admire my daughter and her husband
After a night's sleep they'd missed
Selflessly giving their love and care
Their children, are cuddled and kissed

The going will be difficult they know
For them all on life's way
Yet full of hope for their future
I can proudly say

I'm just one voice, crying in the dark
That's why my words are written here
I never knew about autism
Until it came to the child we hold so dear.

Lavinia Bousfield

EUBANK'S TEARS

He enters the ring in trademark style
vaulting effortlessly over the ropes,
then adopting his unique almost comedic pose
as the MC announces each fighter in turn.
Carl Thompson first, his opponent tonight,
rugged, strapping, the essence of a warrior -
and then it is Eubank's resumé
as the compère relates a brief history
of this champion fighter.

But tonight is different because
tonight, on my DVD box-set, as I watch
for the first time ever I see
something different in Eubank's eyes:
it is not fear, that is impossible,
yes, as I strain to see, what I see is . . .
no surely it cannot be?
Yes - it is tears;
which eventually roll down his cheeks
without a punch being thrown,
floored by nostalgia,
as he knows the end of a great career
must soon be nigh.

He has endured so much,
always emerging *apparently* unscathed.
One opponent, in a wheelchair, ruined for life,
another man, a motorway worker,
hit and killed by Chris Eubank's car, (with Chris at the wheel),
yet still in the midst of all the disasters
I never saw a single tear -
but tonight, as if suddenly everything sinks in
this is a man's life, and these are a warrior's tears.

And I am the same:
put me in my corner, against the ropes,
read out the titles of many poems over thirty years
then watch the tears trickling down;
for my poems were always my boxing gloves
which I used against the brutality of Fate.
That poem is an elegy for my first greyhound,
the other one describes the grief of my divorce
and love for the lady who was my wife.

That one celebrates my love of running
for miles and miles and yet
I am a cripple now.
Those reflect a happy time before
the tragic and untimely death of
the woman I lived for - my mother.
Oh yes, that one you quote
recalls the glory days of a different lifestyle
to now, these gloom-laden times.

So, put me in the ring with Eubank
and give us both a clear-speaking MC.
Put the microphone in his trembling hands
and then watch the tears flow
as nostalgia and emotion strike home,
for we are both at the end of golden eras,
Chris and me: and yet
we were both pummelled by destiny.

The referee calls us into the centre of the ring,
we touch gloves and embrace as brothers-in-arms,
sharing a deep mutual sadness
that only the cruelty of Time can provide.
We were tough, we were warriors,
and we both went out on our shields.
But we were never invincible
and so Fate's blows could not always be slipped.

I watch him now on the TV screen,
I am taken aback by Eubank's tears
but sometimes the warrior and the poet
are the most emotional of all:
they carry their lives with them, and just one voice
can make the tears begin to fall.

Tyrone Dalby

TREASURES

Up in the attic one spring-cleaning day
I found an old sea chest hidden away.
What could be in there - money or gold?
I hurried to open it - what would it hold?

The old lid opened with a squeak and a groan,
It had a presence all of its own.
And what did I find when I peered inside?
Books and love letters all carefully tied.

I sat down to study them and was there to stay
Spring cleaning forgotten for the rest of the day.
Programmes and menus from years long ago
With names and prices I did not know.

Faded snapshots all yellowed with age
And newspaper cuttings with dates on each page,
Out-of-date fashions and reports from a war,
Lying there now on the attic floor.

A packet of letters from over the sea
'Passed by the censor' seemed so sad to me.
They all added up to a life long past,
With a doll, a necklace, a fan and a glass.

And right at the bottom, wrapped up in a sheet
I found a white wedding dress with veil complete.
Who had it belonged to, when did she depart?
Another Miss Haversham with a broken heart?

Underneath was a telegram, a sailor's last trip
It said the good captain had gone down with his ship.

Carefully then, I put all of them back
Into the sea chest each item, each pack.
Then I closed the lid on them tenderly
Back to their memories and mystery.

Pauline Anderson

PURE SPIRIT

A gentle drop of the purist spirit
Pushes boundaries and opens minds.
Quench when burdens feel heavy,
They can be lifted without fear.
When the media fails to nourish,
Honesty replenishes lost souls
Who only cry for love.

John Beals

REVELATION

When I first looked, I could not see,
Second glance, it took to awaken me,
And slowly like, the breaking dawn,
Crystal dew, birds' early morning song,
A touch so gentle, so sweet and new,
I stopped and waited still for you.

Trayce Hamilton

WAITING

In the valley where I wait for you,
Fresh cowslips all around,
Buzzards hover, high above,
Hungrily in the azure sky.
Golden silence,
Save for the murmuring breeze
Gently caressing my cheek.
Impatiently I pace, quietly
Waiting for you.
Before I left, so weary,
Now my spirit, jovial in such a way
I can't explain.
Life is different.
So much to see, digest and enjoy.
Everything I need - yet nothing - here
Waiting for you!

T G Bloodworth

THE AGONY AND THE ECSTASY

Love hurts
Love drives you insane
Love wounds
Love causes so much pain

Love beckons
Love holds you entranced
Love gives
Love is a joyous dance

Love hurts
Love binds you in chains
Love wounds
Love waxes and wanes

Love beckons
Love is a poetic rhyme
Love gives
Love promises for all time

Love hurts
Love cuts like a knife
Love wounds
Love scars you for life

Love beckons
Love is honest, trustworthy and kind
Love gives
Love, the thought, ever present in mind

Love hurts
Love weighs heavy on your soul
Love wounds
Love, endured, will take its toll

Love beckons
Love is silk, satin and lace
Love gives
Love is the smile that lights up a face

Love hurts
Love will tear you apart
Love wounds
Love will always break your heart

Love beckons
Love is whimsical, romantic, sublime
Love gives
Love is a mountain that's easy to climb

Love hurts
Love is a letter torn and burned
Love wounds
Love is a woman, rejected and spurned

Love beckons
Love is a red rose you'll always keep
Love gives
Love, an ocean, unfathomably deep

Love hurts
Love seeks a way to run and escape
Love wounds
Love is a girl to abuse and rape

Love beckons
Love is sensual, secret, divine
Love gives
Love is the rich fruit of the vine

Love hurts
Love leaves you alone in the gloom
Love wounds
Love will lead you to your doom

Love beckons
Love is a dream, dreamt every night
Love gives
Love is a feeling everything's right

Love hurts
Love torments till you die
Love wounds
Love will always say goodbye.

Carrieann Hammond

HAPPINESS IS . . .

Knowing that I'm loved
Freely giving hugs
Fulfilling someone else's wishes
Seeing someone else's joy
A shared hug just as I awake
Forgiveness of my past mistakes
The smell of cooking upon entering my home
The knowledge that I'm not alone
A refreshing shower with a new bar of soap
Melting ice cream on a hot summer's day
And playing cards for 2s and 1s
When skies are dull and grey
Holding my babies all snug in my arms
Their tiny hands within my palms
Freshly washed pyjamas and my soft comfy bed
A glass of Southern Comfort as it goes straight to my head
The trust within my family team
The trickle of water through my toes in the stream
Entwined with my lover through the passion we share
And all our emotions laid honest and bare
The relief and emotion as my tears are shed
Expressing the words that need to be said
To be meet with comforting arms instead
Of the reaction I had expected with dread
Feelings of elation that blossom and bloom
Singing along to my favourite tune
Sung with my sister when I was a kid
Crowing like a cockerel and dancing like a squid
Awaited letters that arrived in the post
Overwhelmed with joy, words stuck in my throat
Passing my exams, doing well in my job
And sucking the butter off of corn on the cob
Gatherings with family and parties with friends
Fridays when finally the week comes to an end
My lie-in on Sundays and my kids getting on
And remembering the moment they first uttered 'Mom'
Licking the lid of a full yoghurt pot
Knowing there's more to come

Entering a spotless room
All my hard work done
Good news as it bursts from the end of the phone
And riding through puddles on my bike coming home
Sledging down slopes with my face all aglow
Hot chocolate in winter looking out at the snow

Running in summer through cool and pouring rain
Munching on chocolate when feelings are frayed
Dancing in my underwear, splashing in the sea
Sitting on the toilet when I've been bursting for a pee
Hot chips in the paper all squashed and piping hot
Sparkling lights on our Christmas tree
With a fairy on the top
Adventuring to different places
Making cakes in little cases
Smell them cooking
Keep on looking
As they Change to fluffy muffins
Bouncing on our trampoline
Reaching up so high
And sitting by an open fire
Looking up at the sky
Sorting through old photographs
Of happy times we've had
I know there will be many more
This really makes me glad
Happiness is the day before tomorrow
And the day after today
The things that make me thankful
That there is always another day . . .
For happiness.

Sophie Mason

FLINT COTTAGE

Flint Cottage with rooms of memory for me,
The days of childhood, adolescence and maybe,
My 'featherbed grandma' so loving and caring,
What little she had was always for sharing.

Photographs arranged and filling the front room table,
Looking at them, guess what? We were able
To know which aunts and uncles were coming to call
For their photos were put at the front to see from the hall,
The picture of Grandad in First World War uniform,
Looking gaunt and proud in fur coat, well trench-worn,
It took pride of place on the sitting room wall,
A fine figure of a man over six feet tall.

The fireplace where chestnuts were set to go pop!
As out from the fire they shot - 'Don't touch, too hot!'
Visiting grandchildren vying to please and placate
As the table legs and cupboard door they tried to negotiate,
Crawling under the table, if I was the winner
Ten pennies in the gas meter for cooking the Sunday dinner.

Grandma whitening the stone step every day,
Inside the cottage, I really must say,
It leads down into the back room from the hall,
The living room with a view of the north wall,
The room where on a Sunday afternoon, with a jug of shandy,
A basin of winkles on the table, a pin each - that was handy!

Newmarket at tuppence half-penny a time in the kitty
Would I win this time? Oh! What a pity!
Grandad sitting in his chair like a lord,
With matchsticks ready by the crib board,
I tried but never understood the game,
But liked to hear him say, 'And one for his nob!' just the same.

The stone copper in the corner of the scullery,
The memory brings wonderful odours to me,
Of washing and Monday dinnertime stew
And suet pudding with lots of syrup too.

The outside lavatory with wooden seat scrubbed white,
I never used to venture out there late at night,
One of my uncles had written 'The Ritz' on the door,
If the Ritz smelt like that, I was glad I was poor.

Sitting in the front bedroom where I was born,
Watching Grandad in bed and feeling very forlorn,
For he was dying and had been ill for a year,
What was dying? Was it something to fear?
Caught him looking at me with eyes sunken in pain,
Oh, Grandad! I wish I had our time again,
I was only fourteen when you passed away,
I wish we had really known one another to say
All the unspoken thoughts we innermost feel,
But cannot communicate or bare and reveal.

Grandma taken ill after Grandad had died,
Sleeping with her, feeling comfortable by her side,
The feather mattress she pummelled every day,
She would not let anyone else do it - that was her way.
The little Dutch girl ornament dressed in orange and white,
She swayed from side to side - 'Touch her gently, she's very light!'
She sat on the bedroom mantelshelf, gazing coyly at the bed,
Now I remember, she also moved her head,
Brass bedstead with one knob turning around,
Who knows if it came off what might be found?

Three sons and sons-in-law, boyfriends always welcome,
Six daughters, daughters-in-law, girlfriends always made 'at home',
Nineteen grandchildren, all loved in every way
A card received by everyone on their birthday,
Peacetime, wartime, peacetime again,
All the different uniforms proudly worn by the men,
One son missing - all gathering there,
Good news telegram arrived - no more tears to spare.

Grandma died a number of years ago,
But, dearest Grandma, I'm glad I was born to your 'Flo'
And whenever I pass that Flint Cottage door,
I'm proud to say, 'I was born at 204!'

Sylvia Olliver

THE TEARS OF A POET

The tears of a poet mean nothing,
It goes with the mindset, you see.
The tears of a poet mean nothing,
They weep just like sap from a tree.
The tears of a poet mean nothing,
Just let them fall,
For the tears of poets mean all things,
For the poets weep for all.

Peter J Morey

62 NOT OUT

Another golden year has past us sped,
Increasing yet again our mounting run.
A stunning sixty-two since we were wed
And on that lucky day became as one.

Though I see promise of yet more years,
Yet is my bliss shot through with secret tears,
Since, with the bard, I cannot choose
But weep to have that which I fear to lose.

G F Pash

TREES

Yesterday I saw the Earth
and it was naked.
Rolling beneath dead green grass,
it screamed and barked like a dog.
'Where are my blooming trees?'
Today, I saw the trees.
A man was reading one,
then he threw it away.

Alvin Culzac

THE 1940S

Two fireside chairs beside the hearth -
That used to be 'the norm'.
The house would not be heated
So you sat there to keep warm . . .

Father read the paper -
Or, perhaps, would write to friends.
Mother might be crocheting
Or mending odds and ends.

There was no television
To bring us worldly news
So we never knew of problems;
Never suffered from 'the blues'.

I used to watch the skylark
Soaring in the blue
Above a field of rippling corn
With thistles poking through.

I climbed up trees; held birds' eggs
And plucked strawberries growing wild
Spent leisure hours 'doing my own thing'
(My wish for every child!)

'Pretty simple living' was our philosophy
How could we know in fifty years
How different life would be?
How 'aspiration' then would shape Man's ingenuity
For he is on a constant search for new technology
To speed things up, to keep things 'green'
'Sustainability'!

All we hear is 'globalisation'
And less 'footprints' in the sky
With touch phones and the worldwide web
I sit and wonder why
We need to travel anywhere?
(And since 'sitting' seems the trend
We could all lead a 'virtual' life -
Just sit back and press a knob
And see a 'virtual' friend!)

Edna Sparkes

DAY - DAY

Net trawling faint light shimmer,
Auditioning still life's calm,
Calibrating shades, arcs and angles,
Half lighting glooms day room - again,
Clay vessels - stirred and still,
Old, impaired, pained.
Street humming reveille
Addressing half-bright,
Days unrelenting want.
Measured strain,
Distract night's dark contemplation,
Of deed - aftermath - pearl sadness.
New light ridding minds unholy discretion
Thoughts of relief and departure,
Forbidden like first fruit,
So pain, still pain . . .
Abide aqua vitae abide
Vessel of abundant medication - still
And timely still - soak he the reverie
Of gold days, sustain once more
Mind image of love limbs imperative touch,
Stay - memories joy
Before a sorrow sip
And memory pile release,
We vessels of purpose of need
As needs must, oh! Aqua magic I sup.
For tone and temper set for
Frail hands uncharted obligations
Driven with callous course concern
This shuffler, faith befriended
You shadow draping our module of propensity
Propels our day with sentiment in ambitious wake
But, no wake yet! My chaperon of sickness
Let you fulfil your sacerdotal pledge
You, full of the logic of life's measure
Living for me, another day.
You allow me to recede
Extract the last visage of
High sun days and star-filled skies
Then like autumn leaves
We scatter them to the wind
In fool's play, touching love's limits
Unscathed in lust's blaze.
Quarantined to life's malady of restricted bliss

Oh! Go leave me your anointed bread,
Leave me your memory, your ghost
Let me consort with my nostrum need,
To accompany me in illusion's cot,
And soften world's pained day.
Tally to my silent wish - please
In tattered dress, scuttle
To what you can kindle, but me
I douse my flickering life
In the barley brew,
Let me pay homage to its deeds
A false want, when all want is gone,
Aqua vitae again, yes again, yet spare me
Chilling unwarranted images of callous acts,
Torpid cringing misdeeds.
Ignorance on a pedestal with pride,
Youth spent as youth can, always
Without fear of reprisal, blind indifference
To the harshest penance wild youth can pay
Knowledge, maturing intellect and sense.
Nonsense craves a despairing antidote
A senseless anesthetization
A selective memory loss.
Total amnesty from pain
Must my soul bear the burden of decaying flesh
As it fought its wanton needs for so long.
Is it the temple of the Lord?
Is it the cross of the soul?
Is faith one long death rattle?
Aqua vitae, take me to your place.

Eddie Byrne

SILENCE TRUE

Silence, no stories to write, only silent mediation.
Yet words come unbidden, stories being silent,
All are placed in boxes within the mind.
This one has a beautiful flower on it so that Elizabeth can
remember where it is when she is not in silence

In silence all is known, all is heard, senses are heightened
As a bee flies by, no eye movement, no reaction and yet!
Deep within the mind the sound of wings
A humming voice saying,
A lovely day for making honey

All is logged silently away
For the humming of a bee carries many tales
Of beautiful flowers open to receive
Humming placed in a box with a bee on it

Here another sound assails the still mind
Of birds in song, greeting another day
Wake up, it is a glorious day to be alive

All is logged silently away
For the song of a bird carries tales,
Of lofty heights, open and clear sight.
Songs placed in a box with birds on it

Oh yet another box with boys' voices
Of innocent speech
This has a sweet perfume of laughter
Of the heart giggling in a lost moment of silence

Two young men stand by seeing her serene demeans

Foot lifted and placed in silent grace
One before the other in hypnotic pace.
They do discuss
I will be the one to find her grace
No, I will fill that place

For Elizabeth is a child at heart
Years have passed away in silent contemplation

All is logged silently away
For the chattering of youth carries much
Of a compliment passed in innocence
This box has a smile upon it
Bringing lots of smiles to a child at heart

A butterfly lands upon upheld hands
The mind ceases the moment
What a story to tell
In that seizure a spell is woven

Only to be stilled
Placed in a box with a butterfly on it
Telling of life's unfold meant in still moments
Nature from her chrysalis reborn

So many boxes of unbidden words
Tales yet to be told

The lid of silence enfolding each moment
Now; the mind knows it knows
Discipline is to stay strong and true
Silent of senses
Non-attachment in all

Santosha of silence in all its perfume
All the sights, all the words one needs
All else superfluous
I am silence

Stilled and silent in sweet repose
The mind knows it knows
No fetters of nature here
Neither bonds of life
Nay, to grow in silence
Let spirit soar the sky's unfathomable heights
Or delve deep in nature's store
To be that central core
Where all words will attest to my fate.

Elizabeth M Procter

GROWING UP

A miracle is made even before you are born,
When two tiny seeds join together as one,
For nine months you grow in your mother's womb,
Then born into this world, you'll find out soon,
Whether you laugh or cry, you'll always know,
Mum and Dad are there to help you as you grow.
To answer your questions and help you understand,
They are always around to lend a helping hand,
Even when they shout when you've been bad,
I know it upsets you and makes you sad,
But they mean well in everything they do,
Deep in their hearts they really love you.
As you grow, you learn something new every day,
So to my mum and dad I just wanted to say,
Thanks for all your love and understanding too,
And with all my heart, I really do love you.

Leah Vernon

HERO

Regular guy, shirt and tie
A good man, risked his life
Wears his heart on his sleeve
He's a damsel's relief

Weighs his dignity on his shoulders
While the world tumbles like boulders
Puts others first
Because he believes in trust

There's just one moment, one way
One man, one day
One life, one heart to give
Or throw it away

He'll be your eyes and your ears
Your heart and your tears
The man who stands
Amidst your fears
A hero.

David Adamson

A NEW DAWN BREAKS

That distant sun,
That rises to the heavens and shadows cast,
New days born, as all flowers bloom in life,
With April showers, of fresh waters given,
For those good, from bad days, in that of all life,
Kiss'd of freshness, on naked skin,
With fresh water, springs and dells,
Where spring flowers bloom and birds sing,
This being the beginning of spring, into summer
And desires of life, we sometimes crave,
In our thoughts and hopes,
Not storms to blight our lives,
As summer comes along, for a new dawn to break
As we start anew,
Of that in life's tangled web of life's ways
And troubled days.

As the sun rises, so we do and go our way
Into the distance and a new day.

Arthur May

I WAS THAT FLY

I was that fly that you harassed all day
When you did your best to drive me away!
You would reach for your newspaper to give me a swipe
And wherever I landed, you exploded with gripe
Yes, for something so trivial you would try to hit me!
After all, I'm not eating a lot when I'm sharing your tea
You ignore my arch fluttering of gossamer wings
A flirtatious offering of such lovable things!
You keep driving me away whenever I land
Don't you think this is getting a bit out of hand?
You could feed me and pamper me, it wouldn't cost much
We would be together and never get out of touch
So if you would reconsider, I'm sure we could try
To be happy companions as human and fly.

Royston E Herbert

KEN'S MARRIAGE
(An acquaintance of my husband)

Hey ding-a-ding-ding,
Doreen's got a ring,
She's married to Ken,
They married at ten.

They quickly dashed home,
No more did she roam;
She fell asleep,
With love he did weep.

She woke up at three,
Said, 'Where can he be?'
He came home at five
And said, 'Snakes alive.'

Hey rat-a-tat-tat,
Who's that on the mat?
Someone's jitterbugging
In my brand new ring.

'Where's my meal?
My hunger is real.'
'There's food on the shelf,
I don't eat, myself.'

'Well cook it, dear wife,
Let's have no more strife.'
Two fried eggs on toast,
Of that she could boast.

Ken slammed down his knife -
My God, what a wife.
But no more she spoke,
Just put on her coat

Roared off in the car
At 70 per hour.
Ken's neighbour appeared,
Disaster he feared.

Next day she returned
And from her Ken learned
That she would win him
With a bottle of gin.

And as she sat there
And plaited her hair,
Pouring out more gin,
Pep pills she slipped in.

'You just doze and tire,
Wife, come light the fire.'
So she got the chopper
And Ken, he did mock her.

He said, 'That's no good,
You've got no more wood.'
At him she did stare
And chopped up a chair.

Ken could stand no more
And he slammed the door.
Then in another room
She came with a broom

Whilst in the kitchen,
Where he was sitting.
Chased him round and round
Till he hit the ground.

How he did regret
The day that they met,
Over weak brown tea
She sat on his knee.

Now ride a cock-horse,
Ken's got a divorce -
Hey ding-a-ding-ding,
Doreen's pawned the ring.

Gladys Burgess

THE PRICE OF COAL
(In loving memory of a dear dad, Robert Fenwick, killed 1969. RIP)

Coal, the cold, black stuff, a coalminer gold
Little does he realise the heartache of many stories untold
How sweet would their lives be for clean working conditions
For nice soap and water, before lunch, what a sweet notion
Instead, gritty bait times, plagued with a few rodents
That's a miner's everyday lunchtime, how would you contend
Through the course of the day?
They have to do what comes naturally
There is no bathroom, to answer nature's call, like you and me
But at the end of each shift, a nice clean shower to cleanse and to clean
Only true miners can face this, ordinary men would demean
Only this strong workforce, if upset by any source of discrimination
Are ready to lay down tools, to help brothers across the nation
Miners and their sons, working by dim torch battery
They have to put up with what ordinary men would call insultery
And spare a thought for many a miner's family,
Left all alone through no fault of theirs
'Cept for a man trying to get an honest day's work done
Can you honestly, hand on your heart, truly say
That you could crawl through dirt, mud and water, day after day
To reach coal production, keep managers' pockets lined
As they sit in nice clean offices, no reason to whinge and whine?
They don't have to scrub away each day, coal dust deeply embedded
Or to wait for that early hour knock, the day you've feared and dreaded
It only happens to others, you never really believe
The knock will come to your door
But yes, my Lord, it often does, like so many times before
The employers and their gaffers, they have the easy part
Never to see the long, hard journey through the aftermath
Come now, my gents, you can easily wash your hands clean
It's harder for the ones left behind, you know what I mean
Just pay up what you think he's worth, just another coalminer
Pass the buck to someone else, no one else can do it finer
But that's alright, ne'er forget, there will be Judgement Day
And never fear, the silent few will be there, just to have their say
And all the things you should have done and meant to, but didn't
I only want to hear you say, how and why, and relish in it
I'm speaking for all the abandoned sons and daughters, especially their wives
To speak out loud and boldly for the men who gave their lives
I've seen how you take care of those so innocently left behind
These unfortunate, unlucky, lacking only in hindsight
Widows and the fatherless, we can never truly repay you

For all the kindness and support you showed us, for some days few
Soon forgotten, like many gone before us, but we will never forget
The poor widow's suffering continues as she struggles to pay the rent
And not forgetting the causes of suffering, the price of coal
She'll be alright when she's sixty, was it really worth it, to reach his goal?
It's been more than twenty years since I kissed my dad goodnight
Do the men of this country truly understand the story of my plight?
Every time I see a smoking chimney, hear the raking through the fire
The only thing I yearn for, unseen grandson's true desire
A widow's days are closing now, her calling is drawing near
To be joined again with her beloved, she goes with no fear
And be embraced in her husband's arms is all she ever needed
To be guided, and protected, if only the managers ever heeded
She'll soon be safe now, soon out of harm's way
No more worrying how to get by, just for another day
Where are all your promises now? Empty words, you said it
You really took good care of us, did you think of us for just one minute?
Did you ever once, after our long bereavement
Call to see how we were or see that our needs
Were even half-way catered for?
Nor did you see that, through the lonely years, the damage done long ago
It wouldn't have taken much to see her into a safe, cosy abode
To those of you sitting reading this, on your conscience now pray
Remember two coalminers killed on Durham Big Meeting Day
It really is ironic, to be taken on this Miners' regatta
It's too late for us now, but not for your working, even on rota
To see far enough into the empty years ahead and don't do the same
Make sure everyone remembers the price of coal, remember their names.

Shirley Atkinson

LIFE'S ENDLESS GAME
(For all those young people who have just fallen in love)

When life has played its endless game,
Will I still love you just the same?
When your face is wrinkled and your hair is grey,
Will I still love you as I do today?
If life's good fortune has passed us by,
Will I still look you in the eye?
Of course I will,
I'll love you till,
The day I die,
That is life's endless game.

Kenneth Jackson

SECOND HOME

An escape from the rat race
Life lived at a slower pace
An idyllic setting they won't be letting
The cottage slumbers
Like the electricity meter numbers
It's early March
The house is dark
They're in Marylebone
Or in Rome
It's a second home

It's a mothballed shell, residential hell
It's a funeral bell, a death knell
For the low-paid locals whose response was vocal
(In the White Rose, before it closed)
But unrecordable
It wasn't affordable
It's an empty place, a waste of space
It hasn't got a phone
It's a second home

People recall that within the walls
Of this second pad lived a mum and dad
With their family, on the settee
They watched Morecambe and Wise, and ate pork pies
In the blue TV light on a Saturday night
And life was pleasant in Woodland crescent
Opening presents, chasing pheasants . . .
But the parents are gone and the kids have grown
Mustn't moan
It's a second home

In the shop the assistant mops a spillage
Cycles to a less fashionable village
And she saved for . . . how long was it?
To get a deposit on a studio flat where you can't swing a cat
And she silently groans and takes out loans
Despite her persistence, she's just living an existence
She says, 'Why me?'

And wishes she
Could spend the days
Where she was raised
Life is tough. Isn't one place enough?
She wishes she could own
That second home

If they want a holiday by the sea
Why don't they try a B & B?
And don't try to build low cost housing
Cos you'll be arousing
The anger of every second home owner
Who'll fly in from Barcelona, or Girona or bloody Pamplona
To claim they represent the residents
A majority of decadents
Don't want to set a precedent
They want a postcard picture
A chocolate-box fixture
In water-colour paint
Want to keep it quaint
Maintain its reputation
Don't worry about inflation
Or minimum wage degradation
Sod the working population
Mustn't lower the tone . . .
It's a second home.

Rob Barratt

TO POETRY

Poetry, thou insidious muse!
You lead me to think I can choose
As mesmerised with pen in hand
I enter a magical mystery land,
As ideas and thoughts enter my head,
Then onto paper and hopefully read,
My desire for my listeners' comments is also there,
Their honest opinion I wish to share,
I want to write of many things,
Ships, sealing wax, cabbages and kings,
Narrative, free verse, limericks too,
Like Wordsworth on his bridge gazing at the view,
Flow on bright muse, while I end my song,
My journey is a river that goes on and on.

Anne Furley

BABY AND THE TWO-HEADED SNAKE

Not so long ago, in a place quite near
A fiery young buck strolled into here
You could tell he was keen for a beer and a fight or two.

He spouted off that he was brave as hell
He was talking hooey, I could easily tell
So I thought I'd go and spin a yarn from the old bayou.

See, in a barely-there dress and cocoa eyes
With a big old snake wrapped from head to thigh
There dances the finest young thing you could care to see.

And along the river, baby does her dance
On the hunt for fools who would take a chance,
But I'm telling ya boy, you best done let her be.

See, the two-headed snake, so long and green
Belongs to her Mama, the Voodoo Queen
And even she can't watch her baby twenty-four-seven.

So the snake, it does all the watching for her
With four burning eyes, it protects her daughter
And sends all unworthy suitors with a bite to Heaven.

In my face, the kid laughed and he slapped his knee
Now, this was a sight he just had to see
And he told me to take him down to that God-forsook place.

In the swamp we waited for at least an hour
When through the reeds danced that lovely flower
I could tell the boy had fallen from the look on his face.

But he shook his head and he made a shrug
'She ain't no great shakes,' said the big, dumb lug
'I've seen prettier faces hanging out of a cattle truck!'

At the boy the snake glared with dark intention
The reptile could speak, I forgot to mention
And with a hiss, it dared the young fool to come try his luck.

The boy made a yawn and declined the offer
'This Plain Jane girl's hardly worth the bother'
He couldn't take her home, for fear she might scare the dog.

At this insult, the snake leapt to the ground
Its eyes growing red, for the boy it was bound
It failed to notice the kid make a reach for a log.

With a swing to one head, the snake made a shriek
And a bash to the other, it could no longer speak
For the creature lay dead and no longer around the girl's neck.

And the boy took the girl in his eager arms
And confessed he had fallen for her obvious charms
All his sass was a trick the proud snake had failed to detect.

With no further ado, the kid got on one knee
And he asked, 'Baby girl, would you marry me?'
And the girl looked in my direction before she would speak.

For you see, girls and gents, Mama's word was law
And I'm the Voodoo Queen, case you weren't too sure
And that uptight snake helped me sort the chaff from the wheat.

If they came towards my baby, all meek and quiet
They soon became part of that big ol' snake's diet
They stank of weakness and that just wouldn't do.

But this one stood tall and he knew his worth
And that's why the snake's going to the earth
My precious baby girl, I knew the boy belonged to.

Within a month and a day, the lovebirds were wed
Never a happier pair, so it's often said
And to that big ol' two-headed snake, I gotta give my dues

'Cause my feet were tired from all of that leading
Young men to the bayou, my soles were bleeding
But they ain't no more, with my fine, new snakehead shoes!

Rachel Connor

EXTREME

I was near to despair,
So slumped on a chair.
Then came the post - I rail -
Surely not more of that so-called junk mail?

No! I see 'Forward Press' - my attention caught -
How great the turn-around from feeling fraught!
More than a million poets inspired -
And their penning by top-names acquired!
Publish - for the meanings of words will always hold sway
Over vicissitudes ever and show you the way.

Beryl Mapperley

JUST ANOTHER DAY

Each day as I gaze at my reflection
I see changes I cannot control
This thankless land is full of chaos
Am I to be a forgotten soul?

Within the twists and turns on this path of life
The hands of time continue to turn
Slowly when we are but a child
Increasing in speed as we age and learn

Stress sails on a fast-moving breeze
Everything changes with uncomfortable ease
It catches me out when I am unaware
Advancing the years with never a care

I wait with impatience for a new chapter to start
Some trepidation and sadness of heart
I age and I tire, I sleep and I cry
For the days of fulfillment now passing me by

Silence is deafening and peace is not all it seems
A house filled with laughter is now only in my dreams
I'm sure it was only yesterday that I felt young
Yet I woke up this morning with a creak and a groan

Seeds of youth fester inside a troubled mind
They say experience fruitfully gained
Will make a person wise
Are there volumes of knowledge behind my aged eyes?

I face traumas alone, no one stands at my side
There is nowhere to run, no hole in which to hide
Flowers in bloom soothe this sobbing pain
Love the coolness of water as I stand in the rain

This time on Earth a struggle in vain
In death will there be peace again?
We all see change as we grow and age
Close the lonely chapter and turn the page

Help remove the misery that has been my shroud
Be thankful for life and shout out loud
I will welcome the dawn and embrace each day
This is no rehearsal but a means to pave the way

We all live to prove that we are worth
The effort God made to put us on this Earth
In the blink of an eye my body changed
Illness reared its ugly head, life was rearranged

Rain washes away all my tiredness
Wind blows the sorrow from my mind
In all I must be truthful
This life, my life, has been kind

For there lies within the churchyards
Deep down in the ground
Many of our relatives
Who wish that they were still around

Each would welcome a headache
Give thanks for pain
Lying underneath the soil
Every day must be the same

I urge you to tread with care
Every bump in the road
This time on Earth is short
The ending is untold

Do not sit in shame, rise up and smile
Give thanks for every breath
For you never can be certain
How many days are left.

Lynn Noone

IN PASSING

Please come home, temporarily or just for a decade or two?
Don't leave this house through a broken window.
Relive what you once knew
And feel yourself respire into tomorrow.

I feel that warmth slip through the hatches,
Passing through rooms of anxiety.
I'm not afraid, only stopping momentarily to see
what only I can see.
God's beauty, in the patience of love and creation -
Deliverance is not cruel or jealous.

Melissa Brabanski

LITTLE OL' MISS FORTUNE

Little ol' miss fortune
Has been banging on my door
Don't want to be in
But she'll come back, I'm sure
Don't deliberate
Over nowt
It will create
Even more doubt
For what you see
Is a crash in progress
And you an' me
Everyone's a victim, I guess
Seen her twisted face
But never looked her in the eye
For it's a deep, dark place
Where taunted souls cry
She gathers in waifs an' strays
With promises of glory
All these are dark days
Little ol' miss fortune's only story
She's got your full name
And looking for you
Wants you to play her game
Break an' beat you black an' blue
At the heart of the eye
Is greed an' a few true needs
And every heavy sigh
Is little ol' miss fortune's seeds
Watered by tears you cry
From your broken hope she feeds
No sun, just dark skies
Destitution all she breeds
Her nakedness is raw
She has no hidden beauty
At your motivation she'll claw
To destroy, her duty
There's nothing that can prepare
For the things you'll come to know
Don't be afraid, but aware
When sinking it doesn't matter how fast you row
Crushed finer than velvet
Brushed away like litter
Got a shoal of regret
Swimming in seas that are bitter

No one counts on you
Only the so-called faults
They stick like glue
Closer than any waltz
Ain't saying I've never been grateful
And that I've never been humble
People though, ain't so faithful
When you start to stumble
Hear the echo of the past
Of where the way was lost
It won't be the last
Never is when counting the cost
Stuck with it, so just get on
There's nothing to stop the rot
Keep telling yourself nothing's wrong
All the way to the grave from the cot.

Mark Tough

ONE LITTLE SECOND

Although it may have only been one little second,
as I lay there beside you
looking into your eyes,
I was aware of every segment of that second.
Because at that moment in time,
the clocks froze,
the universe stood still,
and all I could see was you.
And in that one little second,
I saw deep into your soul,
and I know what I saw was the very same thing I feel for you - incredible love.

But now I don't really know what to do with all these little seconds,
because for some reason,
that I just cannot quite comprehend,
I'm not spending them with you.
I would give anything to have one more little second with you.
And by God would I hold on to that second forever.

Coralee Harrison

ELECTION 2010

You get the government you ask for, it is said, to be said
How you vote, who you want, may not be, who ends up with you in bed
Do not let others in, is the telling tone
Vote for someone else, an acceptable tactic, argue those who advocate
Is it the case that people are encouraged to ignore principles, to cheat?
Are they afraid to lose? Facing dismay, defeat
There is no doubt it is tight, the outcome uncertain
With three main leaders speaking before the final curtain
Have you noticed Brown keeps on saying the same
That they have the answers, the other's to blame
'We are an honest, fairer party, trust us,' while the haemorrhage large, bleeds
There are those who argue early debt reduction is what the situation needs
Labour take the view, early, runs the risk of financial ruin, upon this public anxiety feeds
He proudly misrepresents, with dazzling grin, a feature characterised as that Gordon Brown smile
He has, to his credit, introduced child and family credit, and for many initiatives
Labour deserves the credit, he has said it . . . often
The TV debates were new, and focused minds thinking
All three leaders stood at a podium, Nick Clegg winking
Outscoring the rest, arms outstretched, inviting
The audience to join in and tango, exciting
Cast off the old, looking for something new?
Is Nick's engaging message selling?
His appearance impressing election polls, the shift was telling
The rank outsider enjoying the glamour, joining the race
Giving the Lib/Dems a fresh and recognisable face
The Conservative, Cameron, on TV seemed nervous at first
Telling us we're all in this together, immersed
Needing people to join up, sign contracts with the larger community
Positive thinking, that would mend a broken society
With balloons and coloured T-shirts the big activists cheered
Whilst a passage through the press and media had first been cleared
Open-necked shirt with jacket left behind, the Cameron relaxed style
He's a fit man, jogging at dawn with his companions in line, they file
Vote for change, we will roll up our sleeves, wipe away successful tears
No shortage of ideas and energy - the Tories say, as the way forward clears
Whatever, the future looks bleak with cuts, which no party is telling
'We want the truth,' demand impatient voters, not knowing
The parties delay being open until, that is, high taxes are flowing
The votes are in, a hung parliament, with Tories, no overall gain
The leaders shuffling new cards, involving a power-struggling game
Engrossed they are in talks of coalition

Hard to achieve, like a golfer's hole in one, a prize worth having
Liberals talk to Tories and also have secret contacts with Labour, is this horse-trading or faffing?
It's uttered that it's all in the national interest
TV and media wait with hearts beating, pulsating inside breasts
Press follow men in suits, walking from one building to another
Once caught sight of, they are pursued, pushed, with camera flash smothered
Making notes of statements made, which say very little, except it's time for lunch
But time is fast approaching the deciding moment, the crunch
Liberals join the Tories on the election train, but they go, gone, jumping off at the next station
Now it is Labour's turn to enter the dog fight and form a new creation
Brown at first stays on, in hope an administration will emerge by design
But as the talks break down, he decides to go, and therefore resign
With a farewell speech he says thank you and goodbye
Suddenly people only have good things to say
He, no doubt, wishing Mrs Duffy had not entered the fray
It seems as soon as the Brown family turn the corner of Downing
Cameron with large steps strides up the street
Buoyed by Liberal agreement expected to join forces, knowing Labour are beat
He has with Nick Clegg formed a government, and has been seen
Been to the palace for a chat and proclaimed Prime Minister by the Queen

Ron Constant

CONSCIENCE

C onstantly hounding and butting you out
O pens up your mouth to protest and shout
N udges you when you're unsure of the way
S teps in to stop you make the wrong ones pay
C an't let you switch the channel from the news
I tches your digits to stop painful mews
E ager to do good though it could be pained
N ever doubt it or hold with self-restraint
C old to the protest of your inner mind
E ventual reward of a warm kind.

Claire Rogers

A WINDY DAY

There once was a lad . . .
A rather obnoxious lad.
A rude lad,
A bad lad,
A not very nice lad . . .
Called
Jim.

It was Jim's birthday (he was turning 12)
And he was given a present . . .
A very special present . . .
A kite.
'A boring kite!'
No one else thought it was boring,
They were desperate to see it fly.
After all, it was a windy day.

'It's a wicked kite, can we fly it with you?'
'No.'
'We'll have some fun!'
'No.'
'It's such a perfect windy day!'
'No!'
So Jim went and flew his kite all alone.

At first the wind toyed with his kite,
Picking it up and throwing it down.
It fluttered and fell, fluttered and fell . . . until
A gust of wind took his kite and it soared
Oh how it soared.
Twisting and turning
Swooping and diving
And gliding,
His kite danced to the tune of the wind.
'Look at me!'
But there was no one to look
And a storm was brewing,
The winds were whipping up a delight.

The wind blew him this way
And the wind blew him that way
It buffeted
And it billowed
And it bowled him down the hill.
Then the wind snatched his kite and tossed it
Away across the hillside.
He called out to his friends . . .

'Did anyone see my kite?'
'No.'
'I'm sure it was blown this way?'
'No.'
'Will you help me find it?'
'Please!'

At last they came across it.
The wind had flung it in a tree
Battered and torn and badly worn
For all the world to see.
His kite was gone forever,
The kite he hadn't wanted.
Now caught high in the tree
And he wished that his friends
Could have been there to see
Him
With his kite
Flying free
'Look at me!'

Catrin Thomas

DOWN BY THE WATER

Weary, I hang my head.
This rose, short of petals,
Is limp in your hands like an aged doll.
I am past, I am ended,
I have been forsaken by fortune.

You are uninterested.
Regardless of my dissent,
You find yourself dragging me,
A screaming four-year-old.
You've lessons to teach.
I long to be away from the beach.

Down here, by the shells, in the dark,
He had his way with me.
In the long, hard sand,
I can hear him drowning out the sea.
And yet, here he stands, with age
Bringing his bones out to greet me.
What a strapping man, you say.
What a charming lad.
I retch into the waves.

You have abandoned me once,
Left me stranded in the ocean, and you do so again.
The breeze bites at me, turns my head around,
Begs me to give in to pathetic fallacy.
The waves slap me in the face,
They silence me.

He stands, taller than me, his eyes burn into me.
I can feel his incestuous gaze, his disgusting rage,
I stand. I cannot run anywhere, I have nowhere to go.
He takes steps towards me, grinding the sand with his feet,
Crushing the shells with his shoes.

I remember playing here as a child, briefly.
A flicker of recollection across my eyes,
Where he'd build a sandcastle with me.
Me, barely seven, him not a teen. Oh, how different
We know we are now. I can see him twitch.
He reaches for me, grasps for me, my wild heart
Kicks in.

I tear across the sand, bare feet beating down my memories,
The soaked hem of his dragging me.
He has speed, a night stalker, a predator,
He enjoys the hunt as much as his lust.

I am slow, docile. I cannot run forever.
I know I have nowhere to go; you are gone.
You called me a liar and in that you buried me,
Beneath the sand, beneath the word of your marquis.
He catches up to me.

I am thrown to the waves, my paper skin
Torn from my eggshell bones.
Down there, once again, in the sea,
He had his way with me.
Washed away by the waves,
He drowns his darkened memories,
His violation is my degenerative disease,
My breath is stolen by his decree.

I wash in on the waves.

Mother, mother, mother,
They're calling me home.
Mother, mother, mother,
They're calling me home.

Katey Russell

FATHER'S DAY

A father is who we call in times of need,
To have a game of cricket or football.
He is the one who sowed our seed.
When in trouble we know we can call
Someone we can talk to when in need,
To make better a cut after a fall.
His house is open to everyone of every creed,
We say thank you to them all.
Thank you Father, Dad and God
For being there when we are in need.

Carol Paxton

DONKEY

My mother died when I was born
Which left me feeling quite forlorn,
No one to relate to except the family dog
With whom I could converse or have a little jog.

A 'runt' is what they called me, I didn't have a name,
It was the poor old gardener who really got the blame,
For not being there to supervise when I first arrived,
And Hanna, as my mum was called just lay down and died.

This runty 'donk' must be replaced
By one whose presence truly graced
The orchard in which she would graze
And thus all passers-by amaze.

By market day I find myself tied up in a pen,
A label stuck upon my rump said I was number 10.
Men prodded and poked and looked at this and that,
'Don't think much of this one, not worth feeding to the cat.'

Lot number 10 had no reserve,
Which I thought was quite a nerve,
'Come along gentlemen, what am I bid?
Nice little present for anyone's kid.'

He started off at £50 and couldn't get a bite
Old chap in a raincoat indicated he was right
To have said I'd not be enough to feed the blinkin' cat!
As I only came to 30 quid and felt ashamed of that.

Up in a truck and off we go to a pikey camp I find
What little good I'd ever known, very far behind,
Tethered to a stump till caravans move on
Towed behind a trolley days later on.

A leggy lad leaps on my back, no point to argue now
By the end of the third day
I am resigned to what they say;
At night I drop my head and sleep
And hope I'm brought something to eat.

Once again we hit the road that makes my feet so sore
I'm running out of energy and don't care anymore
I think I've lost the will to live and would like to die
If I could just lay down and let the world go by.

But dying's not that easy without the good Lord's call
Then someone said, 'He needs you, read the notice on the wall'
For a donkey that is wanted for the church's Xmas play
Now I have to play just how to get away.

Wait until they're at the pub then chew my tether rope,
Play upon the vicar's sympathy is my only hope.
Yew trees line the twisty path, past tombstones nearly kept,
Intrepid and with pounding heart, up this track I crept.

To meet a lady taking hay,
To where the Baby Jesus lay,
She said I had been sent by God and must not go away,
And took a short cut to the vicarage with glad tidings of the day.

Who bought me I can only guess but I like my perfect peace
The field behind the churchyard is mine on permanent lease
The stony wall is shelter too, and I get well involved
With all the goings on in church where most problems are solved.

Herdis Churchill

WHAT IS A HUSBAND?

What is a husband? You may well ask
When in the mood, he'll tackle any task
He'll decorate a room, prepare for the worst
He doesn't believe in clearing it first
Will grumble at golfing if I lose a ball
When he's lost five - well, after all
He's not up to his usual standard today
He can't always expect to have his own way
He'll cook a meal that looks a treat
Always good enough to eat
He'll use many a pan and cup
Guess who's left to do the washing up?
He'll mow the lawn with quite good grace
But mustn't be left with plants or seed
He'll pull them up - 'Sorry, I thought it was a weed!'
When food is ready and on the table
Come, let's eat it while we are able
A voice is heard from afar
'Won't be a minute, I'm washing the car!'
After all, you can plainly see
He means all the world to me - of him I can no higher speak
I've written this poem with tongue in cheek.

Olive Willingale

THE CHAIRMAN OF THE BRANCH

Jack tweaked at his tie and let out a sigh,
Then checked that he had a spare pen.
He read his report, which he'd kept nice and short,
For tonight's local branch AGM.

He'd been voted the Chair, at the meeting last year
And been the sole choice at the time.
Since then he'd turned grey, keeping problems at bay
And all of the members in line.

There was Margaret Rose, who would always oppose
New proposals and old ones as well.
And Gordon Dunbar, asleep at the bar,
Until Jack with his fist banged the bell.

And the Lady McNeill, with her dog at her heel,
Whose voice could pierce walls ten food wide.
And farmer Jim Knight, who could go on all night,
About grants and the land 'set-aside'.

And of course, there was Nora, you couldn't ignore her,
Through whom all the gossip was fed.
Each day at her store, selling foodstuffs and more,
She memorised all that was said.

There was straight-talking Horace, who'd bring his wife, Doris
And talk about life in the war.
For him, life stopped still, at the last rifle drill,
He was still trying to settle the score!

I've left out a few, no doubt some you knew
And each one could make their views clear.
They could be quite irate, in a heated debate,
Always careful to talk via the Chair!

There was a butcher, a sailor, a prosperous tailor,
A lawyer, a junior clerk.
A soldier, a teacher, a Methodist preacher,
The attendant who helps you to park.

Not forgetting the plumber, the postman, the drummer,
The comedian, who helps us to smile.
The painter, the writer, the retired prize-fighter;
The list could extend for a mile.

How motley a group, a colourful troop,
Their backgrounds, so varied, of course.
When they meet all together, are they birds of a feather,
United by one common force?

You may think, poor old Jack! What a problem to hack!
He'll be in for some flack from the floor.
But complain though they may, they'll want him to stay;
They themselves won't step in, that's for sure!

David Anderson

UNTITLED

Turning from you, losing all sense of self
a heart filled with hate, all hope gone
your hand holding mine, I try to pull away
inseparable,
touch
gentleness
light on shadow
brokenness
weeping
through torment - the hell of hate
a space . . .
turning to you I see the light
I feel the love
I breathe you in . . .
hope
love
life
your gift
your delight!

I left you in my sleep.

Jacqueline McLaughlin

YOU ARE NOT ALONE

Monday morning rears its ugly head
Suits and briefcases litter the station
Smiles and yawns, a feeling of dread.

Mechanically driven into the town
The business land circus
Umbrellas and clowns
But then
I see you sitting there
Sitting in someone else's ruins
The charred husks of a Friday night accident.

I stand still and watch you whilst pretending to be texting
I watch you emerge like a horror film butterfly
From your burnt-out taxicab haven
You appear like a lunatic Raven
Pecking tears out of eyes of sorrow
Waiting for there to be no tomorrow

Shallow forgiveness
Hollow cough
Nightmare daydream
Mind switched off.

Hiding behind that can of strong beer
I smell your mental decay
Your chronic fear
To you I'm just a moving grey blur
Things can never be like they once were . . .
Down to the pub and home again
Reduced to sleeping out in the rain.
Special Brew numbs the pain . . .

I briefly make eye contact, then look away.
You see nothing but yesterday
I really wish there was something I could do
You're too far gone to wish that too.

So I walk right past . . . that is where you live,
The past, the safe, warm past.

Maybe when your time comes
When the lager runs dry
When you're buried alone with no one to cry
You will go back, to your happy time.
A ghost walking the same road eternally . . .
But for now you stay in your lovely lie
In your liquor-fuelled heaven just waiting to die.

In your burnt-out taxi rank haven
Disguised as the lunatic Raven
Underneath that grubby old mac
Lies a man who wants his old life back
So while you're sat waiting for no tomorrow
While you're forced to beg, steal and borrow
We all acknowledge your hurt and pain,
Though to you it seems no gain,
And, you know,
Tomorrow when it starts to rain
And I spare one moment to think of you
Just then when I pretend to be on my phone
You will never know
But you are not alone . . .
You are never alone.
My poor Raven.

Emma Thacker

A LOVE POEM

If I long to feel your burning lips
Pressing passionately on mine,
To let your breath warmly caress
My skin,
To smell the scent of your vibrant body so close to mine,
To hear your heart pounding in unison with mine,
To drink from the fountain of our desire for each other,
To savour that ecstasy that only with you I have found,
Is this a mere ephemeral passion, or infinite eternal love?

Anna Greaves

THE SUNSHINE OF ALL DREAMS

In a darkened land of sorcery, where daylight was not seen
Where freaks and ghouls and witchcraft ruled by an evil king and queen
With black magic and sorcery they spread fear across the land
The evil king and queen reigned with terror hand in hand

The king he was a demon, the queen she was a witch
The freaks and ghouls obeyed their rules, their souls the queen had stripped
In a castle on a hill is where they did reside
Their subjects lived in fear in the land of terrified

This land was once so sunshine-blessed, this land was once a dream
But then a witch and demon betrayed and slayed the king and queen
With wickedness and witchcraft they put a spell on everyone
And cast the land in darkness so no one could see the sun

In the castle where they ruled, a dungeon down below
Was where they kept the former princess, she was pure as driven snow
This beautiful princess was in reality the queen
Imprisoned in a dungeon, her whole existence a bad dream

Cold and damp and hungry she could sense rats by her side
Terrified, she cried and cried, her hope had all but died
She'd fold her hands and pray in the hope someone would hear
Would a knight in shining armour answer to her prayer?

In a distant forest from a deep sleep he did wake
He saw nothing but darkness, but beside him felt a snake
The snake got closer to him and he whispered in his ear
'My friend I have watched over you, you have nothing to fear

I am no ordinary snake, for magic I possess
My wizardry I give to you now, you are truly blessed'
The sleeping mortal man had become an immortal knight
To fight the powers of darkness and to bring eternal light

The snake told him the story of the real king and queen
Who were betrayed and slayed by evil that before had been unseen
By a demon and a witch who ruled with terror across the land
And an army of freaks and ghouls who obeyed every command

How they stopped the sun from shining, how they cast away the light
And brought eternal darkness, now the days were dark as night
Of the castle where they ruled and the dungeon deep inside
And the beautiful princess whose hope had all but died

Out of the distant forest came the knight with all his power
With his wizardry and magic to be the hero of the hour
An army of freaks and ghouls were sent to battle with the knight
But his wizardry and magic dispersed the darkness with sunlight

The light restored the souls of the army of freaks and ghouls
Restored to normal men they were now no longer ruled
By the demon king and wicked queen who'd lost their evil power
The knight then slayed them both to be the hero of the hour

He then rescued the princess, the rats turned into doves
The dark replaced with sunshine, the fear replaced with love
The knight was now the king, the princess now the queen
Hand in hand they ruled the land, the sunshine of all dreams

Dean Cooper Elston

THE END SHE NOW AWAITS

All her memories are lost now
Familiar faces are all gone . . .
Isolated and not really knowing
Where does she truly belong?
Dull words are exchanged around her
But vacant is her expression.
She utters only a few words
In her state of slow regression.
For this woman still loved and once proud
Is reduced to a meaningless state.
Helplessly dependent on others
The end she will slowly await.
As days pass by so slowly
With slumber and unspoken words.
She watches, but cannot see
And her thoughts remain unheard.
Sitting in her chair surrounded
By people she does not know.
Moments pass by so sadly
Our grieving starts long and slow.
Alas gone is the grandmother I knew
My memories are all that remain.
Of a lady, dignified and gentle
Her warmth and spirit my lasting gain.

Nichola Keel

WORD SEPARATION DIVERSIFIES AT THE SOUL WALL

The inevitability of the appearance of transient grief
As creation's consciousness shows deep anguish of the
weakness of life
That diminishing within as an invisible awareness
communicates with the soul, regarding the soul
An affinity to self
The secret separation liberates one,
yet inhibits the peace of another within
Disassociation of the mind soul, though ingrained and unyielding,
exposes the remoteness and anger of a secretly stripped
but preserved inner soul
Intention being composure, not a continuous, engulfing exposure, causing delusions which
evaporate in reality's direction
Being absorbed incessantly into an immense pre-determined choice
Remote whisperings are regrettably submerged
The vulnerable cannot separate, as an unequalled state exists
Do they ever integrate as one?
A contradicted vulnerability
An inexhaustible anxiety covers stone heart
With tears from eyes that reveal humanity
Salt corroding the distinctive sentiments to near perfection
Defining the essence of dignity and the true identity
which has been ingrained so intricately over time
Silently the immaculate tears, translucent and trembling
in the cobalt eyes - ceaselessly fall
Crevices and core are exposed and washed
Unfeeling stone heart has been illumined and embraced
by being anointed with tears of love
No marker exposed beyond the wall
An intently, desolate, abandoned permanence
To show an uncherished element to society
Man's law cannot separate or identify the truth
from another's heart
Words - a journeying thru - an enduring love
Sculptured fingers that were once delicate, contrasting now
the paper skin and bone fingers of time that tremble
Placing another oil, fragrant paper to lips that once kissed
Clouded eyes watch the line of sight on the horizon
No one must discover the secret now after so long
Stillness suppresses time as breath whispers the words
inside her head

Around and around, never stopping
That voice of silent words, no utterance from the penitent
Yet here, tangible words can go beyond the wall
A stone contradiction separating lost generations
Spidery crevices caress the paper she now places into the wall
at the designated touchstone
Each week at an appointed time she posts her love
into the dry cavity
A feather-light expression descending
Possessing memory - a tool for words
Yet who will read the words?
For now, words are just components of the wall
Her thoughts suspended as her soul receives the closeness
of a pulse - that of an imagined heartbeat
A free spirit knowing limitlessness boundaries of man and time.

H J Clark

I AM

I am the fearless, ever-raging sun
I am the current that with holds the ever-changing sea
I am the grains beneath every piece of sand
I am the heart and soul of every raised mountain
I am the mouth which erupts when angered
I am the ever-patient clouds awaiting to fall
I am the piece to which a puzzle may be complete
I am the moon in the starlit sky
I am the glimmer that can be seen by your eyes
I am the ripple when a lake's disturbed
I am the haunting, ever-silent wind
I am the one that makes you smile.

You are the words in a song that creates a tear
You are the rock that's solid and hard to crush
You are the gentle breeze that can always be felt
You are the oxygen that brings me life
You are the flower that blooms and lies dormant
You are the waves that always return
You are the one that has the key to life
You are the whispers that can be heard a mile away
You are the one who carries so much, yet so little
You are the rainbow that shines so colourful and bright
You are the one who has truly made an impact
You are the risk I would take, my reflection and my halo.

Stephen Timothy

SIBLING TIME . . .

In my 20 months of life
I have accomplished much.
I stand. I walk. I run - a bit.
Don't speak a lot - as such.
But I know where my borders lie;
This whole domain is mine.
This woman - 'Mummy', 'Daddy' too
Danced attendance all the time.
My every wish was granted.
They humoured every whim.
Until that day - I'm sad to say -
They came back here . . . with . . . him!

There'd been something going on
The blighters hadn't told me.
'Til I worked out, before too long,
They'd down-the-river sold me.

With hindsight . . . there was that spare room.
I should've seen the sign . . .
It turned into a nursery . . .
Another . . . ? Just like mine . . . ?

Then all the others bustled . . .
And hairy Grandpa came to stay,
While Daddy and my Grandma
Took Mummy far away . . .

(Don't get me wrong - old Grandpa's
Alright . . . in his way . . .
But a chest to hug at story-time . . .
Give me Grandma's any day . . .)

For days the family came and went
And I kept thinking, 'Funny . . .
Can't share this general merriment . . .
Cos where the heck's my mummy?'

Well - she came back home soon enough
And everyone's delighted.
Except . . . she'd brought this extra guest
Whom I had not invited . . .

'He's got your eyes . . .' 'And Toby's nose,'
I heard these people saying.
And telling me, 'What friends you'll be . . .'
Don't tell me that . . . It's staying . . . ?
I'm older now - and wiser too

By all of seven days,
I've grown up fast - this one week past
And I think I've learnt the ways . . .

Of showing how I love the brat -
Cos that's what Mummy wishes.
I'll smile and give his head a pat
Until some time propitious.

Her guard will drop - and off she'll pop
To make a cup of tea . . .
Then I'll 'take care of him' alright . . .
Just leave him here . . . with me . . .

Tony Douglass

DEAD AS .

Nah! Don't believe in that,
When yer's dead, yer's dead,
Ain't no such fing as a spirit, ghost, whatever,
That rises up and goes to 'eaven,
Nah, when yer's dead, yer's dead.
Yer bones an' fings just rot in the muck,
The worms come in an' finish yer up,
Yer just become earth an' bits,
Then trees, an' flowers, an' carrots
Can grow (in yer like) yer can live again,
In that kind of way, sort of, but
When yer's dead, yer's dead.

Nah, there ain't no such fings as ghosts,
They're made-up fings to frighten kids,
Don't scare me,
Don't mind seeing 'em on the flicks though,
Me an' me bird went to see a zombie one once,
She got scared an' cuddled in, close like,
Great; she sort of likes scary fings,
Me - nah, when yer's dead, yer's dead,
No God, no ghosts, zombies, spirits,
Least that what I fink, don't you?
But when me da died, in the army like,
Me ma, she sort of knew, said she saw 'im,
Makes yer fink,
Don't it.

Sandy Phillips

ONCE UPON A RAINBOW

Once upon a rainbow
Across a cloudless sky
I came upon two angels
As they were flying by
'Where is it that you journey?'
I asked of not one but two
'We travel to perform our miracles . . .
But what of that to you?'
'Well I could use a miracle,'
I hastened to reply,
'Won't you stop and perform one
Instead of flying by?'
The angels seemed confused
At the request I bid them do.
They looked at each other mockingly
Then came closer within my view.
'Do you not have two arms?'
One asked me rather stern,
'And also two legs I see.'
The other then had her turn.
'Yes, but I could do with money
To buy my better home . . .
And I could go on holidays,
Oh I do so love to roam.'
The angels sat beside me, each on opposite sides,
Their wings seemed to wither
And tears then filled their eyes.
'What is it that's the matter?'
I asked with not much concern.
'You, my dear mortal,
Have so much you need to learn.'
They took away my sight,
So the blind man's world I saw,
Then took away my legs
So I could no longer walk.
'Now tells us, Mr Mortal . . .
What would you wish for now?
Would you still ask for money . . .
For you to spend, and how?'
I no longer wanted riches,
Just my sight returned to me
And I would want to walk again,
To run so far and free.
The angels granted my wishes

And gave me back my health,
And once I could see and walk again
I felt I had much wealth.
I appreciated what I had
Instead of wanting more,
I had taken things for granted
Whilst thinking I was poor.
The angels stood to leave
They had much work to do
Granting miracles to the needy
Instead of just me and you.

Kriss Simone

THE ANCIENT BOWLER

There, playing bowls, he looks endearing,
Eighty-plus and hard of hearing,
Portly, stooped, movements sedate,
White hair surrounds his sunburnt pate.
Dim of eye, long-toothed and gummy,
Cruel, the rumbles from his tummy
And during tea, he's not alert,
There's half a cuppa down his shirt.
Give him a nod, but don't go near him,
It's from afar he looks endearing.

Robert Keith Bowhill

POLITICIANS RULE OK?

They talk without really saying much
Their undeserved power they hungrily clutch
We put them there in that high place
They abuse their position, it's such a disgrace

They are there to represent me and you
They float through life, they haven't a clue
They say vote for me, I am the one
But we know they're not right when the others have gone

We swap one bad for another and then they gloat
They're in number 10, it's all our fault
Maybe this lot will help, hope springs eternally
But they don't give a damn when they have the key

The others voted out, what a mess they leave
It will take 10 years to sort out the others plea
And we buy it once more, we're really quite dumb
We allow this deception, they take the last crumb

We've never had it so good, they drum in our ear
We're the best in the world, they've made that quite clear
Taxes and laws they build dwarf Babel's Tower
We bow under the strain, it's really quite dour

What rubbish we're told and we swallow it
They've dug our grave, we're in a pit
We obey like zombies, our minds brainwashed
To resist is futile, we're all kyboshed

Our freedom eroded, it's for our own good
ID cards accept, terrorism conclude
Cameras spy and follow our every move
A necessary evil they try to prove

More databases needed, they haven't enough
If we complain they shrug, too bad, it's tough
Mindless beings taking control
The streets, a secret force will soon patrol

We take the toys towards us they thrust
Digital TV, broadband is now a must
These worthless playthings are a smokescreen
To keep us at home is their furtive scheme

When toys aren't enough, awkward questions we ask
They instill thoughts of a doomed planet and set us a task
It must be saved from global warming or all will be lost
By any means, anyway, whatever the cost

And how do they combat this perceived threat?
By introducing more stealth taxes, yes you bet
A microchip inside your bin
Now 'fines' for excess rubbish can begin

Turn your heating down, it will save energy
We're told bills will be smaller, just trust in me
But big business won't suffer, go cold, that's OK
Their prices rise, the less you use, the more you pay

Tax this and tax that for the environment it's good
No one sees through it all, it's time that we should
Eventually we will break under the burden
Big business and government win, that's one thing that's certain

So what can we do? We moan all the time
Our liberty erodes but they promise less crime
And what happens when we're lost? There's no turning back
The politicians will just shrug and say, 'I'm all right Jack.'

Barbara Lambie

NEVER AGAIN

Oh what a headache, never again,
Thump, thump, thump, such a dreadful pain.
Yesterday I felt just fine,
Why oh why did I drink so much wine?
Under the covers glued to the bed,
Cannot move my poor sore head.
Stomach churning deep inside,
Snuggle down further trying to hide.
Oh no, oh no, there goes the alarm,
Mustn't panic, try and stay calm.
Important meeting at work today,
What it's about, I really can't say.
I've lost my memory, that must be it,
Perhaps I'll feel better if I try to sit.
Rush to the bathroom feeling sick,
A glass of water should do the trick.

Recovering slowly from memory loss,
The office party, out with the boss.
Laughing and flirting, dancing so slow,
He looked embarrassed and wanted to go.
I really was having the time of my life,
But I shouldn't have kissed him in front of his wife.
Was that before I sank to the floor,
Waving my glass and shouting for more?
I cannot remember who brought me home,
Thank goodness I woke and was all alone.
I sneak into work ignoring the looks,
Bury my head in a large pile of books.
'Good morning Miss Brown, I hope you feel better,
Come to my office and take down a letter.'
My mouth's so dry I can hardly swallow,
But I grab my pad and meekly follow.

He's not quite so handsome in the cold light of day,
His coal-black hair's now streaked with grey.
I sit there in silence, my head bent with shame,
And then I say sorry and take all the blame.
He's such a nice man, what must he think,
'Don't worry my dear, I know it was drink.'
I lift up my head and meet his eye,
I wish I could simply curl up and die.
His fatherly gaze is friendly and kind,
He says he was flattered and didn't mind.
'It certainly was a wonderful kiss,

One that I wouldn't have wanted to miss.
I'll order some coffee, strong and black,
Please don't worry, I won't give you the sack.'
What else did I say, what else did I do?
My mind's blank again, I haven't a clue.
Glad to be home and to climb into bed,
Cymbals still crashing inside my head.
It just wasn't worth all the heartache and pain,
So all I can say is, never again.

Susie Field

SPIRITUAL DIMENSION

Lost in the seven veils of deception,
To complete the 7th generation prophecy of perception,
11 days, 11 times and 11 hours,
Need to refine one's powers,
Complete and utter submission,
Time to make a decision,
A heart that weighs heavy on my soul,
The need to regain control,
Inability to see through haze,
Need to focus to navigate through this maze,
Cautious words carefully said,
People cunningly misled,
A cloudy reflection,
Guided protection,
Hand given, an oath taken,
Thought of this temporary world forsaken,
Spiritual enlightenment received,
Elevated to the next level because they believed,
Signs shown,
Hidden secrets become known,
Clues given,
To the extreme, patience is driven,
A vow to obey, honour and respect,
It is control over emotions one has to perfect,
Past mistakes admitted and forgiven,
In the depths of darkness sorrow is hidden,
To become hard-hearted is forbidden,
Intentions faltered on the grounds of good,
The spiritual code is still misunderstood.

Farah Ali

DREAMS OF SARDINES, POEM OF CLICHES

Now that's what I'm talking about
Nice one
Put it in the back of the net
Lovely
Best one yet
So beautiful
That's my whoo
Everybody
Put your hands together
Shout!
That's what I'm talking about
So good
A work of art
From the heart
Just right
Good night
Action!
Sunrise, new day
Emmm - ah
That's what I say
I think I'm dreaming
Fashion gown
Bring the house down
Look so fine
Sound so sublime
Let it swing
Make me want to sing
Like a fine wine
Love you to the end of time
Alright
Well that's alright!
Mean machine
What a team
Know what I mean?
The dreams of sardines.

Graham Peter Metson

YOU'RE MY APPLE ON THE TREE

I'm happy that you are here,
That you will stay by my side,
Through the tears and the rain,
I know you're here for the ride.
We'll name the distant stars,
With you here, so close to me,
As though it could be a beginning
Of our plot of a love story.
When you play with my hands,
Teasing me with your toes,
My heart skips a beat,
And yet I don't think you know . . .
It's the simple things I love,
The things that make you . . . you.
They are the things I dream about,
Not the fancy things that you do.
You're my heaven on Earth,
My moonlight walk on the beach,
You're the apple on the tree
That seems just in my reach.
You're the one that makes me smile,
The one that holds my hand,
The one that knows just how I feel,
The one who helps make me stand.
Because of all these reasons,
And because of everything you do,
So much that it all can't be mentioned,
But from my head and heart . . .
I know that I love you.

Sarah Penrice

THE SHADOW BEHIND ME

Wherever I am I can feel him
Burning into me
Like a flame
I look
I see nothing
Though I sense something more
I carry on.

When I am lonely it gets worse
Turning around to find something
I look, I look
Turning back sighing
Nothing there once more
In my mind he's there
Why not here?

Walking by myself
Trying to clear my head
That scary feeling arrives
I know how I feel
I look, I look, I look
Nothing.

Suddenly two sparks of light
I see what's been missing
A black shadow
With two burning red eyes
I look
I can't breathe, I can't see, I . . .

I am the shadow now.

Alexandra Martin

MY SCAFFOLDING BODY

The bones in my body
Joined like scaffolding poles
My knees joined together
With self-tapping screw holes.
My hands and my fingers
Where calluses grow,
Match my hardworking feet
With an aching big toe.
My skin is all sunburnt,
I'm as brown as a berry;
My nose sticks out from my face
Like a big rosy cherry.
My skin stretches over
Each bone in my body,
All wrinkled and ageing
With a scaffold that's shoddy.
The head scaffold is weakening
And falling apart,
The grey cells are dying
And affecting my heart.
When my body is dismembered,
You, you'll have a good laugh
When they recycle my uni-joints
And that's only the start.
Anyone can have a new scaffold
When their body falls apart.
Reconditioned remoulds, I call them.
I should know, I'm falling apart.

John Hickman

A JOURNEY - SEPTEMBER 3RD 1944

We rode in trucks through countryside,
Our destination still unsure.
No cars, no people to be seen,
It really wasn't like a war.

But suddenly the word had come,
By jubilant outriders spread.
'We're off to Brussels - the Germans have gone.'
'There should be some fun,' we all of us said.

Soon people appeared to welcome us in,
They clapped and waved their flags in delight.
We pressed on to Brussels amid growing din,
Where crowds were singing with all of their might.

Soon the column of trucks was brought to a halt,
As garlands of flowers now festooned us all,
And the citizens climbed in to hug and to kiss,
For the people of Brussels were having a ball.

The officers knew they had only one choice -
The word passed along, 'All off duty 'til night,
Then report to the camp in the royal park,
But make doubly sure you don't end up too tight!'

Two pals with myself were hauled off our truck
And carried with laughter inside a large bar,
Where free drinks were offered and had to be drunk.
I tried schoolboy French but did not get too far.

One of my pals, Jack, spotted a girl
Who gave him the eye and walked up the stairs.
Lothario Jack did not need schoolboy French -
He followed - ignoring our warning, 'Take cares!'

We finally left and went back to our truck,
But a young girl called Ghislaine now brought us away
To her family's flat, where her mother awaited
The heroes who'd freed them on this special day.

The mother was charming, her English so good,
And the meal she provided was really first class.
The talk was of Germans and how they behaved.
They asked about us and the time just flew past.

Then Ghislaine, the daughter, went out to locate
Her father, who'd gone to a bar for a drink.
But when she burst in, from the look on her face,
It was bad and our hearts began to sink.

Her father was dead, shot by mistake
By a revelling Belgian, too drunk to know.
In shock we were glad to leave the flat,
We knew that all we could do was go.

So ended our visit to Brussels that day -
A mixture of joy and sadness we'd met,
As on to the camp we gloomily trudged,
A time of our lives we would never forget.

Eric Savage

SKY-CLAD

I'm sky-clad beneath the cool moonlight
I can feel the breeze on my skin tonight
The earth beneath my feet, soft and comforting
I am now at one with nature, calm and serene

I listen to the night sounds
I close my eyes and drift away across time
Through space
I'm floating
In a state of ethereal grace
Until
I hear the policeman shout
'Sir, put your clothes back on
and get off that roundabout!'

Grant Meaby

SCARECROWS AND CHARACTERS

It's not only the scarecrows
That have strange, eccentric ways,
The owners who created this lot,
Their eccentricities leave us in a daze.

First there is Bill Lawley,
Every veg contest does he win,
But the only flower he does adore
Is that petal named Dame Vera Lynn.

There's Chris, his giant butterfly reveal
On his newly-acquired plot,
A good job that butterfly isn't real,
Or it would gobble the bloody lot.

Then there is Lady Brenda,
The gladioli queen.
If those blossoms were a melody,
Then glad-all-over would be the theme.

Next there is our tea boy,
But this hides other earthly skills.
There is no veg he cannot grow,
Provides gourmet dishes fit for a king.

My plot neighbours, Michael and Theresa,
With both veg and flowers excel,
But I won't mention their rhubarb,
It's a secret I cannot tell.

There's Norman with his family crest,
Of which he is very proud,
His pride does grow with his veg,
From their past the seeds of knowledge sown.

Then there's Don the digger,
Is he digging for victory?
The hole he is digging never gets bigger,
It is all such a mystery.

Next there is our Jason,
The allotment super-man,
Everything he grows is A1,
To say nothing of his frying pan.

Then there is little Eric,
The big-hearted Scot.
I asked him for some haggis seeds,
But I think he must have forgot.

Last, but not least, there is our Keith,
To forget him would be a sin.
Another heart as big as his plot,
We are all so lucky to have him.

This poem must end with emotion,
Thinking of those come and gone.
Thanks to their devotion,
The Ley's allotment carries on.

W H Stevens

A STRANGE FIGURE

A strange figure
sitting by the wayside
attracts attention
takes perfect little mirrors
out of a hold-all
holds them up to the faces
of the curious who stop to look
they hate what they see
then they lapidate
the poet falls
the mirrors lie shattered
they rush forward
reassured, they pick up a few pieces
the broken fragments
reflect the same thing.

Elaine Harris

THE 1970S

Platform shoes, long hair and flares,
Tank tops, maxi skirts and bright shirts,
Slade, Sweet and T-Rex topped the charts,
As well as The Carpenters, Mud and Gary Glitter,
People didn't seem to have a care,
But then there was the three day week,
Britain joined the EEC,
Some felt this shouldn't be
The path that the country followed;
Decimalisation changed the currency,
Heath clashed with the miners and they went on strike,
Bombs were exploding in Northern Ireland,
And the USA was still in Vietnam,
Wanting her to become like Uncle Sam;
Nixon was disgraced by Watergate,
Was replaced by Gerald Ford,
And the Cold War was abated by détente.
'Love Story' was on at the cinema,
'New Faces' made unknowns into stars,
And Shaft was a TV hero.
Muhammad Ali won many fights,
And talked on 'Parkinson' about 'The Nation of Islam',
At the Munich Olympics some Israelis were shot dead,
But the Games continued nevertheless
Although the Israeli tragedy was publicised greatly
by television news and the press;
Arthur Ash was the first black player
To win Wimbledon in 1975,
Borg dominated the game in the mid and late '70s,
While Olga was the prodigy of gymnastics,
Her performance was filled with so much drive;
The Beetle was in vogue and so was the Chopper bike,
And then there was a craze for the skateboard,
Which some parents couldn't afford
To buy their children.
Punk blasted like a rocket onto the scene,
Spiked hair and piercing became the fashion,
And punks appeared on TV who didn't sing but scream,
Some felt that they were really obscene;

There was The Silver Jubilee,
When many held street parties,
But this time of glee,
Was ended by the winter of discontent,
And Thatcher and the decade of greed
Was on the horizon.

Sarah Sidibeh

SATURDAY NIGHT

The Modern Man exits to the stage left,
Out the front door, feeling almost bereft
Of hopes, of dreams, of ivory towers
With nightingales a-chirping in the bowers
And dragons fiery and knights in armour
And sights that make you ever calmer
And all the chivalry of Camelot,
And all the people who care not one jot.

Bereft, we say, the Modern Dreamer felt;
Yet he takes all this with a pinch of salt.
He dreams compulsively, 'tis said, for he
Must just do so; he cannot stop reality
By making frozen angels in the snow.

No; he knows he must build his world up high;
So he goes downtown: bars, clubs and pub golf.
That twinkle starts to light up his eye
As he knocks back with gusto every half . . .

Later, later; how much later?

Dunno.

Stagger on the pavement. Seeking refuge.
Streetlights blurry, mind a flooding deluge
Of emotion. When did it creak? When did
It crack? I'm still chasing dreams, as I bid
More emotional capital to Fate:
I reach out, across the networks, late,
For the whisper of my dream.

Fergus McAteer

UNTITLED

I'm trying to forgive and I'm trying to forget,
I'm trying to move on, but my heart won't let,
Is it my heart? Or is it my mind?
I'm looking for answers that I cannot find,
You make me angry, you make me sad,
You make me scared, have been so bad?
You remember our past with a perfect rose tint,
I remember your eyes with that sneering glint,
You hit me, you hurt me, you manipulated, you lied,
You punished me outside, you broke my insides,
I stoically took what it was you gave out,
My scars can't be seen, but they're there without doubt,
I'm hurting and angry and want to let go,
I wish it were different and I want to know,
How could you ravage this beautiful child,
Who now is woman with tears in her eyes,
You've made your excuses and reasons quite clear,
I am where I am because you brought me here,
We have nothing in common but our family tree,
I am who I am, not by you, but of me,
A phoenix rises from ashes to a pure new life,
I want to lay down this trouble and strife,
This mental anguish that tears me apart,
These scars that you've left across my heart,
And now, you're old and alone and you want to be friends,
There's nothing to do to make good amends,
I'm resentful, revengeful, remorseful to you,
I'm better than this, tell me what should I do?
I try to enjoy and tolerate your presence,
I make the right noises at your awkward presents,
But they're there all the time, these feelings inside,
Bubbling and oozing into the outside,
And now; I have a precious child of my own,
A family, a husband, a place to call home,
A home that is made with love, trust and care,
A child who is nurtured and given her share,
A husband who loves me for what I've become,
Who's journeyed with me through the dark to the sun,
Who's held me so close to help soothe my fears,
Who's raised me up in praise and good cheer,

So: because of this good, it only seems right,
To: tolerate the old woman and see her plight,
To: try to be good, and caring and true,
To: be what you will, just be true to you.
Some questions don't have answers,
Some answers shouldn't be heard.

Lisa Livingstone

BABY

Baby, do not throw that book
Come, sit with me and take a look
At all the worlds these pages hold
Look, here's a smiling sun, a boat,
A caterpillar eating toast,
A little girl just like you,
A star, a wish, a dream, a view
Of other worlds you'll never see,
Of laughter, joy and liberty.

And as we turn the page in years
You'll read about new hopes and fears,
Worlds discovered, worlds unknown,
Worlds where books are often thrown
Into fires, burned with hatred,
Worlds where girls like you are fated
Never to read contentious books
With words that make you stop and look,
With words to challenge, or excite
Passions for humanity's plight.

For when you turn a page and look,
Even in this first nursery book,
You are opening up your mind
To all that makes us good and kind
And bad and wild and reckless too.
But without the books how will you
Understand the human race
In all its complex, muddled state?

So baby, do not throw that book
Come, sit with me and take a look.

Fran Hunnisett

FEET

Feet,
I love my feet,
They help me to walk along the street.
Without my feet I couldn't stand,
They help me to balance on the land,
To resist the wind that gusts and blows,
I love my feet
And my ten toes.

Legs,
I love my legs,
They are my faithful, needy pegs.
Without my legs I couldn't walk,
Despite my feet of which I talk,
To resist the winds that blow and gust,
I love my legs, they are a must.

Hands,
I love my hands,
They help me measure with ten-inch spans.
Without my hands I couldn't grasp,
They help me greatly in my tasks,
Fly kites in the wind that ever lingers.
I love my hands
And my thumbs and fingers.

Arms,
I love my arms,
They move about and keep me warm.
Without my arms I couldn't throw,
They are my upper strength, you know,
To fight the wind that rages then.
I love my arms, yes, both of them.

Torso,
I love my torso,
It's full of parts that I love also.
Without my torso I'd never be,
It's filled with vital organs, see,
To face the wind that might extend,
With limbs fixed firmly, sides and end.
I love my torso, my faithful friend.

Head,
I love my head,
It holds my brain from where thoughts are fed.
Without my head I'd have no brain,
Decapitated, without saying.
My head has eyes and teeth and mouth,
And orders for my body, south,
To withstand the wind that gusts and blows,
From tip of nose to tips of toes.
I love my head, it makes complete
This amusing poem, entitled 'Feet'.

Peter Ridgway

HENRY GIBSON

Acres of newsprint afforded to some
Often lacking real talent in a world often glum
Yet little written about you
You stood on Rowan and Martin's Laugh-In TV show
Holding flower, reciting your poems
Whimsy in a gentle way, perhaps
But guaranteed to bring an affectionate smile
John Wayne was a fan
On one of the shows he gave a supportive look-in
You acted well
Being swell above the musical din in Nashville
Now you're gone, missed by this one
Perhaps a final poem might have been:
'I hold another flower
Better than another shower,
By Henry Gibson'.

Barry Dillon

GREATEST OF 'EM ALL

Cassius Clay, the man they say
was the greatest of 'em all
he fought real well
in the ring of hell
as he watched opponents fall.
He was black and so laid back
he could dance the rhythm and blues.
The man from the south
with a very big mouth
had 'em quaking in their shoes.

Before a bout he'd curse and shout
and deliver words of pain
'If you think your clout
will knock me out
then you'd better think again
'cause I'm the king of the golden ring
and I float like a butterfly
I sting like a bee
I'm the best you see
and that's the reason why.'

Now Henry Cooper, he was super
which no one can deny
but on the day
he fell to Clay
and kissed his chance goodbye.
This man called Clay, back in his day
was always on the ball
and just like me
you must agree
was the greatest of 'em all.

Stephen Guy Craggs

IN MY 90TH YEAR

I watch from the window - I don't open the door -
Cars rush up and down and strangers appear.
There is fear all around, of what I don't know,
Is it bombs, knives or guns?
They come and they go.
I have lived in this house for 64 years
And the road is familiar, but some folks are queer.
Times have changed and our peace may never return,
What's gone wrong in this country?
What's wrong with the world?
Or is it my age, and strength that has gone?
I don't know what's ahead, only that I might fall.
I look where I tread. I walk with a stick,
I have to be careful and I'm slow - never quick,
Because if I'm careless I might lose my head,
And then I'm in trouble and I'll soon be dead.
So I watch at the window - people walk up and down,
I cannot go out much to look at the town.
Since I've been a widow, I've lived here alone,
I look after my cat, and this is my home.
I don't want to die yet, cos where will I go?
I have no idea what is 'Heaven' - above or below?
If it's just 'doing nothing' it will not appeal,
So I'd rather stop here where I know it is real,
Helped along by my family, friends, coffee and tea.
With paper and pens and books I can see.
Where I'm reasonably happy and definitely free,
Whatever happens will have to be.
But I doubt if I shall get any choice at the end.
I count my blessings every day that God sends,
And I pray to God He'll look after me.
Well - up to now, faith has been the key.
I'm still here!

Doris E Pullen

AN ENCOUNTER IN TIME

A boy came up and raised his perky head,
'Please, do you have the time, old man?' he said.
So I replied, 'I've not much left, it's true,
As, when you said, 'old man', I thought you knew.
Your 'please' was nice, but 'old man' rather bold,
Though inoffensive when you too are old.
And do I have the time for what, my dear?
Of that, I think we're equally unclear.'

I could have sworn his boyish face was pained,
'You do not understand!' the boy complained.
I told him that was frequently the case,
For understanding rarely stands the pace.
If he could do it two times out of three,
He'd almost be about as good as me.
He asked, 'Do you have a time-piece on your person?'
I told him that my name was Jock McPhearson.

Then, after showing him my dangling locket,
I took my watch from out my waistcoat pocket
And bad him spy it with his boyish eye,
For being old, I might mistake or lie.
Why, even then, was it run-down or bust?
There's precious little in this world to trust.
He merely said, 'Oh, jolly good - hooray!
It's three o'clock - I've one hour more to play!'

I said, 'Play on and do enjoy yourself,
For boys, an hour to play is wondrous wealth.
Remember, when you get as old as me,
You'll find it's nearly always time for tea.
Or always time for getting washed and dressed,
Or wondering if it's time to feel depressed.
It's always time, because it flows so fast;
Its speed is hinting that it cannot last.'

He heard me not - he'd vanished to a spot,
Caring neither tittle nor a jot.
I'd pulled his leg, perhaps unmercifully;
My sense of humour is a curse, you see.
I'd answered literally - it was my plan,
To punish his, quite literally true 'old man'.
But if he'd listened, he'd have learned a lot,
Like how to treat a geriatric clot.

Well, he, like me, may reach his 'Man's Estate',
True meanings he will learn of 'love and hate',
Of 'playing a straight bat' and 'give and take',
He'll try to work out really what's at stake.
It comes to all of us in Time, God wot,
To wonder just what is and what is not
And if one does retain some lingering doubt,
It can be irksome when Time's running out.

Frank Sutton

MAJORCA

With its many sandy beaches and quaint little bays
Majorca offers everything for perfect holidays
Go by train to Soller and pass by the orange groves
Or visit Formentor with its rockpools and coves.

Pollensa, in the north, is a lovely place to stay
Or you can go by bus and spend a pleasant day
With its pretty harbour, shops and sandy beach
Restaurants and cafés are never far from reach.

Then there's Palma, the capital of this island
With its fine cathedral, port and many shops at hand
Visit C'an Picafort and Alcudia, again both lively places
Roam around the markets there, meet the Spanish people
With their friendly, smiling faces.

The picturesque mountains surrounding the bays
The beaches upon which you can happily laze
Majorca has everything you could wish for
Go on, book now and take a tour!

Lisa Pease

1918

Such humps and bumps of cobbled way
Are lost in concrete slabs today
Where once a lady's lifted skirt
Prevented soiling in the dirt
And lackeys stood by phaeton door
To help the gentlemen aboard
All in a mist of days long o'er
Elegant days that are no more
Maids with baskets on their arms
Dimpled faces, winsome charms
Coyly catching some man's eye
Then blushing when he passed by

Matrons in their bombazine
Beaus who stand aloft and preen
Urchins gather in their marts
Through the crowds they duck and dart
Gathering up the fruit that's fallen
With grimy hands all chapped and swollen
Beggar maimed and home from war
Selling matches at the doors

Young girls in their cotton dresses
Toss their heads with ringlet tresses
Rich and poor the great division
Each treat the other with derision
Nannies wheeling perambulators
Fops with trews and buckled gaiters
Child in rags delivers laundry
Without which she would go hungry

Gone these days as in a dream
Only for the rich it seems
Were they times of much and plenty
Different those with purses empty
Squalor reigned within the home
To which ragged children came
Glad am I those days no more
Exist where poverty knocked on the door

Margaret Hickman

CLOUDS

When the Lord God created Earth and Heaven,
Either His 'writer's' minutes weren't quite straight,
Or God missed clouds out of the Bible
And remembered only when it was too late!
Alone, without the clouds, the sun makes deserts,
Relentlessly breaks down rocks to sandy grain.
A cloudless moon comes crisp and cold, with stars
Lighting the holes for later spots of rain.

When the morning sun has widespread wisps of cotton cloud,
It dawns a lovely mix of rose and mauve to end the night.
When the evening sun has cooling cloud and dust,
On a huge canvas, it paints gloriously with light.

The other cloud scenes, which not everybody sees,
Are still clouds, silvered by the moon, when day is done,
Or brisk, high level winds, send the scurrying clouds,
Like smugglers, stealing darkly homeward, from a 'run'.

The weather pundits see grey clouds, touching hills,
'Black over Bill's Mother's' - making a profession
Of threatening rain, high water, rising floods,
Creating 'prison' of a deep depression.
We all see the ominous 'thunderhead' clouds,
Grey-white, expanding, silver-edged, no wonder
When they bump, with muscles flexed, like Sumo wrestlers,
Torrents of rain ensue, lightning and crashing thunder.

The clouds look best to the boy lying in a hayfield,
Glorying in the patterns of a near-still 'mackerel' sky,
Or, against the infinite blue dome, sees the procession
Of white summer clouds, as they eternally drift by.

Perhaps the untroubled boy has yet to meet the worldly worries,
That induce the rest of us to walk with downcast eyes.
Why do we treat great clouds like faded wallpaper
And make tuneless 'musack' of the ever-changing skies?

'I will lift up mine eyes unto the hills,' the psalmist says,
But lift them higher still, to find tranquillity,
For often, up there, in the movement of the clouds,
Are beauty, optimism and serenity.

Robert Collins

SPIRITUAL LOVE
(Inspired by Sister Mercy)

I know that it is time for bed
But still my head is reeling
With these words which spirit sends
They are given with great feeling.

I must put them down on paper
For all the world to see
And hope they will bring comfort
To others, just like me.

I too have lost a loved one
I found it hard to bear
But now my life is straightening out
And with you these words I share.

Put your trust in spirit
As you go from day to day
And always remember
Your loved one is just a thought away.

As you get on with your life anew
And your new pathway you find
There is one thing to remember
Be good and true and kind.

With love sent from the higher plane
You know you cannot go wrong
Your loved one is there to guide you
And to help you get along.

Remember you are not alone
There is one who is always there
Just ask for spirit's help
And they will show that they still care.

Joan Fowler

IT WAS NOT TOO LONG AGO

It was not too long ago, a man looked from a train
And saw a million buffalo, roaming on the plain
And the evil and thoughtlessness of Man came to him as he thought
Of the chance to make big money
By killing them for sport

And it was not too long ago, in the forests of Brazil
The tiger and the ocelot, Man's weapons soon would kill
And the evil and thoughtlessness of Man
Came to him as he wrote
The contracts to supply the skins
To make the rich Man's coat

And it was not too long ago, in jungles the world through
Man saw the birds of paradise, parrots and cockatoo
And the evil thoughtlessness of Man
Came to him seeing that
And they killed them for their feathers
To adorn some rich female's hat

It was not too long ago, on ocean fishing trips
Man first beheld the mighty whales that frolicked round their ships
And the evil and thoughtlessness of Man
Came to him through his toil
And he hunted them relentlessly
For their skins, their meat, their oil

It was not too long ago, the world was rich in game
Birds, fish, animals with strange exotic names
But the evil and thoughtlessness of Man
Wreaked havoc in their midst
Soon there'll be nothing left but pictures
And for me they'll be sadly missed.

Don Woods

MY FRIEND JOHN

The old station wagon had bitten the dust
The big ends that unknown to us were
In terminal decline had consigned our friend to rust.

So we waited there, me and him, two lads far
From home in the land down under
Two young strangers, both to ourselves and each other
We are still there now, me and him, waiting
The passing of the years going by like cars.
After some time, the waiting ended and we filled
This space with laughter, you opened a book
And read aloud poems that turned language
On its head, what was it that Lennon said?

We travelled as brothers, the caboose all about us,
Sharing biscuits we stole in some station down line.
Played poker with locals and others of kin
And held the sun's zenith in our hearts, not in sin.
The old engine eating the distance in hunger,
The tracks clanking in rhythms, speaking in tongues,
About dreams full of magic and romance discovered.
We had history that joined us in armour and songs
Our fidelity a bond that we fostered between us.
We slept once in a freight car outside of a town,
Sat waiting for her in the hours that surrounded
Our friendship between us in silence not sound.
We picked tobacco in the heat and found solace in
Laughter, that held us aloof from dangers abound.

Then, on a beach, we discovered some lessons
And drank milk and consumed sour green tea
And smoked roll-ups like chimneys puffing united.
We looked to each other and were loyal, you and me,
Then you left me alone, to travel down south,
To the girl who was heading for death with a smile.
I then met someone who murdered my purpose,
Who took me again to my weakness with guile
And dressed all the lies that she used to control me.

She loved laughter so sweetly and captured my soul,
She left me dejected and completely unhappy,
Desolation surrounding I accepted my role.
She gave me her stars, but I lost and conceded,
A bargain that no man can really survive
And Sandy, you knew that the moment I met you,
That I was the pilot and you were the skies.

John D'Arcy

MY BROTHER, JAMES

A little boy sat on the stairs,
Trying not to cry.
I was just a baby,
He was waving me goodbye.

I went on to pastures new,
James was left behind.
But the memory of the parting
Stayed always in his mind.

He grew up and joined the forces,
A handsome, smart marine.
Fighting for his country,
Not always a pretty scene.

There were many miles between us,
As I understand,
He met and married Anna
And lived in another land.

Years have come, years have gone,
The daughter born to me
Was playing on the Internet
And found my family.

We travelled off to Africa,
And in this other land,
The first time in 74 years,
I shook my brother by the hand.

Although I was adopted
By a wonderful mum and dad,
It was great to meet the family
That I didn't know I had.

Thank you for the welcome
You gave to Trudy, Bob and me.
God bless you, James and Anna,
And all the family.

Peggy Howe

HEAVENLY CUSTOMS

When our life on Earth is over and
we travel the road back home
Let's hope we've done and seen it all,
leaving no reason left to roam
Then we should approach the gates,
wait to be invited into the hall
We might be a little surprised to read the signs
up there on the wall

Green area, 'nothing to declare',
red area, 'something to declare.' We choose
I'll wait a while, quietly watch the race for green
whilst I stand and muse
Try to think back and judge for myself, honestly,
which line I should join
This honesty thing proves harder than I thought,
maybe I should just toss a coin

I think for me it would have to be red,
I doubt I got everything just right
There was never any malice in anything I did
so I hope my future is bright
I am sure there will be pushing and jostling to be seen
at the front of the green
Just like in life, self-denial, inflated egos won't disappear,
still there to be seen

No passports required, the relevant paperwork
supervised long ago, gone on ahead
It would be much easier to pick the right line,
if we knew what these papers said
Angels on the gates have heard all the excuses,
if you need one, it had better be good
Better try them on with the truth,
be as humble as you know that you should

Once the gates open I hope we will find everyone is equal,
all under the same care
Pardons granted to those in need,
we can join our heavenly families waiting there
Happy reunions, no apologies required,
forgiveness in abundance we know we'll find
Peace and tranquillity, everlasting love all around,
contentment of the angelic kind

I hope to graduate to the higher level of the afterlife,
facing up to any wrong deeds
Accept it's time to take stock, answer unrehearsed questions,
do whatever it needs
To achieve what is required to progress
with the knowledge that my earthly life was blest
And if this is God's plan for me,
I will graciously embrace my share of His eternal rest.

Morag Grierson

OUTFLUENZA

My love he rang
with a bubbly streamy.
Sneezy early he will be.
Homing red car, stumbly stairway,
undercover time for tea.

My love he lies
with a sorrowful drooping,
aching jointly, creaking too,
for such it leaves a terrible weakness
trembling fingers cannot do.

My love he sneezes
a nosy tingle,
and sweats through soaking slumber drift.
Unseen weights pull downward lashes.
Heavy eyelids briefly lift.

My love he aches
in a red-eyed stupor,
hypnotised by pain to sleep.
Two days dozing, drinking, dreaming,
back to normal he will creep.

My love he thrives
in the arms of caring.
Daily duties nudge once more.
Leaning limply on the laundry
yawning nurse-maid shuts the door!

Doris Townsend

VIETNAM

He strolled toward his homestead
Just home from Vietnam
He was pleased and happy
Going to see Dad and Mam
His mother ran to meet him
'My son, my son!' she cried
Hugging and kissing him madly
'We had word that you'd died!'
'No, Ma, they didn't kill me
And no bullet held my name
And look at this, a Purple Heart
Ma, your son won fame'
'What is that you have in your hand, son?'
'This, Ma, is a hand grenade
When I pull out this little pin
The enemy sure do fade'
'Show me how it works, son'
'OK, Ma, step out of the way!'
Then, ripping out that little pin
He threw the grenade away
It blew up the outside toilet
His mother got quite mad
'You shouldn't have done that, Sonny Boy
I think you've just killed your dad!'
After the dust had settled
A tattered figure was seen
Covered in all sorts of business
He definitely wasn't clean!
Looking at his ma and son
He did splutter and cough
'Good job I didn't break wind in the bedroom, Ma
I would have blown the ceiling clean off!'

George Edward Bage

HEAVEN SENT

Our little bundle of joy
was born on Christmas Day
the most wonderful baby
that ever came our way
marvellously perfect
what more can anyone say
in the coming years
she grew and grew more lovely
happy, friendly and cheerful
extremely beautiful too
there was no one
that we treasured more
the perfect addition
to our happy store
but in her early teens
brought a nasty change
her activities
and loss of charm
caused us both alarm
looking older
and feeling colder
our terrible loss
soon came
the doctor's thoughts
unexplained
but we knew the reason
why we'd been
knocked off track
Heaven had just
lent her to us
now they wanted
her back.

Martin Selwood

THE CLIMB
(An unexpected experience climbing The Bwlch)

Lost the right route across the fields
(guess that's what senior memory yields!)
followed the fence at forestry edge,
used fencing-post as supportive wedge
to steady through bog and lumpy grass,
thought time stood still but time did pass.
Soon the forest ran out on me,
turned an angle - no gate could see;
the only way to reach the top
was climb the scree and just not stop.
So, pack on back and pole in hand,
tested balance, viewed the land;
onward, upwards, yard by yard
the climb was steep and very hard.
Grabbed the fencing, used the stick
(daren't look down or might be sick!)
Climb got steeper metre by metre,
wind got chill but needed no heater
as effort made the body warmer,
silent singing helped feel calmer.
Upward, onward, keep looking ahead -
one wrong step: could end up dead!
At last the uppermost rock was reached,
road on top - the challenge breached
as safely then on level ground
could find fresh breath and friends astound
when tell the tale of what achieved -
but first: walk home before relieved!
Down the main road, mile by mile,
enjoy an ice cream, rest awhile
until at last, three hours from start,
hot tea, hot bath, and rest the heart!
The unintended climb was good
but next time - use right path as should!
The Bwlch is rough and steep and high -
unless prepared, don't even try.

This climber was lucky this time, no doubt,
was careful, had whistle, no need to shout;
but novice climbers take heed, beware
of unexpected dangers there;
when walking out, especially alone,
remember, just in case, your phone!

Ann Voaden

THE PERFECT LIGHT

I took my soul to the one
Whose heart was black as night
I offered it as the price
If I could cease the fight.

'No rest for you,' he said with glee
'Go back and sin some more
Then come back to me
And maybe, I might unlock the door.'

So I gave it to the one
I had loved so dearly
He looked at it and sighed
And said, 'I don't want this really.'

Then I took it to my friend
Who said, 'Dear soul, be still
And you will see it all will be
Put right in the end.'

So I took it to my God
And told Him of my shame
'I've sinned,' I said, 'It's not quite bright
Now I must bear the blame.'

Then He held it in His hand
And weighed it carefully
'It's had some wear, I must admit
But it's just worn and weary.

Around this soul, I see a band
Of gold, that's shining bright
Of love! And that's the only thing
That gives the perfect light.'

'So, come you in and rest awhile
And I will take the burden of your sin.'

Joan May Wills

APPLE OF DISCORD

An apple and the Earth, which came first?
A round, green-reddish fruit
An apple was found just after mankind's birth
Attached to the Tree of Knowledge in the Garden of Eden
A pleasant snake-infested paradise
Adam and Eve, hand in hand, in promised land
Eat an apple
'It's alright,' said the snake
Never trust a talking snake, or any other speaking reptile
Cold-blooded, cold skin, don't perspire under pressure
Hide under rocks, hide emotion
God angry
Banished from the Garden of Eden
Banished over an apple.

Years later
An apple falling on someone's head, led to the discovery of gravity
An apple simply fell from a tree
Chain of events
Isaac Newton ponders
Discovers gravity
Yet again an apple's at the core
Yet not a fictitious poison apple that nearly caused Snow White's downfall
My pomaceous fruit hypothesis continues with the science of gravity at the core.

William Tell didn't bow to Gessler's hat
The hat on a post in town, a matter of fact
Yet again, an apple involved
Whether it was Granny Smith
Golden Delicious or Gala remains unsolved.

Four apples from a tree in polystyrene holder, wrapped in clingfilm, aisle three
An apple is grown on a branch of a tree, surrounded by dirt, elements and insects maybe
What next?
Wrap the whole tree in clingfilm maybe?
Recycling issues caused by an apple
In my pomaceous fruit historical research I continue to dabble.

Years later
Busy nightclubs
Drunken people
Drunk on cider
Yet again an apple involved
My research has evolved and evolved
The apple is the only fruit at the core of history
If you don't believe the hype
Listen, trust me.

Mark Anthony Love

THE GARDENER

We all have roots, some deep, some shallow,
Our lives are a garden to be hallowed.
We all have gifts to use and to share,
It's good to find them and learn why they are there.

To walk in a garden offers tranquillity and peace,
Respite from a busy world of noise and speed.
A change of thought to ease the mind,
Among plants and flowers of every kind.

Brilliant colours among shades of green,
Leaves large and small blend in nature's scene.
Trees swaying in the breeze give shade and shelter
To the birds who come here, summer and winter.

A garden is a haven for those who enter,
If you don't come back - will you always remember
The Head Gardener has many gardens to tend,
Likewise many hearts to mend.

Kathleen McBurney

TRIBUTE TO THE ENGLISH POETS

I am amazed as I go through your songs and sonnets;
Oh Shakespeare! Your verses even mentioned the linnet,
With such majesty and grandeur you penned your emotion
And revealed your prosaic power unfathomable as the ocean.

When nature mingled with imagination to put forth,
Had to be Milton's poems or the lyrical ballads of Wordsworth,
You possess the power to touch us emotionally,
The sharp critical perception painted so beautifully.

The sunset on a mountain edge seen from a high bridge
Brings back memories of the Genii of Coleridge;
Regarded as the great Unitarian poet of spring,
The freshness of flowers is what your lyrics bring.

Your writings gift us with immense happiness,
William Blake or Robert Southey who wrote with elegance,
The generation of Romantic poets to create such epics,
From history or an uncommon issue of politics.

One might perceive Lord Byron as the poet of oriental tales;
His poems come like music that floats from mystic dales,
His verses, so articulate that bring hours of joy,
Lucid as a stream that Time can never destroy.

Blending pragmatism with ideals, we hear a new voice;
Percy Bysshe Shelley is undoubtedly a unanimous choice,
Despite the death of his loved ones he created great poetry,
Imaginative and timeless; beyond the limits of magical territory.

To John Keats, death appeared to be attractive and fair,
Dreams were always important for Walter De La Mare,
Odes of Keats enchant me with strange metres,
I love the mystery in De La Mare's 'The Listeners'.

It is Alfred Lord Tennyson with poems mostly lyrical,
That's why they are a pleasure to read, somewhat musical;
The list is endless with Rossetti, Stevenson and Kipling,
And also D H Lawrence, Masefield, Noyes and Browning.

What to us is just a fancy that appears,
You threw the spotlight on the future years,
The beauty of nature that the earth conceals,
With the intellectual light, your verses reveal.

How I wish I could write a bit like you!
To play with the words and change its hue,
I grew up with your poems from birth till date,
This is my humble tribute for you all so great.

Paramita Chakraborty

MY SPECIAL FRIEND

You are my very special friend
And very dear to me
I love you with all my heart
And this is plain to see

No matter what is going on
You're always there for me
To reach out a helping hand
Or lend a shoulder if need be

With troubles you always help me see
By guiding me along
You're always there to give advice
And help me to stay strong

We can talk and laugh together
And share a tear or two
We're never very far apart
Our differences are few

You're always there to give support
Which I'm willing to receive
You're showing you believe in me
And this helps me to achieve

You share in all my glory
And never have looked down
Even when you don't agree
You never wear a frown

You always have a smile for me
And I have one for you
We have a bond that's very strong
And a friendship that's quite true

You are my very special friend
Thank you for all you've done
You are my very special friend
You are, of course, my mum!

Julie Preston

ETERNAL

From birth we are laid in a hearse
Death unites life, unseen in our curse
Fallen dreams as above become below
Unaware of what waits to taint the soul

Mysteries forgotten, hypnotic awaken
I am taken cyclical, chaos bound
Lessons not learnt, never-ending continuing round
Born yet I am born again

I reach divinity though cannot muster speech
I seek in present, a spiritual time
Yet inside I am many, but divide in two
One side won't relent until it rules

The planet is a crossroad, existence a test
The end brings failure, so continues the test
Once taught I am lost, the demon awakens
Living life, wondering, who am I?

In silence it creeps, disturbing one's sleep
Words not mine, behaviour untrue
By the power of light, be gone into the night
Hormones erupt, therefore easily corrupt

From knowledge, there is only survival
Words from the Bible bide me time
Even if freed, this world hinders me
One so fallen, descends humanity

Looking back with age, naïve my path
Symbols of math, dictated the path
The number two, rendered me a fool
I am the demon's tool

The truth of Eden, is we are the fallen
No memory, in death we remember
Then transcend again
Touching the left, restarts our breath

The test starts again
Exorcised demon, yet around are more seeds
Life to death is the purpose I seek
I am Adam eternally weak

A puzzle of confusion
Life of delusion
A wrong conclusion
New birth, new illusion

Louis Cecile

WHO YOU ARE

It isn't what you have
That makes you
Who you are,
It's not money
In the bank
And all that swank
In this materialistic world.
It's the smile
On your face,
The gentle touch
Of an embrace,
The twinkle in
Your eye,
The compassion
To forgive
Another's mistake,
The sensitivity
To show you care,
The guts to go
That extra mile,
That's what makes you
Who you are.

Penelope Kirby

REACH TO THE LIGHT

'I have seen the light'
Never before have I questioned this statement
For it is true. There is light.
I now see light and colours again, once washed into greyness;
for before the light is the darkness.

Inside the darkness, 'I have seen the light' means so much more . . .
The light to escape; to run, to be . . . no more.
Crazy loneliness; feeling despair.
Nobody loves you; nobody cares.
You don't understand. You don't want to help me. You're all against me.
Feelings so real, they have to be true?
People will stare. Why are they looking at me? Why can't I run and hide?
Because I'm a mother.
The torment inside.
I have to go on.

The family suffers, you push them aside.
Not caring or thinking what goes on in their mind.
A selfish reaction for hurting within
Destruction and pain are the trail left behind you
A trail you don't see
Until
Until the light seeps though . . . !

Slowly . . .
You start to feel again.
You see . . .

My partner still loves me, he didn't give up . . .
The children still play, and life carries on
Now; time for apologies.
The hardest of all . . .
So easy to run; to start a new life.
But what if they did care? Did I push them away?
Will they ever forgive me?
What if the darkness falls to take me again?
What if . . .

But the light shines though.
Hope and love will live.

Don't give up; don't run away; don't let the angels take you.
For there is light waiting for you . . .
You just have to wait . . .
And time
Time
Time is the greatest healer of all.

Wendie Hayes

LIVING IN THIS WORLD OF MADNESS

Living in this world of madness
Ruled by clocks, time and day,
Night the essence of my sanity
In my darkness I sit and pray
For forgiveness, for all my sins
Errors I continue to make,
In searching for the love I need
The love I want, how I will break
Every rule known to Man
To feed the craving, to make me whole,
The black and white rainbows
Outside my window
Are but negatives to my soul.
How I dream of bright colour
To shine a light on this dark place,
Free me from the lonely shadows,
Sadness be a forgotten trace
Of what is here, of what I'm feeling
Hidden behind this broken smile,
Love counted in minutes and hours
Stands no test, doubted worthwhile.
For I am but the one who's counting
Breathing hours that pass me by,
A heavy heart wrapped in silence,
The hands of the time keep ticking by.
I'm living a life upon a stage
Full of pretence and make-believe.
The audience applauds me for staying,
Yet my conscience beckons me to leave.
A leading lady where red roses
Fall at my feet, left to die,
My heart is but an understudy,
Where black and white rainbows fill my sky.

Lisa Mills

UNFORTUNATE

Now I'm going to tell you a story
And believe it or not, it's said to be true
It was told to me by a friend
And relates to a couple she once knew

It's about a house-proud woman
And her husband, poor hen-pecked bloke
For the wife in no uncertain terms insisted
That outdoors was the place if he wanted to smoke

But one day it was raining stair-rods
And she was out shopping and he fancied a fag
He thought while sitting on the loo
That he'd have a crafty drag

Now the wife had just cleaned the bathroom
And with detergent given the bowl a spray
But he never gave it a thought
As he sat blissfully puffing away

Till he heard the front door opening
Then thought, hell, I'll be a dead man
So without the slightest hesitation
Dropped the half-smoked cigarette down the pan

He rose with the immediate explosion
Crying out like some demented creature
As a red-hot, burning sensation
Attacked, one might say, his best feature

His wife on hearing the commotion
Shot upstairs in a hell of a hurry
To be greeted by her husband dancing about
His face sick with pain and worry

She soaked a towel in cold water
And said, 'Till the ambulance comes, this will do fine
Now stand still and keep it pressed on,
While I go down and ring 999'

The ambulance seemed to take ages to arrive
When told, the men had big grins on their faces
In fact they laughed so much that they dropped him
And broke his leg in two places

So now he's hospitalised and immobile
And his visitors come in laughing and joking
But he doesn't think it's funny at all
And he's definitely given up smoking.

Edwin David Bowen

LOOK AROUND

Have you ever paused for breath
Taken time to look around?
Do you skim the surface of your world
Oblivious to sound?

The birds on high
Sing so sweetly
They bring such joy
Fitting with nature neatly

While you rush through each day
With work and worries
This leisurely world
Is not in a hurry

Time stands still
Not like you
But the day will come
Your indifference you'll rue

You miss so much
With senses closed
Your internal musings
Never exposed

The light each day
Brings treasures new
But to a blind man
Have no value

You are not blind
Wake up and see
Your introspection
Worries me

So stop and look around
Appreciate while you have time
Rushing through life
Really is a crime.

Sonia Richards

THE 11TH HOUR

I was shopping in Sainsbury's on Sunday, when the two minutes silence began,
To remember the dead of a century's wars, that unique invention of Man.
I covertly looked around me at the shoppers, all silent and still
And the checkout assistant, with head bowed, in front of her idle till.
And I marvelled at just how quiet it was, where just a few moments before,
The place was alive with the hubbub of sounds, that abound in a crowded store.
And as I studied their faces, some lowered, some staring ahead,
I wondered just what they were thinking in this mark of respect for the dead.

Some young ones perhaps were impatient, to get on with their shopping again,
It was so long ago when it happened, they hadn't experienced the pain.
But the elderly lady beside me, was secretly shedding a tear,
She'd known the horror of wartime and suffered the noise and the fear.
Perhaps she remembered a loved one, who went away not to return
And looking around at the world of today, she wondered why they never learn.

I was too young to know what had happened, when the Second World War was declared,
Just eighteen months old, a mere toddler, I hadn't yet learned the word 'scared'.
I didn't notice the shortage of food; I barely remembered my dad,
I suppose it's quite true that you really don't miss the things that you've never had.
And the sacrifice Mother had to make to ensure her family thrived,
I knew nothing about till long after; then I marvelled at how she'd survived,
I was eight when it finally ended and Dad arrived home at last
And started to rebuild our lives again and tried to forget what had passed.
As a family we had been lucky, for none of our loved ones were lost,
But I remember the tears in my mother's eyes, when they talked of the terrible cost.

My image of war was fashioned, by films and by books that I read,
I read of our glorious exploits and revelled in enemy dead.
I saw 'The Dam Busters' and cheered with the rest, as the water gushed out in full flow,
I didn't think of the thousands who'd drowned, in the stricken valleys below.
When I played, if it wasn't Red Indians, it was dastardly Germans I shot
And like in the films, they died cleanly; it seemed not to hurt them a lot.

In real life, of course, it's not like that; they don't die without any pain,
As a shell rips a limb off, or bullets tear through, they cry out again and again
And lie in the mud for hours on end, with no one to render first aid,
Till death puts an end to their suffering - and another poppy is made.

The voice on the tannoy says, 'Thank you,' and the hubbub resumes once more,
For life must go on for the living and the tills have to roll for the store.
We have made our annual gesture and I wonder how much it's achieved,
I fear, for the planet in general, the message is still not perceived.
For during that two minutes silence, the tide will not have been turned,
Many more have been killed the world over - and all because Man will not learn.

Bryn Strudwick

THE BUCKET AND SPADE

There was plenty of sunshine at Redcar,
On Bank Holiday Monday to boot.
There were families playing and splodging about
And girls in bikinis - quite cute.

There were sandcastles, deckchairs and towels
And not much spare space on the sand,
Old folk with hankies tied up round their heads,
Saying, 'By gum, but isn't it grand.'

There was one little lad who was being a twerp
And spoiling the fun of the rest,
Kicking down sand pies, swearing out loud
And generally being a pest.

A chap sitting right by the toerag's domain,
Spoke to the miscreant's dad:
'If you're wanting an end to his mithering
Get a bucket and spade, me old lad.'

'A bucket and spade?' said the father, bemused,
'Reward him for being a sod?
That doesn't sound like the saying,
Spare the child and you're spoiling the rod.'

'Nah, what you do's easy,' the watcher replied,
'Though it looks like a reet sticky wicket,
When kids are being a nuisance,
A bucket and spade's just the ticket.'

'But how will that stop him?' the other chap said,
'When he's being a right little thug.
If his mother weren't here to see it,
I'd be belting the bugger round t'lug.

So tell me this miracle cure of yours
And show me how bucket and spade,
Can bring us some peace and some quiet,
Cos my patience is starting to fade.'

'It's easy,' replied the old chap, wi' a grin,
'A bucket and spade's what he needs,
I saw it once - some sort of problem,
On a Sunday school outing to Leeds.

Make sure the bucket's a big'un,
Be certain it's pretty strong made,
Shove it down on his head, past his lugholes,
Then give it a smack with the spade.'

Brian Morton

THE PARTY'S OVER

The party's over, let's call it a day
Those loving words about trust and fair play
Was it just a dream of a love that could not be?
Did I believe too much in her?

The answers are hard to find
Perhaps I never will
Her sweet, soft words will remain with me;
Forever and a day.

Her enigmatic smile, was it true or one of guile?
Her sweet words haunt me night and day
Her delicate beauty did me enthral
The party's over, let's call it a day.

It is said that 'silence is golden'
I don't think that is true
Non-communication has made me feel blue
Requests have been in vain and this caused pain.

She will always remain so special to me
'Forever and ever' has been so brief
Does she too feel some grief?
The party's over, let's call it a day.

Was it love that could not be?
Did we fail to grasp reality?
Who can find the key to love;
Perhaps only God above?

What more can I say?
Love once more has slipped away
But my love for her still holds sway
Yet the party's over, so let's call it a day.

Roy Mottram-Smale

THE FOX-WOMAN - ODE TO KIRSTIE MCCOLL

She lives in the urban park, the fox,
The little vixen, with no shelter for her head,
Under the sooty trees, in the scraggy grass,
The daily roar of a great city in her ears,
And the shouting of boys flinging cans in the dark.
She feeds from boxes discarded around, finds
Scraps of food, laps pink-tongued from puddles
And sleeps curled up, thick tail over nose,
Her coat ruffled by wind and wet in the dark,
At the side of a bench with her old name carved.
Think fox, and you think thick red fur, bright eyes,
But she is dull and matted, and somewhere she knows
That once she was loved, but it comes and goes.
At times she feels that her hair was long and groomed,
That her eyes, once blue, shone from out a smooth white face,
That her teeth, now stale-breathed fangs, were even,
And smiled at crowds as she swanned serene.
But her foxy brain blurs and the memories fade,
Glimmers come seldom as she sinks with age.
What was it that passed, in a cast-off life,
That caused her to sink and die, fighting for breath,
In the bright waters of a far-off land?
She remembers being pushed and thrown through stars
From across the world on the racing jet stream,
Impelled tumbling and breathless, to find her home,
Falling into this forlorn beast with the russet fur,
Hair the same shade as hers. They set this bench
As memorial for a dead girl, her friends,
And here she will live until one morning,
One of too many mornings of winter chill,
Will leave her stiff and gone, again.

Liz Davies

SMILE, SAY, 'CHEESE!'

Teeth, we need 'em for sure.
After their first invasion of the jaw,
We clean 'em, lose 'em.
Then we get some more!
My little mum had dentures,
Her mouth was always sore,
So she kept them in a lace hanky in her apron pocket.
Her 'best' set she kept in a secret drawer.
Sod's law made her forget which one.
Then the fun started, all light-hearted
To find the Demon Gnashers.
They'd appear triumphant to cause pain once more.
This ode is to my dentist who was on my side.
'Open wide,' and so it began, a monetary adventure to keep my self-respect.
I didn't expect the worse, as the money evaporated from my purse!
My cards whizzed through the machine with some frightening pace,
As first it was crowns, then veneers, as my little mum sneers,
'You're not a film star, you're not even on TV. You don't even laugh
Much these days. It'll all be in vain, your teeth will end up in Steradent, just like me!'
I tell her, 'I'll be famous one day, wait and see.'
It was a declaration of war, as I sit in the chair once more.
'Implants now,' he says. I nod, okay.
I take out a loan to pay.
Friends admire them, scrutinise them.
'You've done right, they're so natural, you can't take your brass with you, good on you. Hooray!'
I'm tempted to join some Am-Dram, or even learn to sing,
But I can't hold a note or now remember lines,
So I'll just smile as I think of my lovely Mum all the while.
Maybe some 'Time Team' dig will find me in a forgotten space.
People will see me on TV. My lovely teeth and me! Maybe?
My little mum will be pleased as the cameraman goes, 'Wow!'
The hand-painted notice with me reads, 'Barkhill Clinic, Wonderful for Teeth!'
They position me for the cameraman with a reverential tease,
'Come on, Madam, smile for the photo, say, 'Cheese'!'

Joyce Hefti-Whitney

WHAT REALLY MATTERS

It took a long time to learn from the books
all the things one needs to know
and how to interpret those telling looks
and inflections, that matter so.

It took a long time to get to know well
the best way to tackle a task,
when to keep quiet - get on with the job -
and when to question and ask.

It took a long time to find a true place
in the hierarchy in which we live,
the right times to say those words, yes and no,
and when to refuse or to give.

It look a long time to carve out a niche
for a future that's sunny and bright,
a home and a family and all the things
that make life worth living and 'right'.

It took a long time to write down these words
as I am both frail and old.
But now, looking back, I know the real worth
of much more than diamonds and gold!

It took a long time to realise just what
was meant by a welcoming smile,
a loving kiss, a consoling embrace
and a gentle chide - once in a while.

It took a long time to find what matters most
in a lifetime of heartache and fun.
While possessions are lovely to have and admire,
true friendship is the only one . . .
that matters!

Fredrick West

LIFE AND ITS DREAMS

Dream is not just thinking to do
It should be a manner to preview.
It is capability to look beyond things
Without fearing of losing if something rings.

It is making a strategy in your mind
And keep telling your heart, everything is fine.
It is bringing your thoughts to procedure
Enjoying in-between turn and twist it features.

Life is about realising your potential and rewinding your will
Because nothing stays until you hold it with thrill.
It is to accept achievements and defeats with equality
Balancing everything with regularity.

Courage is in learning each day till life ends
And facing challenges that it sends.
With each new task done your new potential is realised
And improvement becomes a part of your life.

It is also self-confidence that matters
And all other complexities wants you to scatter.
It is about trusting yourself and people you like
Since environment plays a major role in life.
As we are humans to be more precise.

Life is also about satisfaction
Giving mind the necessary relaxation
Without involving in irrelevant deeds
And removing the over expanding greed.

Impossible looks a very tough task
Just remove two words from the start
And making a vision to make it possible
As it depends upon you
What credits you want to give to anything unusual

Dreams are not to make burden that takes away sleep
It's about madness in work that does not let you sleep
Sometimes few thoughts keep pondering your working
Block that area and fill it with fully refreshing

No one owns you, it is a battle between you and your desires
Whether you win or lose, both should be admired
You are born alone in this world with unique individuality
You will die alone without taking any collectivity
Leaving behind your fulfilled and unfulfilled dreams . . .
And *the real connectivity* . . .

Abhilasha Tyagi

HALLELUJAH
(The survivors of breast cancer)

We are here.
We are many.
We can be touched, seen, heard, smelt, loved and hated.

Hallelujah! We are here.

Dismiss mythology
Make no talk of legend or noble deeds;
Do not raise hoary old Amazons or the fighting spirit.

Death is the reality,
And the spectre of death
Is neither folklore nor an old wives' tale.

The Spectre is
Cruel and powerful:
Robs me
Of my children's future,
Digs a hollow
Where, once,
Love held sway:
Steals the wind, the sea, the flowers.
The Spectre empties my mind
Blinds my seeing
Smothers my senses.
Makes me no more.

Wait.

Hope is reality.
Hope is no mere spectre,
Yet comes in terrible forms:
Oncologists, chemicals, burning skin and falling hair.
Scalpels, surgeons, amputated flesh.

Yet these, all these, shrivel the Spectre
(That, yes, will one day come.)

But hope, and skill and trust
Crowd the emptiness,
Diminish the fear,
Push aside that Spectre.

Hope and skill and trust bring to us
Wild joy
And pain and life.

Hallelujah! We are here.

Tessa Paul

WHEN THE WORLD HAS GONE MAD!

Rage! Rage! . . . Oh, apocalyptic rage!
White-burning letters dancing upon cra-zed page!
All-consuming chaos inflaming this carnal cage -
When the world has gone mad!
War! War! . . . Oh, glorious, raging, Armageddon - war!
Searing souls of the burning man - more and more!
When the world has gone mad!
Gladiators of God and sons of Satan - swirling . . .
In maëlstroms of passion and mayhem -
What shall become of me
In these battles of destiny?
When the world has gone mad!
Fire! Fire! . . . Oh flaming furies of fire!
Higher and higher burns this blinding funeral pyre!
When the world has gone mad!
Insanity! Insanity! . . . Oh boiling - reality - insanity!
Cooking cauldrons of poison ink profanity reality!
Oh wherefore art thou now, all honour and integrity?
When the world has gone mad!
Righteous incandescent indignation!
Of serial killers and saints!
Burning incense to the gods of my complaint - and damnation!
When the world has gone mad!
Pity! Pity! . . . Oh pity this raging inferno of calamity!
I have become . . . my own worst enemy!
Trapped in the walls of society's sobriety -
And humanity's cold - cold cruelty;
And the winter's chill falls upon the disenchantment, of -
My desire . . . !
When the world has gone mad!
God! God! . . . Oh, Almighty Great God!
What salvage salvation for hypocrite or liar?
Drowning in the quicksands of this midnight hour!
My God! My God! . . . Am I . . . the Messiah?
The world has indeed gone mad!

Paul R Denton

FLOWER POWER - 10FT HIGH AND RISING!

It came from an ordinary packet of seed,
Let's give it a whirl, we all agreed.
So, out by the greenhouse, a sunlit patch,
We planted the seed, and sat back to watch
Our sunflowers.

They burst through the soil, they were green and small,
I didn't suppose they'd grow very tall.
As they sat in the ground, poking out from the dirt,
They suddenly put on a magical spurt.
Our sunflowers.

As they jostled for space, hampered by the weeds,
It was fast becoming the battle of the seeds.
But the two frontrunners reached up for the top,
Was anything, anyone, going to stop
Our sunflowers?

Onwards and upwards they continued to flourish,
With Miracle-Gro their roots to nourish.
Out came the tape - measuring six foot, seven, eight,
They showed no signs or wish to abate,
Our sunflowers.

At last one decided to go it alone,
Pulling clear of its mate, and second to none.
Above all support, even our highest cane,
And the greenhouse ridge, and the weather vane!
Our sunflower.

Finally the whole thing came to a head,
Let's bring forth the measure, someone said.
It passed the 11 foot mark with ease,
Its yellow head nodding in the breeze.
Our sunflower.

As it swayed there gently, top of the pile,
You could almost see the big face smile!
In time to come I'll still be amazed,
As I think of the monarch of all it surveyed,
Our sunflower.

Brian Fisher

THE BRIDEGROOM'S MOTHER

I am the bridegroom's mother,
I'm feeling excessively grand,
The sleek cut of my dress
Cannot fail to impress
And I'm careful to pose when I stand.

I am the bridegroom's mother,
I'm noticed and people agree,
Dignified and demure,
Not prudish but pure,
This elegant lady is me!

I am the bridegroom's mother,
Curvaceous, distinguished and tall.
Oh, the bride is quite sweet,
And her mother petite,
But I am the belle-of-the-ball!

I am the bridegroom's mother,
Breasts thrust and firm like a girl's,
My skin clear, as you see,
Pretty well wrinkle free,
And my head is all covered in curls!

I'm the bridegroom's mother, I'm charming,
My figure is held in a vice,
And do look at the smile,
Fixed, yet oozing with style,
Such perfection was cheap at the price.

I'm the bridegroom's mother, I'm gorgeous,
Never pretentious or loud,
I am cultured and gracious,
Not at all ostentatious,
And quite understandably - proud.

Rosa Johnson

A STRENGTH WITHIN

Brimming over with happiness she looks to the future
The oncoming birth of their beautiful daughter
The first day of school for their eldest son.
Their first family holiday
She was too happy. She was too secure.
She was wrapped up in an endless intoxicating love
Having loved him from the first time they met.
She could still feel that uplifted feeling of love in her heart
Was still flooded by ecstasy when he walked through the door
Snubbed. She felt alone and abandoned
He had spoken cruel words
Denied her any understanding
A selfish carelessness in his manner
A nasty attitude never before seen
Knowing he loved her no more
The pain and anguish
Of a broken heart for the first time felt
Putting on a brave face while her heart bleeds
Emotionally shattered and torn
Completely broken inside
The emotions drain away, dripping away from her like
a light shower of rain
Forced to face the harsh reality for the sake of their children
A numb emptiness descends upon her
She forces herself to confront her future, alone
To step into the light
She finds her inner strength
She finds her inner pride
'I want to try again'
She feels nothing but distrust
How can you truly love when love has gone?
Knowing she can't let him break her again
She starts to hope for a better man
He'd look into her eyes and tell her she's beautiful
With eyes full of love
Always there when she needs him
Someone who will never leave
They carry on normal to the eye
But she has been shattered by the ignorance of man
Rebuilt as a fragile shadow of her former self
Stronger, less in love and distrustful
Waiting for the day he decides to leave her world.

Gail Charles

THE FIRST TIME

'Wrap up warm,'
My mother said,
'Or you'll catch a chill.'
There I would stand
In my hat, coat, gloves and scarf
Ready for the big game.

As the time came,
With my mother at my side,
We approached the gate
Along with the comrades,
Ready for battle,
Ready for war.

I can still see the battlefield,
Lit up by light,
The soldiers coming out
In the different uniforms.
I'm backing those with gold and black might
To win the day, and send them away.

The army repel any attack,
Before advancing forward
And the love affair began.
The ritual of the meet,
The comradeship of brothers
In victory and defeat.

Even after all this time,
I'm still drawn to the battlefield
Of great events played out before me.
When the memories have remained,
Even when the trenches are gone,
And replaced with new heroes and comrades

Some days, I wandered the streets alone.
Wondering what may have been.
And on others, sung and danced
To the joys of a carnival.
But nothing compares, to
The first time I walked through those gates of gold.

David Blakemore

WATERCOLOUR CLASS

'Listen, ladies catch my drift,
Take your colours for a walk
And give your pictures lift.
It lets the subject talk, talk.
Now bring those green leaves over there
Not sprouting rigid at the base.
Let combinations sing together, sing, sing
To make the almost perfect space.'

'Always let your background dry
(But fear not the odd 'cauliflower',
Be patient, blow with your hair blower)
Then wet in wet, or wet on dry
With lights by darks to emphasise
The depths and heights you'll realise - no rush
With your number 16 brush.'

'Try your tubes on a piece of rough,
Begin with experimentation,
Assure the shades be good enough
For heavy innovation.
Not every pigment in the spectrum
Will glow and start to glisten
Save for the novel combination!
Of course trees are not always green!
And seldom true 'as seen'!'

'Pursuing your art therapy
Will need some walls and boundaries
But do not slave on every brick!
The brain fills in, it's a simple trick
To indicate the shape and hue
And only paint a significant few.'

'When finally your work is done
And the last stroke happily in place,
All masking fluid rubbed away,
You're only waiting to hear friends say
(As if their opinion should count)
What a difference it makes with a mount!'

Laila Lacey

HE WANTS TO GO WALTZING TONIGHT

There's the echo of gunfire inside his head
He wants to go waltzing tonight
There's a dance hall downtown
Where you can wear your blue gown
And it's a thousand years away from the fight.

He's weary of violence and of death, little lady
He's just got back from the war
And he's learned the military skill,
How to hide, how to kill
Though he never knew why or what for.

And the reason he was sent there to fight, little lady
Was something he never could get
But the politicians know best
And he could not protest
And now he can't sleep or forget.

He wants to go waltzing downtown, little lady
Away from the sun and the sand,
And the screams and the silence
And the blood and the violence
And other things he never could understand.

They were fighting the tyrant, at least that's what he believed,
But lately he can't see who was right and who wrong
But he can see people dying
Hear them screaming and crying
And he can't forgive what he's done.

He wants to go waltzing tonight, little lady
But somehow he can't seem to stand
There's a terrible pain in his side
And he knows now that they lied
When they sent him to that foreign land.

And his gun falls to the sand in slow motion
And he realises he no longer can fight
And in that last deadly hush
He cares not for Blair nor for Bush,
He just wants to go waltzing tonight.

Trevor Leah

LOST TO THE STREET

It was only a poor boy's dream,
An escape to another world,
A fantasy, a mocking bird,
Hope slipping past the word:
He was just seventeen.

Escape was the master key
To a youth born to poverty,
The bright lights and company -
He thought it was all for free:
He was just seventeen.

Didn't know there was a price to pay,
That promises have feet of clay
In the world he chose to play
Where the password is 'Betray':
He was just seventeen.

He tried too hard to be smart,
A stolen car was his art,
A silent shadow in the dark,
He was ready bait for the shark:
He was just seventeen.

The rules of the street never bend,
Youth is not there to defend,
And mercy is an absent friend,
A fool always pays in the end:
He was just seventeen.

He wanted too much too soon,
A greedy boy out of tune,
Suddenly familiar with the knife-edge
Of reality, life:
He was just seventeen.

He found he was no more use,
A liability on the loose,
No one heard his silenced screams
On a street of forgotten dreams:
He was just seventeen.

Colleen Biggins

GNOSTIC

What strikes between the pen and page,
Between neurons firing action potentials,
Those vast electrical charges that gauge
The measure between words and offer us
The insight allowing for imagistic totems?

What spark within causes the questions
Marking this long, laborious human quest
From time's beginning? As a spark of flint
Once bringing into light those first fires of
Primitive Man, who howled at the moon.

Who planted this vast spark, which some
Call spirit, this gust of life's quick breath,
Starting up the first infant heart, a chicken
Or perhaps the egg? In the darkest hour
Of our brief history, how did it come to be?

Does this spark, between pen and page,
Also cause the myriad stars to glitter in
The black firmament, on which all of our
Origins are anchored? Does this account
For a poet's fascination with their light?

Does this spark also account for his lack
Of belonging in this world, who looks at
Stars for answers and thus feels no place
Within a prison, material, lush and green,
Seductive, but a curse of all that is finite?

Could this spark lead to the knowledge
Of a self known wholly and completely,
In a pledge of inquisition by the scalpel
Of his pen, to see his form in the mirror
Of poems written within its celestial light?

I see only that I must be receptive to it,
To perhaps allay my fears of a sea quiet,
Black and eternal waiting for me in death,
A hard light of the poet put in infant limbs,
Causing me to write my own immortality.

Paull Hammond-Davies

COLOURS

Nature from her palette chose to paint one day
All the birds and varied things offered on display
Daffodils and daisies, mimosa, bright and gay
Fluffy chicks and sunlight, the sight of new-mown hay
Ears of corn a-ripening, canary birds that sing
These she painted yellow for the joyfulness they bring

Nature in her wisdom chose to paint one day
With one stroke she painted fields and grass and leafy way
Reeds and rushes, mossy stream and cooling forest glade
Waving ferns and paths that led to avenues of shade
Fragrant, fresh with foliage that makes a leafy screen
For the coolness of a day in spring, these she painted green

Nature with her skilful hand changed the scene one day
Into the loveliest picture far as summer came to stay
Delphinium and foxglove, hyacinth and lupin rod
From slender necks the bluebells their global heads will nod
The sky a shimmering background, so delicate in hue
For the happiness the skylark brings, these she painted blue

Nature knew the time had come to clean her brush one day
She washed it in the churning sea and splashed the earth
with spray
And everything was cold and damp and misty all around
Smoke from chimneys filled the air and toadstools could be found
The sky with leaden clouds on high, the kestrel with his prey
The sleet, the sludge, the crumbling clay, these she painted grey

Nature, with her natural flair, was so inspired one day
With outline bold she sketched the scene and brought her skills
to play
Exotic plumage, robins' breasts, the beech in autumn hewn
Blazing logs and embers glowing bright with colour strewn
The heat that greets geraniums risen from their bed
Melting warmth and radiance, these she painted red

Nature took these colours and mixed them up one day
Then she cast them all astray in glorious disarray
But as she flung them carelessly, not knowing where they'd fall
A kaleidoscope of colour formed as the sun shone over all
The colours mingled one by one, the shades to merge and flow
Nature looked at the glowing sky, and this she called Rainbow.

Alma Sewell

HIDE-AND-SEEK

I listen very cautiously,
From this carefully picked spot,
I'm hiding right underneath the bed,
But scared, I am not.
I may be a tiny bunny,
But I'm growing every week,
And I'll tell you something for free,
I'm the *best* at hide-and-seek.
She'll never find me here,
I'm practically invisible, you know,
Camouflaged into the carpet,
Except for this stupid bow.
She insists on tying it round my neck,
She thinks it looks 'sweet',
I wish I could pull it off
And have it as something to eat.
But like I said, it doesn't matter,
Stupid bow or not,
I'm still the best at hiding,
I do it an awful lot.
My heart starts hammering
As I see her huge feet,
She peers under the bed, calling me,
Bribing me with a treat.
Apple slices and carrot pieces,
I could have maybe missed,
But she knows me too well, I guess,
Bunny chocolate I can't resist!
I slowly shuffle from my corner,
Dragging my little bunny feet,
I can't help but feeling
Sad at my defeat.
I'm disappointed she's found me,
But she greets me with a cuddle,
I return the warm welcome
With some poop and a puddle.
She shouts something I can't understand
And puts me on the floor,
I head under the wardrobe, excited,
I guess it's time to play once more!

Sammy Wells

FROM HOUSE TO HOME!

Having lived in different houses
In Britain or abroad,
Large, small, old or new,
I found across the board
You have to make it personal,
For a house to be a home!
Adding your own touches
Before it is your own!
By adding small mementos
From everywhere you go -
Filling your house with memories,
Always there on show!
Some may call it clutter,
But it makes your house unique,
Each treasure holding memories
Whene'er you take a peek!
Nothing need be valuable
In a monetary sense,
Just priceless in sentiment,
While causing no offence.
Then, if in later years
You are left to live alone,
Your life is all around you,
Right there in your home,
Bringing you great comfort
As the years pass by,
Recalling happy past events,
Where e'er you cast your eye.
Thimbles in their houses,
Pictures on the wall,
Tiny plates on a shelf
Displayed along the hall.
Teddy bears sit on the beds,
Albums of photographs,
Vases, jugs, ancient stones,
Quirky ornaments for laughs.
It takes a lot of dusting,
A labour of love to me,
Making my house a loving home,
Where there's always a cup of tea.

Evelyn Eagle

NATURE'S INSPIRATION

Beneath the surface
Thy heart feels worn
But keep thyself embraced
Feel thou not forlorn
Seek the heavenly light within
Giving thee a bright outlook
Taking away doubt and all sting
Feeling gentle as a rambling brook
Seek thee nature inspiration
Thou find thy life guided
Thy heart filled with emotion
Days' pleasant and contented
Sadness enters the life of everyone
It is comforting to know
The shining light within comes
Giving spirit when thou feel low
Beneath the surface
When one suffers sorrow
Nature inspiration offers faith
Through days that follow
Starting each day breezy and fresh
Gives a sparkle to the eye
Folk thou meet feel impressed
Respond and are without sigh
With nature inspiration in sight
To face each day
One feels inwardly bright
Even when skies are grey
With all doubt feeling
Thrust thy soul upon nature
Taking away all sting
Giving a beaming heart so pure
Beneath the surface
Keep warm thy heart
Look upward a bright outlook to face
Encouraging folk with a laugh
When time to go with emotion
Thou know thy life endured
Experiencing nature inspiration
Offering folk a life so pure.

Josephine Foreman

A SURVEY OF SURVEYS

It popped through the front door this morning
Before I was feeling my best.
I dropped it right there on the table
With the bills, the junk mail and the rest.
I started to read through the paper
As I drank my first cup of tea,
But my eye fell on that square folder
And I knew full well what it would be.
Another of those dratted surveys.
I glared, but it stared back at me.

So laying aside my paper
I slit open the folder, and there
Were pages and pages and pages
Of a neatly laid out questionnaire.
But I never intended to read it
Over my toast and my tea.
I scanned the first innocent pages,
No more than perhaps two or three.

Then the questions became quite intrusive
And I certainly didn't like that.
Why should I reveal my assets,
Or say what I fed to the cat?
Or tell them who were my insurers,
Or what washing powder I used?
Such details are my private matters
And I, for one, wasn't amused.

Well I tore it in little pieces,
Through the front door the survey came in.
With hate it went out through the back door,
And I filed it away in the bin.
The result of my survey of surveys
Was to hundreds of people like me,
A sheer waste of time and it ruined
My morning toast and my tea.

There's just one good thing to be said though,
It gives work for the postman to do,
And plenty of work for the dustman.
As for me, I've enough work to do.

Barbara Dunning

ANNABELLE

Miss Marion,
Your lips rust, a rough grain that scrapes as we kiss.
As the whirring of your cogs gets depressingly slower
Pessimistically, the world seems less important without
your movements.
Your majestic cogs which are jammed as you circle endlessly
Round and round the same lightless path
Your cosmetic limbs dangle almost lifelessly.
My Marionette,
Harken to the Puppeteer.

In the gauche house I found you
Without life, destitute and alone.
Cedar wood extremities painted with simple colour,
Pale whites with black pearls, that stare blankly
Upwards as your rotting corpse sits and waits.
The colour is so striking. The muddle of peach and white
Woodlice find sanctuary in your faux skull.
Black hair threaded and tied there, knotted after years of abuse,
Long since been washed or combed,
So I found you in the gauche house.

Your eyes screamed volumes,
Your body was broken and battered,
The life you lived left harsh superficialities
And the cords that breathe life into you are tangled.
The twine twists and traps the torment of your turmoil,
Warps the social distortion as you take the centre stage
The shabby wooden cross of manipulation needs restoring.

Patiently I kiss your rusted lips and reassure you,
Care for you, tend to you.
I know you don't want this.
I gaze at your hidden beauty;
Nothing a little paint and oil can't fix.

I traverse the sky holding you in my arms,
Spreading our false wings out and grasping at the thermals.
I cut your ties, sever the servitude.
Once I found you in a gauche house,
Now you go to tea . . .
Annabelle.

Stephen Shimmans

THE LOST YEARS OF SOLDIER JOHN

Kneeling in the Afghan dust, with sweat upon his brow,
The young man, only in his teens, is a warrior now.
The green hills of his Yorkshire home seem a million miles away,
But they are always in his thoughts, by mom, by night, by day.

He dreams of loved ones in his sleep, which is in short supply,
The enemy is all around, and to kill him they will try.
The trailing smoke from mortar shells, high above his head,
Makes him quiver in his boots, and fills his heart with dread.

Two friends were killed by mortar blast, they were not
a pretty sight,
And sometimes in the early hours he calls out loud in fright.
Around his head the bullets fly, and shrapnel sears the air,
The choking dust and searing heat, he has to grin and bear.

He fires a shot and ducks back down behind his flimsy shelter,
And when grenades fall all around it is like a helter-skelter.
Men dive for cover just in time, and the air is filled with smoke,
As what was once an armoured car, ends up smashed and broke.

A silence deep and so profound falls on the weary men.
They grin and call out to their mates, now all is quiet again.
The Taliban have gone for now, but they are never far away,
They will be back with gun and bomb to fight another day.

They call that godforsaken place their homeland, theirs alone,
And they will fight to their last breath, until their enemies
have gone.
So who is right and who is wrong, it is so hard to say,
Why should men die for no reward, could there be a better way?

There are no winners, no one gains, blood stains the barren clay
And politicians shake their heads and frown, but look the
other way.
The poppies in the killing fields, thrive on the burning sun,
They do not care who lives or dies, for they go on and on.

The speckled fields of flaming red draw men from near and far,
They labour, fight, and die in droves, what a vain and
senseless war.

T Stuart

THE CIDER-MAKER'S DEMISE

Over the orchards I have known,
The storm-tossed winds, contempt bemoan,
To wrestle, with a burthened groan, the hapless apple tree,
Whilst here and there, a-spatt'ring sound involuntary hits the ground,
'Tis goodness that the wasps hath found, the maggot and the bee.

'Tis autumn and old Dan's awake
And Tom and Dick and one-eyed Jake -
And mustered, gives each tree a shake, with ladder, pole and spit,
'Tis what they've done for years on end, and what the rustics comprehend -
The countryman's most vital friend, and they wants more of it.

'Tis cider and they licks their lips, the staff of life, like fish and chips,
They drool and on stout poles they grips and whacks the trees the more,
They're dreaming of strong scrumptious wine, extracting from the fulsome vine -
'Ere' round the barrels they do dine, wi' tons of cheese galore.

With 'Oo' and 'Aa' and 'Ee' they toil, to grapple from the grassy soil -
The fruit, more precious than black oil, more precious and by far,
The wasps and bees, they grapple too, the maggots will enhance the brew
And for some action duly drew, all eager for a jar.

There Tom and Dick and Jake and Dan were in the cellar to a man,
Watching the syrup as it ran, contentedly somewhat.
Each took a glass and took a swig, Jake spitting out a thorny 'twig',
Then joining hands, they danced a jig, collapsing on the spot.

Four men collapsed and three men died, one man survived, the one, one-eyed,
The police, they said, 't'were homicide, but couldn't prove a thing.
Jake lost his friends, Tom, Dan and Dick, dead from a little arsenic -
'N' which four wasps - that made them sick, were covered, wing to wing.

He's not the man he was, is Jake and of his friends, he'll never spake
And neither will he cider take, just flash a hand or eye.
Where once his garden was his pride, where now the bees and wasps reside,
He'll never spray a maggot's hide, just lets the world go by.

Each Sunday morn, all dressed to kill, he's walking up the church's hill,
To eulogize 'bout ev'ry ill, to worry and cajole.
A worthy man who's seen the light, a second chance! a second sight!
No . . . Dan and Dick and Tom's his fight, have mercy on his soul.

Derek Haskett-Jones

GRANDMA AND GRANDPA

Grandma and Grandpa need an iron.
They're such a wrinkly pair
I am sure they weren't that crumpled
The last time I was there.
Grandpa is bald and Grandma is grey,
Grandpa says Grandma has chased his hair away.
Grandpa has no teeth, Grandma has a few.
Grandpa can wiggle his teeth, when he looks at you.
Grandpa can't remember a lot of things that have been said,
So Grandma has to shout, to get it back into his head.
I love them both; they're very kind to me,
I wouldn't like to be without, Grandpa and Grandma, you see.
Grandpa grows veg in his vegetable patch,
Grandma can freeze it to make it last.
Grandpa says Grandma cooks such lovely grub,
Grandma says to Grandpa, 'Let's eat, then go down to the pub.'
Grandpa has a pint, Grandma has a sherry,
After a few, Grandma gets quite merry.
They talk about the olden days and the things they used to do,
Before I was born, and before my mum was born too.
There was homemade ginger beer,
Not like what you get now,
In those days, they said it was tastier, somehow.
There were coalmen with carts and horses,
Rag and bone men too, coming down the road
Shouting things to you.
The children were playing cowboys and Indians,
Hopscotch, spinning top, skipping and ball,
Some were just sitting on a wall, talking and laughing,
Making jokes and having a ball.
You made your own entertainment.
Grandma could play the piano and Grandpa the spoons,
They used to swoon to each other's music,
They played wonderful tunes.
They said the days were longer with lots more to do,
I love to listen about the things
Grandpa and Grandma used to do.

Pam Lutwyche

THE VIEW FROM NUMBER TEN
WRITTEN 28TH MAY 2010

No, not that one in London, and I do declare:
No politicians, journalists, doctors of the spin are lurking here
No wrought iron gates, security and passes
No budgets clothed in red; no policies to level down - or up? - the classes

No, in Number Ten, penultimate in Tining
Close we have but people, a plethora of talent
In remotest Shropshire, the county where good dining
If urban literature is to be believed, is quite a rare event

Let me dispel this strange illusion, bred of uninformed
And, I fear, as a once-born Londoner, I must
Label it as simple crude confusion; here, in the Marches
Between Old England and Old Wales, the lust
For life and literature and even love still lurches
Through the shires; living, breathing, feeling, forming

Patterns which in a microscope would engender wonder
What do we here, in the not very far North?
We think, we act, we use each pregnant day
To engender something new; a silent thunder
Of ideas. Here there is no dearth
Of inspiration; here we can still be gay

Without a sordid meaning. Yes, there's sex
And sometimes mindless limbs play
The eternal dance. But here, too, there
Flickers the beckoning candle of hope

Here, though we sometimes doubt their words
We listen to the Coalition Men
Perhaps, just for once, egos, needs, demands
Ambitions might work together . . .

Westminster's knights now have no swords
But a sharper weapon is the wordsman's pen
We will not heed establishment's commands
We shall our thoughts express, again, again, again . . .

Geoffrey Speechly

THE GIFT

A tatty, old brown dining table
Given to me by my mother and father
When they bought a new one because
They did not treasure it as I did.
It had no meaning for them
For them it was just a table
A table to dine on
A table to write on
A table to play games on
A table to sew on
A table to cook on.

But to me it was special
It was my first stage
From the moment I was born
I needed a stage, an audience
Applause, reciprocation.

My table is not used to dine on
To write on, to play on, to sew on
Or to cook on
It is a keepsake.
My most treasured possession
Like an old, ragged doll among new
Treasures, it stands - scruffy amid my antiques
But it is for me, the beginning of my life.

From this table I progressed to the theatre
To open spaces great and small
Some with stages, some without
But there was always an audience
Even if it was only an audience of one.
An open space, a table, an actor, an audience -
The beginning of theatre
And my beginning too.
The ending is my love of literature, of words
But rather to be spoken or acted, rather than read silently
And an education almost as precious to me as my table is.

Sheila Bruce

BEFORE AND AFTER THE WRITING OF POETRY

Before

What? Me? Write a poem? Don't be silly
I can't write a poem, willy-nilly.
I'm no poet, pale-eyed and sad.
I can't write a poem. Are you mad?
I'm no Wordsworth, I'm no Donne
I can't write a poem just for fun.
It's much too difficult, much too hard
I'm no Shakespeare, I'm no bard
Writing a poem would be a waste of time
As I have no way with meter and no way with rhyme.

What? Me? Write a poem, write a verse
Write an elergy or worse
Write a haiku? It can't be done.
I never write anything unless it is fun.
I can't write a poem, don't you see?
I can't write a poem, it just isn't me.
I could write a story, might even write a play
But, write a poem? Sorry, no way!

After

I have written a poem, lend me your ear
I have written a poem without trouble or fear.
I have written a poem with meter and rhyme,
I might even write a haiku if given more time.
I will summon my muse and the poets of yore
Whilst observing the parameters of poetic lore.
I may be no Wordsworth and truly no Donne
But, I have written a poem and it really was fun!

And yet, am I a poet? That is something I ask.
I can say I'm a poet but am I up to the task?
I gave birth to a poem without labour or pain
Now, the test will be . . . can I do it again?

D M Griffiths

FOSSILS OF YESTERYEARS

Harpies sang on the rocks at Newbiggin,
sang to me of seaweed forests
shrimps, eels, deep red anemones
that remind me of Jelly Ju Jus
in a shop at the corner of my street.

Between all this, a hermit crab scuttled
its shell-type house overbearingly large;
upon a rock, baby barnacles clung;
bonsai seaweed trees of silver, brown, purple,
strands of moss like the skirting of
Grandfather's beard, lying below.

Behind, a North Sea roared, leapt,
music lingering as pebbles rolled forwards
chattering then lulling a calming, calming
till foam hissed soothingly on a pancake beach
where boats, like mussel shells, lay waiting for a tide.

Beyond the needle's eye, St Mary's lighthouse,
its beacon beckoning on and on, closer still;
the port of Blyth, where once a welder's flame
threw its gold upon iron ships.

Still, as deep as a pool when clouds block a sun
further beyond; heather blossomed across Cheviot's landscape,
it rode through carpets of green to a sea's edge,
where castles Bamburgh, Alnwick, Warkworth and Dunston
rested teapot frames of past legends,
of saints, kings, love, battlefields and tyranny;
battlefields as red as the sunset of poppies,
as lipsticks on a dressing table,
as balloons on a Christmas festive night; and mellow too,
as mellow as an ancient wine after its first exploding exuberance.

Fish bone, coal dust, shells, pink and ivory, white,
castles, beaches, moors and church steeples,
they would always come -
always come in the dawning of my Northumbrian morn.

Diana Robertson

PROGRESS

Years ago, the light from a tallow candle lit
The faces of friends and work we all did . . .
Working with wood and shaping the stone,
The lace and the crochet for collar and bib.

Next with the soft glow of lamplight -
We read of the saints and the princes of good and bad;
The work underground of children, not grown
Being pushed up the chimneys of grander-style homes.

Times change for the better; so we understand,
With gas lighting in streets and houses, some grand
The homes are built better and wars that were won
To make life worth living for everyone?

Now the power has been harnessed, to make brighter the light
Called now by candle power 60, so bright
Nights now can be made as bright as the day,
Will the world now be happy and thankfully pray?

The power from the horses in engines now run
Faster and faster, where are we headed? Why can't we slow down?
Does anyone notice that beauty abounds?
How a smile lights the eyes and all faces around?

With gadgets so clever and machines
That now work doing most of the jobs once done by us,
We should all be happy, but this is not so
Less work - means less money and so people steal
And they hurt cos they are angry and nowhere is peace.

How, where and when will it all ever end?
Somehow all the 'improvements' from all the years past
Have not made for more happiness nothing now lasts -
Don't pretend.

Yet the sun is still shining, birds all still sing,
The moon and stars will be there and bells will ring,
Prayers will be said and children be born,
The sadness of death and the brightness of dawn.

Peggy Morrill

THE LONG WINDING ROAD

Who would have thought of stopping here,
At the hotel of horrors down Winding Lane,
It looked so nice and ordinary,
Until entering the lobby and ho! What a scene,

There were great big murals of ugly people,
There on the wall, for all to see,
It couldn't be true, it couldn't be me,
It couldn't be you, alternately.

So if you think I stayed the night,
You must be joking,
It gave me a fright,
So much so, I turned around.

And made a sound,
Of disgust of all I could see.
All these faces looking down at me,
Please don't think I am a sham.

Because if I am truthful,
I think I am.
Never again to enter this way,
You would have thought it was another day.

Because I felt confused and amazed,
That people stay every day,
Loving the murals upon the wall,
Looking at them with admiration,
It takes all to make a world

Of them I have admiration,
Ugly is not for all,
But some see beyond the wall,
At paintings by artists all.

Clever and no regrets,
I will never come this way again,
I will take the turning way past this one
And pretend the journey never began.

Iris Crew

FRANKIE

Don't ever leave words unspoken
Don't just walk away
They'll never know the reason why
Your thoughts are darkest day.

Of solar eclipse is the light you see
It's midnight at midday
Let sunshine pass moon's darkest hour
And speak the words

I love you.

You're a hard man Frankie
Scarred by your father's promiscuity
Your mother is mirrored in every girl who's got something
But still you can't say

I love you.

To say those words means something to someone
But what is something when something means nothing to you,

Who is hurting?

She loved you
She loves you
He loved you
He hurt you

Control your hate man or it might fight back and cut you
It's that face again, the one that won't forget you
It's chasing you down old cobbled streets
Each cobble a slab from the morgue
You've lived your life looking over your shoulder
Dazzled by the blade of a sword.

You've been cut deep is not a melancholy metaphor for love
You've been cut deep and you're bleeding
Lie down Frankie and take it, it's over
The life you've lived, we'd never be so cruel
To wish upon another one.

David Ord

THIS IS LIFE!

The hot flush of youth has departed
Passion! Is more in the mind,
Love very steadfast and loyal
Most satisfactory - I find.
No flaring tempers - no tantrums
This comes with the passing of years,
Few recriminations
That always brought on the tears.
Age has many faces
Including a fair share of pain
And memory tends to come and go
Every now and again.
Mind is always willing
But body not quite what it was,
So though inside you feel twenty
You are just not fit - because -
You're short of breath - your knees are stiff
Your hearing's getting dull,
Glasses are needed for your eyes
And you often have to mull.
Am I going - or coming back?
Have I been or went?
Did the pension come today?
Or is it ready spent?
Did we have our dinner?
Or is this meal our tea?
Is it time to go to bed
For weary you and me?
Face all wrinkled - craggy
Hair turned snowy white,
Deep within is the certainty
That all will be alright.
Years of living together
With a love that does never cease,
Has brought these loving OAPs
To a time that is lived in peace.

Dorreen Young

CAVERNS OF MY MIND

I looked for you today,
In the caverns of my mind,
Where memories often stray,
But are never left behind,
Your voice is slowly fading,
Like a worn out recording,
Through my memories wading,
The process is rewarding,
A memory emerges,
And seeks to breathe again,
With my mind it merges,
And I remember when,
When you would walk through the door,
With a funny little greeting,
That simply made us laugh more,
As the phrase we kept repeating,
Memories I have many,
Tucked safely in my mind,
Worth more than your penny,
I'm sure that you will find,
Can I tell you that I miss you?
That it's no easier to bear,
That I want you back it's true,
Though I know it isn't fair,
I wonder if you see me,
From your place high in the sky,
See the sorrow and the glee,
As time goes racing by,
Can I tell you that I'm fine?
That time is flowing fast?
As a star you'll always shine,
In my present and my past,
Although I miss you very much,
You've not been left behind,
Upon the memories I can touch,
In the caverns of my mind.

Adele Rawle

BLOODSHED

No man can be said to be free
While he dons the suit of a warrior.
He forfeits his freedom completely
In beckoning peace to come nearer.
Jingoism rings out loud and clear
When we battle with foreign powers.
We use it to overcome our fear
And when adorning graves with flowers.
One must learn to live with war
As a consequence of the quest for peace.
How our hopes and aspirations soar
When hostilities finally cease.
Amidst silence we begin dreaming
Of creating a life of freedom
And in celebrating whilst grieving
Shed tears of hope that soon blossom.
'Never again!' we always say
From the depths of our grief-stricken hearts.
As life once more continues, we pray
For diplomacy before the next war starts.
When will we find no more use
For the bullet and the bomb
And seek out an everlasting truce
That peace can eventually spring from?
Until that fateful day arrives
Let it be the goal of everyone
To spare civilian and soldiers' lives
And learn to live as one.
So let no one warmonger in our name,
Let us preach the futility of war.
It's high time humanity grew tame
And shed our blood no more.
Yet our valiant do not perish in vain,
We are not guilty of hypocrisy.
In graves all over the world our dead have lain
The ultimate price of democracy!

Arthur

THE FOREMAN

He scurries around the workshop
With his little, fat, ugly frame,
His bald head shines in the sunlight
As much as it does in the rain.
To everyone who knows him,
He is a flaming pain.
His constant argy-bargy
Is driving us insane.

He creeps about the storehouse
Every single day,
We wish he'd take his money
And bloody go away.
He hides down the racks
To jump out on our backs,
To try and catch us out,
With his little, fat, hairy snout.

He walks with a stoop,
And the hump on his back
Is where he puts his awful hat.
If he reads this poem
I'll get the sack,
We all think that he is a prat.

You can always tell
Where he has been,
Because the poisoned dwarf
Turned all the lads mean.
To work with him, it is a sin,
The state this warehouse is now in.

So look around, when you pass by,
If you look hard, you might just try
To see the humpty-back foreman of the factory,
With a little luck, he'll go away,
But don't hold your breath
Or he'll dock your pay.

David Watkins

THE BUSINESS WOMAN

I am a business woman whose dreams could not be clearer
I work all day to earn the cash and buy goods that's dearer.
In each top hotel around I wine and dine my clients
On my large expense account, it isn't rocket science.

You want to know what I do to have this marvellous life,
Well firstly there's no man around, no room for all that strife
And basically I drive around in my big, red car
Picking up unsuspecting fools, I really am a star.

I take them all out to dinner and wine and dine them hard
There is no limit to expenses on my business card;
And when they are feeling mellow I start to talk a loan,
Little do they know that I will take everything they own.

I tap into their little dreams, hidden inside their head
And they are so gullible, they're very easily led.
We talk about a bigger home or super business plan
Or a university degree for each dog and man.

And when they're burning nicely and their brains are all afire
I tell them all about our loans and how they can retire.
They start to shake and eyes light up when contracts then appear
As long as they can repay they have nothing left to fear.

Then with sweaty, greedy hand they sign on the dotted line
As we celebrate over drinks I thank them for their time.
When I say goodbye I promise that I will be in touch
They are so thrilled; they shake my hand and thank me very much.

As I walk away across this luxurious carpet
I think about my bonus without one single regret,
Even though I know of course they will run into great debts
As sure as today is today and jelly always sets.

Then in a month or year or so when I am far away
Their house and car will disappear when they just cannot pay.
As for me I'll be even richer still and moving on
To yet another sucker with my glistening, loaded gun.

Sue Gerrard

THE SECOND COMING OF THE RT REV JESUS CHRIST TO THE CITY OF MANCHESTER

Dog collar glinting sequinned in the sunlight
Crafted for the occasion by the Guild of Craftsmen,
As a special 'thank you' from the church.
The open bus moved slowly down the centuries old,
Smoke-blackened street of the dirty old town.
Flags were waving, old men smiled,
Benignly, kids threw stones
And empty bottles and puked.
Someone threw in a pile of greasy fish and chips
Wrapped up in yesterday's newspaper
And shouted, 'Feed the world!'
The hot dog stands were all doing well
And the ice creams were selling fast.
The three betting shops,
The four mobile phone warehouses
And the four Starbucks coffee houses
Had shut for the afternoon in the city centre
As a mark of respect
And with great honour from the big, fat dignitaries.
They filled the bus, all faltered by too many beers
And free official banquets,
Dwarfing the diminutive figure of the Rt Rev Jesus Christ,
Given the title by the Church as a great honour.
He was sitting in the back of the bus,
Hidden by someone's massive stomach.
It began to rain.
Someone suggested that, 'He would stop it if it comes on too heavy.'
Someone said, 'Get him to walk across the river.'
Shrouded in six umbrellas
And dwarfed by massive town hall and police staff,
He entered the town hall and was gone!

Philip J Loudon

WATT AM I?

I am in every house,
In every place,
The speed of light
Is my pace.

I cannot be held
And oft' go to waste,
I am the modern world
And can always keep in the race.

I need to be greener
And come from sources that are cleaner,
I am not consistent across the world,
I can be inter . . . mittent,
But always flow from high
To low.
I can be lethal,
So be forewarned,
Handle me with care,
Or risk being scorned.
I bring light to the
Darkest of places
And prolong life,
In the smallest of paces,
I am attributed to
A great British mind
But I am the right
Of all mankind.
I dazzle spectators,
At the North Pole,
I am universal but,
Do not feel the cold.
As long as there are electrons
I shall continue to flow,
I permeate the universe
And to its ends and beyond I shall go.

Omer Ahmad

SAM

How do you tell a small seven-year-old boy
His mother has died and you can't stop the pain . . . ?

When only this morning he waved her goodbye,
The wind in her hair and a glint in her eye.
She stood at the gate and off he went to school,
Clasping his pack-up lunch and strawberry fool.
She had blown a kiss, saying, 'From me to you,'
Sketching a heart in the early morning dew,
Promising tonight they would watch together,
His new DVD, no matter the weather.

How do you tell a small seven-year-old boy
He will never see his mother's smile again . . . ?

She will no longer be there to stop the hurt,
To wipe his nose and to wash his grubby shirt;
To cheer on his game on the football pitch
As he clears the ball and scores without a hitch;
Nor help him with his homework when it gets tough,
Or plan his outings and treats and other stuff;
And those quiet moments of secrets and talk
Before he snuggles down to sleep in the dark.

How do you tell a small seven-year-old boy
He will never hear his mother's voice again . . . ?

No breath, no life, nor sparkle in eyes of green,
No laughter, no mischief as they plot and scheme
Together, no songs or dancing round the room,
For him she was the bright sun, the stars, the moon.
Tonight when the TV mayhap be switched on,
He will watch alone for his mother has gone.
No arms to wrap around him and hold him so tight,
To whisper, 'I love you' and wish him goodnight.

How do you tell a small seven-year-old boy
She will no longer come when he calls her name . . . ?

Gwendoline Douglas

GETTING VALUES IN PLACE
(Isaiah 55 Verses 1 & 2)

I'm looking down my shopping list, the cupboards are quite bare,
The supermarket is the place, it stocks all kinds of fare.
I've been on overload this week, all sorts of angst and stress,
I need my peace to be restored, my life is quite a mess.
I haven't had much time for prayer, (in goes another 'need'),
Two minutes, that should be enough and I'll get through at speed.
I'm looking at the shelves right now, at all the 'value tins',
I want my goods at half the price, does God do that with sins?

My basket's getting pretty full, it's feeling heavy now,
All 'value packs' without a doubt, my life's like that somehow.
I've also gone for bargains and the 'two for one' looks best,
Buy one and get the other free, it makes up for the rest.
But what about the time I give to 'top up' my own need?
'No time to stop, I've got to rush, too much to do,' I plead.
Ah, here's the bread counter at last, the basket won't take more!
'Please stop,' a voice calls in my ear, 'and listen, I implore!

You're missing on the vital food, chose busyness instead!
It's Me, your Heavenly Father and you need your Daily Bread.
You're hungry now, my busy child, stop by and taste of Me,
I'll take your emptiness right now and fill you, just you see!'
'Lord, thank You that You called me and I'm glad I heard Your cry,
Just feed me on Your precious word, on eagle's wings I'll fly!'
And gradually, I'm back on track, priorities in place,
Please Lord, give me Your Daily Bread, by Your amazing grace!

My budget balances again, true value's found in You,
Now I've no need to 'penny pinch', only the best will do!
I'm reaching for the finest goods, no money can provide,
The basket's full of nourishment, I've Jesus as my guide.
He writes the list and highlights things I failed to see before,
My great Provider God who has the best things in His store!
There's everything I'd ever need, a bountiful supply,
So I'm inviting all my friends to come in here and buy!

Gillian Humphries

MEADOW ROCK

The film flickers before me in stabs and bits
Of colour and sound, some in sepia and red
And others a slashed black and white.
You are there lying back in the tall grass
Laughing with a satchel beside you with books
Showing like the contents of our past
And beside you, alert, is Monty, staring full
Into the camera wagging his tail away.

I was there of course and drove the car back
To the house and cooked supper while
You bathed and sat out in the garden to read
The poems I had been working on all
Those months of the long hot summer.
I didn't think it would be like this with
Everything so clear and detailed in colours
And sounds bouncing around and about
My head and seeming to be nearly there.

I say nearly for I can pass through forms
And stop the music with a snap of my eyes
And Monty sometimes isn't beside you
But somewhere in the distance as a blur
Careering around fields and lanes separate
From you in the tall grasses with hot sun
On your face and a crinkly smile on your lips.

It stops altogether in the dreamtime of half sleep
When I have no thoughts, only sensations
Of being and having a presence and a past.
You are never far from me and I will always
Remember the stream and its water running
Forever between us and you calling across
With your arms raised towards me and then
My running as the film slowly spluttered
And with a cancerous whisper just quietly died.

Dave Slater

UNE ANNÉE AU SOLEIL*

Sheen sheets of metal
Slice an expanse of foreign sky,
As seagull-grey wings
Slip through chiffon clouds.

Now engines slur
Permit brakes to imbue ear-popping melody
Incessant sun pounds

Tarmac.
L'année à Nice avait commencé,**

Se promener, to stroll,
The meandering ribbon of prolific palm trees
Courting a crystalline ocean.
Perpetual breaking waves

Washing up memories to stain a porous shore.
Vin rouge drenched nights
Diffuse into sultry delights,
The aromatic trickle of fresh café

Throngs the balmy air.
The languid are aroused
And all the while

Time rushes by

Whispers its mocking chant:
The gale raging in our ears.
The shadows of our before
Seep into the intensity of our now,

And the ever pensive balcony,
Whose wrought iron boundaries
Never will our secrets tell.

*A year in the sun
**The year in Nice had begun

Ciara Duggan

THE CREST OF THE WAVE

Drifting on the crest of dreams,
The music washes around my ankles.
I stand and stare
Into the horizon: colours merging,
Fading, becoming hazy waves
Of memory.

The gentle tug of breezes,
And ripples emerge. The colours are gone:
Light radiates, and each nuance -
Broken chords, rising and falling,
Melodies, twisting through dreams,
Spiralling into consciousness -
Each nuance is crystallised,
Captured,
Hovering partway between
Waking and sleeping.

Floating six inches beyond the present,
The future glistens, touchable;
Each new note is breaking
On the shores of wakefulness.
Gently, the echoes
Slide the present back into perspective.
A brief cadence;
Past, present and future are synonymous.

The spectrum opens its wings before me;
A kaleidoscope of possibilities
Silvered with moonlight,
Dancing in the golden warmth of
The untouched morning.

On the crest of the waves, the shore;
A sliver of reality
In an ocean of dreams.

Laura Cheshire

HAMLET'S MIDNIGHT WORDS

Fragments written across the pages,
Italic scrawl,
Words of wisdom, music and laughter,
Lyrics to those songs that might as well
Be a part of you,
And quotes that sum up your entire existence
In a single sentence.
Pen to paper and the words flow,
Bring me sunshine, light and day,
Or darkness, silence and shadows.

Late night stretches on,
And still I cannot sleep,
So on I write, let the music play,
Let the shadows dance in flickering torchlight,
Minutes slip away, hours passing by,
Tiny planet, tiny world, spinning,
Lost in such vastness studded with diamond pinpricks,
That are so very far away.

Breathing in the stillness,
Breathing out the words,
Ticking clocks disturb the peace,
And the distant late night rumble of traffic,
Moving ever onwards.

Pages turn and the pen still writes,
But at long last, my eyelids droop,
Lead-heavy,
Drowsy, dreams are beckoning,
Pulling me down,
So book aside, let the pillows
Take my weight,
And sleep . . .

To sleep, perchance to dream . . .

Glynnis Morgan

THE CHANGING WORLD

Do you remember as a child
When you were free as any bird,
And with your playmates running wild
Your joyful laughter always heard,
When fun was making daisy chains
And watching rabbits scuttling by,
The scent that followed gentle rains
And buzzards wheeling in the sky?

Do you recall the railway line
With giant engines flashing past
And how we couldn't understand
That anything could go so fast?
Can you think back to Pressley Wood,
Our very favourite place to play
Where primroses and bluebells grew
And birdsong could be heard all day?

The little school where we were taught
Complete with noisy clanging bell,
The morning hymns we had to sing
And water drunk straight from the well
Our teacher with her bamboo cane,
And fingers which she struck with force,
The shame of tears in front of girls
Who never got the cane of course?

Our little village offered much
To children in those years gone by
When things moved at a slower pace
With expectations not so high
Unlike today when all is speed
And no one has the time to spare
For all unfortunates in need
Of friendship, love and tender care.

Roy Hobbs

TO THE SPARROW FROM MY WINDOW

It was such a delight today
To watch you from my window,
you and your many friends
gathering like an early morning assembly.

You flew to a clipped willow
in next door's garden.
We were close enough to touch.

You looked handsome in your ebony cap,
beige and brown winter outfit.
You danced a hip-hop from
slender branch to slender branch
until you reached the top,
masquerading as King of the Castle.

Your friends scattered,
black acrobats, silhouetted
against an icy blue sky,
leaving just the two of us.

Then, what you left me, was one of nature's miracles,
a golden trinket for my old age.

Whenever you opened your beak in chirpy call,
a puff of your warm breath,
as it met February's frozen air,
was transformed into a delicate silver ball,
fragile, like a seed head of an autumn dandelion.

I'm glad I did not blink,
because, as quickly as this filigree orb appeared,
it mingled with your song,
then disappeared
into the bright frosty morning.

And to think, you didn't even know I was there.

Dea Costelloe

THE RIVALS

Said Mr Clegg to Mr Cameron
'This is Gotterdamerung!
In this pickle this is what I see.
That other blooming lot
Left no money in the pot
There isn't even gum up that there tree!'

Said Mr Cameron, 'Dear Nick
Though it cuts me to the quick
I have to say I can't help but agree.
I really cannot joke
We do seem to be broke
That, of course, is just 'twixt you and me.'

Then Nicholas said, 'Dave,
We really must be brave
We'll have a coalition, you and I.
Our differences we'll sink,
It will save us from the brink
And all that doom and gloom we will defy!'

Said Dave, 'Oh, well said Nick,
That ought to do the trick,
Together we will make a common cause.
A coalition's just the thing,
All the bells will ring,
There'll be long and long and long and long applause.'

Says the poet, 'Yes . . . well . . . hmmm,
I see, dee-dah, dee-dum,
And so, I think, say all of us,
I don't want to sound too fractious
But I feel that there'll be taxes!
Let's lock up all our wallets, at a guess.'

Martin Harris Parry

DECKCHAIRS AT SOUTHWOLD

Still, oily heat
Crisscrossing the surface of the sea
At Southwold,
England's most eastern point.

Stacks of deckchairs
Break the view of the sea huts
Which ripple the colours of the sea.

Beneath the eyeglass of the sun
Pink-patterned lace seeks wisdom
As seagulls cut the air in sharp loops.

On the pier, the ticking clock shaped as a bathtub
Strikes on the hour and on the half-past
Its wheels in tune with the propelled water.

No turning back for mums dressed
In the colours of the azure
As their offsprings gulp chilled fizzy water.

Exhausted on opened deckchairs
Experienced bodies sail siestas
As the sky blushes even stronger.

It is business as usual at the end of the pier
Amateur anglers check the horizon
For silent moving shadows and hidden waves.

The sky is weighing its blue
Over the deckchairs in animal print
Over the maze of men, women and children.

With nothing to do, but rest and shop for
Buckets, spades, and fish and chips
Against battleships of seagulls . . .

Mariana Zavati Gardner

SUPERIORITY - INFERIORITY SYNDROME

I can assure you that had I had a good start
Things would have been so much different for me.

You see, firstly, if I was able to do things
On my own, I would not have become so

Dependent on others doing things for me.
Even though I am fully aware of my patterns.

You see, it serves my purpose having others
In servitude to me. It helps me perpetuate

My 'lifestyle' that I am so accustomed to
In this world that I find so uninteresting

And boring, to the extent that I need to
Event dramas to bring my whole world alive.

You see, it all goes back to a much earlier
Time when I felt ignored and insignificant

So much so that I vowed that if ever the
Opportunity arises for fame, then that will

Be me, first. You see it doesn't really
Matter whether I was born first, middle or last.

The fact is, I was born to be superior
Even though somewhere along the line there

Is this gnawing feeling of feeling inferior.
That I find myself constantly battling.

It had dawned on me recently though, that
If I focussed on the world in terms of two people

Instead of only one, I might gain an understanding
Of where my relation to the other begun.

Jennifer Hooper

THE OLD OAK

'Can you all feel it children, sprinkling gently from the sky?
Absorb every drop you can, else it quickly passes by.
Attention my brave soldiers; straighten up each sun-scorched blade;
Your uniforms will be as green as troops billeted in the shade.

Be ready drooping beauties to open your petals up:
Shape them like drinking vessels, to fill for each quenching sup.'

'I can feel my roots tingling,' squealed a grateful beetroot.
'The earth is getting softer; now I can sprout a new shoot!'
That made the old oak chuckle, causing his branches to sway.
'I can see a huge dark cloud; the wind's blowing it our way!'

'I thought I would die for sure,'
Whimpered the weeping willow.
'Oh, she's blubbering again,'
Scoffed the evergreen hedgerow.

The greenhouse plants were grumbling,
'We can't get as wet as you!'
'But you get watered daily; we've had to wait, so we're due.'
Rambling rose rattled her thorns as she danced in the warm breeze.

A cucumber retorted, 'That plant spray makes us all sneeze!'
'Now, now!' the old oak chided,
'Settle down and have some fun;
The rain is now abating; let us bask in summer sun.'

The old oak called his charges, 'The sun will be setting soon,
It's time to rest, my dear ones, 'neath the night-light of the moon.'
As a young sapling, he was ravenously keen to learn,
Now mentor-protector, his hunger continues to burn.

The leaves had their last rustle; then the flower petals closed.
He mused about the 'morrow - more challenges he supposed.

Janet Hewitt

MOVING ON

We are moving house today,
we are moving house at last.
I must not turn my thoughts around
and think of all the past.

This little country cottage
we have lived in all these years;
the city life a-beckoning
with all its many fears.

My friends all say be positive,
it may not be so bad;
at least the house you're moving to
is near your mum and dad.

Is there time to change my mind?
I fear not - feeling sad;
perhaps to live the city life
may not be quite so bad.

With lots of shops and more to do,
it could be rather funny.
Of course to live that kind of life
could easily eat your money.

Well, it's time for us to go;
I've just picked up the clock.
It made the house seem quite alive
with its very loud tick-tock!

The furniture is on the van,
it's time for us to part.
I will miss this little house
from the bottom of my heart.

Stephanie Foster

FAVOURITE FLOWER

When the people were asked to make a choice
Of the country's favourite flower
Most thought the rose would stand supreme
But another has risen to power

The nation's choice is the lily
Favoured by the French of old
Are we allowing them to dominate?
Along with the marigold

My own choice would be the sweet pea
With their blooms on high
Stretching the artist's palette
So pleasing to the eye

In narrow-waisted crystal
In our sitting rooms
In the hands of brides
About to wed their grooms

Climbing up our garden walls
Reaching heady heights
Tendrils gripping on the way
To burst forth in delights

Perfumed and such subtle shades
This perfect little gem
It reaches up to face the sun
The garden's diadem

Sweet by name and nature
Giving us much pleasure
A garden's really not complete
Without this little treasure.

Len Peach

SWALLOWS

We have a lovely family
That come to us each year
It is the swallow family
In mid-April they appear.

The swallow is a small bird
With nice long pointed wings
It has a pretty forked tail
And is a bird that never sings

They stay here for the summer months
And are as busy as can be
Building nests in outhouses
Or barn lofts, but never in a tree

The swallow has dark feathers
With a little breast of white
They fly away quite quickly
And soon are out of sight

When the swallows dive down low
Catching midges as they fly
The weather's cloudy and rainy
But in good weather they fly high

They have a special instinct
In autumn they move on
To a warmer, sunnier climate
With their families they are gone

They have no map or calendar
But they know when to go
We have so enjoyed their visit
Although they do not know.

Nell Thompson

Another Place, Another Time

When you gently take my hand
A million warm winds cross our land
And when your lips kiss me once more
They carry me to that distant shore

You and I have sailed close to the warm west wind
And have been as flotsam on that shimmering beach
Drifting in those currents of love
Floating never more out of reach

For every moment your eyes meet mine
I know you are my love, my only one
Carrying me to another place and time
On the far side of the sun

Many will never understand
They mock and are quite blind
I will whisper once more my love
Of another place and another time

Feelings grow from strength to strength
All barriers come crumbling down
So kiss me once more my love
In this beauty that we have found

For true love will never die
Feelings of peace and beauty carry on
Across the oceans of time and space
To the far side of the sun

So gently take my hand once more
And again let your lips touch mine
For you and I will travel on
To another place and another time.

Jim Wilson

THE COMPUTER AG(U)E

My computer has a new life
But it's a life of its own!
Whatever key that may be pressed,
It prints another (just in jest!)

It has a way of sabotage -
As proved by this, my poem -
Which was to be a work of art
But thence behove itself to roam!

Its own idea of monochrome
Is more a shade of pale mauve,
Although attempts to choose a font
Are not one it seems to own.

Thus, its Word grows hot and bothered -
As do its operators.
Even now it's in sleep mode,
Which seems its preferred status.

Its memory's as good as mine -
No back-up will restore.
Whatever I typed yesterday,
By now it has gone astray.

And so I dropped it on its head,
The keyboard's all askew,
Only to find its guarantee
Is no longer valid and new!

Now I rest in my own sleep mode,
Without a care in the world.
No thought of Word or McAfee -
Just a twinge of regret from me!

Jo Allen

CAT'S EYES
(Dedicated to beautiful Dillon my cat)

I see the rain
What am I to do?
I want to go out
I stare through French doors
Waiting, watching, thinking
Keeping in
Keeping out
Keeping up
Miaow, miaow
Sun is coming out
A rainbow's appearing
It's time to go
Smell the new air
Daisy, daisy
Going slow
Going fast
One hour to wait
One minute too late
It has been said
I am streetwise!
Whatever
That's why I'm on the sunny side of the street
With my tail in the air
I don't have a care
Popping in
Popping out
Last to my post
Here I feel secure in my armchair
Miaow, miaow!

Georgie Ramsey

SO IN LOVE

In a park,
On a lovely summer's day,
My baby and I,
Have many a long, loving kiss;
No breath to speak or say.
Warm and comfy,
In each other's loving arms,
We succumb to each other's loving charms.
We are such a loving couple;
So in love;
Whilst in the trees,
Up above,
Birds and squirrels look down with awe,
At this loving couple,
Kissing and cuddling,
Upon God's lovely green floor.
Leaves drop around us,
In the shape of a heart,
This loving couple,
So in love
And can't bear to be apart.
Finally, we rise,
Constantly looking into each other's loving eyes
And holding hands and loving arms entwined,
Beneath the lovely sunshine,
Walking off;
Stopping every yard or two,
For another loving kiss and cuddle
And uttering those lovely words,
Darling, I love you!

Jason Pointing

QE2

Having travelled and flown for many a mile
For my homeward trip in a liner of style
I'd waited so long before getting aboard
But the picture of her in my mind I had stored
It was evening time before she set sail
And all we could see as we glided away
Were the lights of New York along the quay
So smoothly she glided away out to sea
The ocean this time so smooth and so calm
With the sun shining down to add to the charm
The Atlantic now was just at its best
With hardly a ripple of showing unrest
The ocean, it seemed, we had to ourselves
Save small sloop complete with sails
It is so hard to believe until taking a trip
That everything needed is there on the ship
A walk around on deck, at the shops you amaze
And then wander up deck, at the shops you amaze
And up deck to enjoy the sun's blaze
The dining, the swimming, the music, the fun
But I think best of all is to lie in the sun
The ocean, the sky and the tang of the breeze
Softly caressing a trip of such ease
Those days, so perfect, passed as they had
Back to old England once more, I felt sad
I'd left her once without even a tear
Travelled to other lands, far and near
But now I was back, rather sadly I fear
After a wonderful year
England looks so drab and so drear.

Thelma Jean Cossham Everett

ZONING IN AND OUT

Ah, the waiting, the pacing
The yearning, the gazing
For my tube to chug along
Its own sweet song;
And open its doors
With its slippery floors;
Warning me to *mind the gap* -
As I enter - the doors close - *snap!*
I look left and right for a seat -
Gaining one is such a treat!
I read my paper and check my make-up,
Giving the others a little shake-up!
On goes my iPod and off goes my mind,
Meanwhile, my tube leaves stations behind,
Zoning in and out of towns,
Some snort, some shout - and some frown!
As it's time for me to alight,
I ease up on my seat upright.
I check my watch and the maps above,
Ignoring the faces which show no love!
I get up and clamber over feet and bags,
Saying, 'Sorry,' 'Excuse me,' as my momentum lags;
Some are polite, some smile -
Some make me wish I'd run a mile!
My stop arrives and I leap out - minding the gap -
The doors shut - *snap!*
As I switch off my iPod and turn on my mind,
My tube leaves the station behind;
Zoning in and out; some hug, some smile
And I look for the exit aisle.

Sudakshina Mukherjee

A BATTLE BUT NOT QUITE

Your face is like a mirror,
Reflecting on my thought.
Am I trying to escape,
Or have I already been caught?

Your eyes are the deepest blue,
Swaying like the ocean.
Can I still sail away,
Or has the boat been set in motion?

Your mouth is full of danger,
You use it like a gun.
Has the firing already started,
Or has it not even begun?

And I, I seem to be,
The only innocent one.
This is no battle we are fighting,
Because you have already won.

Joséphine Kant

SUMMER NIGHT

The sinking sun sets slowly over the rooftop ridges
Its fiery orb paints blazing brushstrokes across summer sky
Leaving the dusky world to nocturnal creatures of the twilight domain
Elusive screech of owl, ghostly moth haunts in street light haze
A snuffling hedgehog shuffles his well-trodden routine way
Under the arch, heady scented with fluorescent rambling rose

Whisper of wind rustles spiky crest of dense matted phormium
Its feather-fingertipped silhouette spires gently stir
The monotone hum of distant traffic reverberates in still, sultry air
Above me, the twinkling, lunar-lit, star-dusted sky
I breathe the heavy night air still warm from the heat of the day
And close my door on the world of darkness and cats on the prowl.

Shirley Clayden

THE GIRL CALLED 'SARAH JANE'

She was a typical middle-class Victorian miss,
Endlessly paraded but must not be heard,
Her skittish thoughts to her immediate family.
Her father a disciplinarian general practitioner.
Leech bleeding, cold baths and sundry opiates.
He must protect her from the outside world.
Groomed to make a good wife from birth.
Try to marry her into one of the noble families.
Trained in the art of crocheting and darning,
And painting in water colours in the parlour.
Acutely lonely, for she had no other siblings,
Her mother untouched since her trying birth,
Spent much of her time confined to her bed,
Feigning sickness due to female problems.
Sarah tried to please her dear, distant papa.
Various private tutors saw to her education.
She spent much of her time downstairs,
Mixed with some of the servants' children.
These youngsters set themselves a mission,
To show her the delights of being a child,
Though life was extremely harsh outside.
God or Darwin never meant her to be,
A fragile fern who resided in the shade,
For she was to be a bloom of great beauty.
Like a popular, opulent, buxom Bourbon rose.
A hybrid of European and Chinese origins
Let the passionate actress/songstress emerge.
To throw off the shackles of her upbringing.
Let the whole globe see her performances,
Young Prince Bertie made her his paramour.

Julia Pegg

STABLE

My dentist says my teeth are stable;
He hurriedly hands me my dental
Chart then says if I need to
See him I would know where he
Would be; for he is very busy, he has
To look at a lot of people's teeth all
Day long.

The dental nurse opens the door
And then quickly smiles, for she too
Is very busy and she has to smile at
A lot of people all day long.

I wait at reception and think how
Lucky I am that my teeth are stable,
For there are a lot of people whose
Teeth aren't stable and this gives
Them a lot of pain and expense.

I hand the receptionist my chart and
Money and she quickly hands me my
Receipt then answers the phone
For there are a lot of people who
Need to speak to her about their teeth
And this keeps her busy all day long.

I go out into the street and when no
One is looking (not wishing to offend) I spit blood into the
Gutter then walk home thinking, if
They really knew or even guessed,
That in the whole of my life some
Thing that I have never felt is stable.

Brian Grace

SEA OF BLUE

Away, away to the bluebell wood,
Over yon' distant hill,
In through the wood,
Walking mossy ground,
Hear the skylark's shrill,
Garlands of lichen
Hang like lace,
I push my way on through,
A sea of blue assaults my eyes,
What a sight to view!
Bonny bluebells everywhere,
An aromatic smell,
Down the bank clear water springs
From a shallow crystal well,
I'm away, away to the bluebell wood,
Sweet solitude lies there,
Imagine you are here with me,
This moment we can share.

Winifred Curran

I LOVE YOU . . . UMERSIDDIDY

Where is the tender touch of light
To soothe the shadows from my heart?
I like awake,
As your memories stumble from eyes in the darkness
Awaiting a glimpse of the yawning sun.
I'm missing you.

Usmaa Umer

CYCLE

Our lives are sand upon the shore,
Swept out to sea and back once more,
In constant flux, these sands of time
And when we're gone the stars still shine,
Upon the place we used to be,
Where pictures fade and memories flee,
To disappear amongst the crowd,
Of wispy visions that like a cloud,
Are blown away by windy breath,
While hand-in-hand we walk with Death.

And yet the cycle carries on,
It doesn't care that we are gone,
It never slows, it never stops,
They plant the seeds then gather crops
And what is it we've left behind?
Our bodies gone, our hearts and minds,
Just our children and theirs that follow,
Who have our eyes that see tomorrow,
The sands still shift before the tide,
The cycle cannot be denied.

Robert Brooks

AUTUMN LEAF

Falling
Gliding
Tumbling, slowly
Cast adrift to trip and skip
At the wind's will.
Floating motionless
On air waves
Tossed in a torrent
Of swift surrender
A last brief shaft of life
That ends quietly
Underfoot.

Greta Robinson

EMPTY NEST SYNDROME
(Dedicated to couples whose kids flew the nest)

Life is empty,
They've all gone home,
No more fun,
No more moans.

My daughter and son,
Were here to stay,
Not forever,
For a holiday.

My house is so quiet,
My house is so bare,
All I can do is sit and stare,
At four empty walls,
It feels so unfair.

Once so noisy with my children's laughter,
When in their bed my children would natter,
About the old days, good or bad,
How they behaved when girl or lad.

Life is empty,
They've all gone home,
No more fun,
No more moans.

But cheer up, they'll be back
For a holiday,
Maybe next summer,
Or another year,
My house will be full again, of family cheer.

John Murdoch

MOTHER (LETTING GO)

The flicker of the hospital light
Bleeping of machine
Pulsating out hope and restless fight
Preacher preaching his mechanical words
With incensed fingers
Braille like in their search for reason and truth.

Yes, I still speak her name
And see within the shadows
That last flicker of life
Till the dark engulfs my vision
And hearts and souls entwine
In fevered salutation.

Your unspoken words
Aren't meant to chide
Just a farewell from
Within the silence
And white light
And hence we wait
For Heaven's gate
To be unlocked
And your entry
Guaranteed.

And what remains isn't hope,
Or light,
A future not born
All that remains; and can ever
Be,
All that remains is love.

Mark Boardman

THE ANGLER

The sun was shining o'er the river bank
Along its edge the cattle drank
O'er the rushes and the reeds
Dragonflies hummed upon the breeze
'Neath a shady willow tree
A lonely angler sat at ease
Trousers rolled up to his knees
The day was hot, not a thing did stir
Except those dragonflies flitting there
The weary water jogged along
Down to the salty sea
The lonely angler soon did nod
When something pulled upon his rod
No, not a fish a-hanging there
An old shoe, not a pair
He roused at once from his sleep
And flung it back into the deep
When suddenly a sound did stir
A moorhen was swimming there
Then the croaking of a frog
In the rushes by a log
And the droning of a bee
Blended together in harmony
A water rat came nosing out
To see what it was all about
The day wore on - with still clear heat
When over all a haze did creep
The angler rose to his feet
And homeward tread for tea and bed.

D Carr

DUNKIRK - 70 YEARS ON

It wasn't clear now
but I knew we had entered Dante's Inferno,
every foul fiend in hell screeched there.
The beach, once empty as it may have been
but not today, no not today.
No asylum could have offered such scenes,
though the insane were wandering between those
many abandoned shapes of sculptured metal.
Man-made pterodactyls screamed above,
releasing their lethal eggs as the tide rose.
In pain I stumbled into the all-enveloping smoke
that stank of oil and gripped your throat.
The mind plays tricks, this place must be Hell,
perhaps the Devil's joke,
not a place to dwell.
Suddenly the pain subsided,
then I saw her standing there
in the shimmering haze.
The wind was blowing her hair,
'Come on son,' she whispered,
'You'll be fine.'
Then her shape shrank and faded
into the darkening skyline and was gone.
Out to the boat we waded,
how we survived is a mystery,
the rest history.
Funny thing an exhausted brain,
Or did my mum come back again?

Colin Burnell

LIES

Is trying to figure out somewhere in my brain why people lie -
I can't quite understand why.
Is it because you don't want to fight, don't want to hurt me,
Make me low and make me cry, break me down and make me blue?
Don't tell lies - please be true.
Do you know that one lie leads to another and then another?
You will get found out - somebody will tell me
And then I will know for sure who you really are -
There I was thinking you were my rock,
My star, even my world,
Now it turns out that that was just a fake disguise,
You were dressed in to win my respect -
Do you deserve it? I think not.
I must stick to the pride that I have got left and let you go,
Walk away and never look back,
Keep on going down that path, find a new direction,
A destination from this situation that I got into.
I'm gonna get back on my feet and admit defeat,
Surrender while the going is good,
Get a job, a life, my sanity back,
Leave the past behind me and don't look back.
In years to come this will be funny, not fresh and raw,
And not so sore upon heart.
Let's make a start. The future's ahead,
Lead me the way, let's use it instead.
Give me directions to a better life,
Lead me the right way, not the wrong - give me a map,
If needs be I'll find a way that in the end will surely pay.

Julie Paton

UNDERSTANDING

I understand now more than ever
That what I most believe in is myself.
I am my own god, master, lover and carer.
To worship myself and fill my body with pure light,
In the form of wisdom, knowledge and insight
Captivates the true sensory of the mind.
The natural crops, grains and fruitful treats
Enrich and sweeten my skin
And allow that glow to shine
From me onto others so effortlessly.
To treat my fellow man, woman,
Animal and world around me
With that tender touch and that great warmth
Which I crave from others;
And to keep learning and educate my soul.
I know that society, not life,
Will try to corrupt me
And scrape the vitamins from my eyes
With both hands shaped like claws.
But I must stick to my bible of I
And withstand all that may face me
With open hands and open palms.
If not, what shall become of me?
Who will save me from the darkness,
The screams and temptations?
Who will care?
Only time will unravel the truth for me,
The truth for us all.

Shane Jordan

FOO

Light shines
eyes bright
I remember you
Soft skin, warm fur
a little cat called Foo

At home
Playful times
Until day would enter night
Quick chase, learning grace
a little cat called Foo

Curled small
I hear your call
you must leave this life
Strong fight, fading light
a little cat called Foo

Rest now
playful miaow
we remember you
perfect puss, lots of fuss
a little cat called Foo.

Alison Williams

SO DEAR

A land of ancient beauty
Steeped in history
Surrounded by many secrets
Hidden in a cloud of mystery
So dear, so wholesome
Mellowed with time
A land now of plenty has
Withstood the test of time.

Richard Mahoney

WHEN DEATH BORROWS LOVED ONES.

Here and now, beyond and above,
This earthly-bound creation place
Hurt hearts seek God's unending love
And will depend upon His grace
When death borrows loved ones.

To experience deep sorrows,
For sweet times that could be tainted
By harrowing lone tomorrows,
Is painful for all acquainted
Who give thanks for lost loved ones.

Faith and time will mellow sadness
Then all past shared pleasant days
Will become sources of gladness,
Joyousness, and of happy praise,
Not grief, for dead loved ones.

In our confusing sense of loss,
Yet aware that through Christ's release
Death was defeated on His cross,
We know our souls will not cease
But rejoin heavenly loved ones.

Ronald Rodger Caseby

BACKYARD LIFE FORMS

Confined by space;
Looking like distorted white slugs, undisturbed
They can survive the rain.
Glowing into the night sky,
And repelling those who use the backyard.
If a house owner found the nerve,
He'd use a bucket of water with a brush,
Or a handful of salt.

Thomas Baxter

WORLD CUP 2010

The sun is out, the sky is blue,
from our hotel window what a view!
Shower taken, jet lag forgotten,
it's down to breakfast dressed in cotton.
It's time to go now, be on our way
to a very important date today.
Driving past happy faces
through the dry and dusty places,
Our destination looms in sight,
oh my goodness, what a wondrous sight.
We park our car then we take our seats
with excited fans shouting and singing,
Waving flags we feel so proud
to be a part of this happy crowd.
The waiting is over, the time has come,
here comes the England team,
the roof is raised with thunderous applause.
We stand with pride, with a lump in our throats,
singing the national anthem full of emotion.
The handshakes are finished, the whistle blown:
'Come on England,' bring the cup home.

Sandra Leach

ESCAPING THE PATH TO DESTRUCTION

18 and lost, it shouldn't be like this,
calm yet twisted in some romantic bliss.
Tired yet restless, reaching for gold,
drenched in fear and feeling so old.
Collective with wisdom, reflecting in none.
Clutching to memories that should now be gone.
Banishing anguish, an ugly phase,
deep within the poison haze.
With light a hand points the way,
to show a clearer, brighter day.
A bed of roses awaits my feet,
and avoids the beautiful that caused deceit.

Maria Howson

SONG OF THE SPHERES

As many grains of sand are there
As scattered stars in the heavens.
In each there lies a secret code
Which creates this wondrous world.
Is there any man who can count each strand
And exactly name the glistening points?
Which man can leap from star to star
And proclaim that they are blesséd?
Within the cold and dark, black void,
The planets erupt into song.
Oh, that we could only hear and capture
The crescendo of the melodic line.
This paeon of praise, this anthem to His hand
Which with the waves, extends forever
Unheard, mysterious with enigmatic tongue
Their unison continues to the utmost.
The melody, the Earth can only sense
No orchestra or conductor leads.
Yet still in chorus the spheres chant well
Dreaming while they carol, in silent space
Turning and burning, the intensity grows
Brighter and dimmer, the singers spin with grace.

Anne Szczepanski

SAMMY THE DORMOUSE

Little Sammy Dormouse
Lived in a little house
He spent his life
Looking for a wife
He hunted in ditches
And under bridges
In barns stacked full of hay
Where rats catch their prey
Alas, that was the end
Of little Sammy Dormouse.

Elizabeth Bevans

GROWING UP

I used to shoot Indians
From a sofa that was a covered wagon.
I flew cardboard box rocket ships to the stars
Alongside Flash Gordon,
I battled aliens from Mars.
When I was growing up.
With a sword made of wood
And dustbin lid for my shield.
I was a knight in short-trousered armour.
Mother's pride always falling out of trees
Arriving home with cuts and bruises to alarm her.

Clockwork trains
Subbuteo figures that were always breaking.
Boyhood memories from yesteryear
Summer's halcyon days,
Where we played in innocence without fear.
When I was growing up.
No thoughts past bedtime
Tomorrow was always a day too far away.
Growing up was the last thing on my mind
But sadly, grow up I did,
Like we all have to do in time.

Keith Tissington

MEMORIES

Memories are dreams of the past
Something that's there, and will always last
Memories are a smile and a goodnight kiss
Full of love and utter bliss
Memories are something no one can take
Memories you know are not fake
Others are bleak and sad to recall
Best maybe forgotten if possible at all
Keep your good memories close to your heart
The unhappy ones, let them from you part
Life is too short to dwell on grief and pain
Try letting go and life may be complete again.

Jennifer Parker

DOUBTER

What makes you so angry
that you fight with your soul?
Childhood memories - sexuality,
what will make you whole?
Take one problem at a time -
relax your mind.
Erase all the jealousy
and a solution you will find.
Think of all your good points
and work on them.
Remember the times when you were happy
and believe you'll feel that again.
Bitterness destroys you
and won't allow you to move on.
It distorts your feelings
and becomes your number one.
Use your intelligence
and decipher fact from fiction,
only you know -
how to stop this addiction.
For that's what you are following,
a fictitious path.
Your thoughts are warped
and you suffer your own wrath.
Nobody's out to get you.
The opposite is true.
You're very much loved.
The only doubter is you.

Anne Leeson

THE TRAIN

The station's quite full
We get on the train
Find our seat
I'm near the window again
The train leaves on time
As we settle down
Sad as we leave
This quaint little town
Fast as it can
The train takes us to
Lots of small stations
And wonderful views
Countryside, cows grazing
Pylons and roads
Much larger stations
Then canals and boats
Rivers and lakes
With houses nearby
White fluffy clouds
And lovely blue skies
Having a snooze
Well just a short nap
The train racing on
Along the rail track
Soon it will be
The end of the line
It will be great
If it gets in on time.

Jeanette Gaffney

THEY CALLED HER A WITCH

Their ignorance called her a 'witch'
        She lived alone,
          Knew ancient ways
    And herbal law,
    Could 'charm' a wart,
    Your 'fortune' tell,
    Make 'lucky charms',
    But never curse
Or injure, as they said she did.

For what can earn that title 'witch'?
    One différent,
    Who dances to
    Another tune,
    Therefore becomes
    Rejected, feared,
    By 'normal' folk,
    Who toe the line
That happens to be fashionable.

Was she a witch? They thought she was,
    One day they grew
    Hysterical,
    Burnt her alive
    From zeal for God -
    Who I am sure
    Stood with *her* and,
    Sharing her pain,
Atoned for those who claimed His name.

David J C Wheeler

THE 3AM KICK OUT

Two mute meat merchants detonate the exit doors
An army of flailing arms sweeps us into the night

The glass you've been holding hostage under your jacket
is finally released to the ground,
showering our shoes with little rum-coated diamonds.
You don't notice - your hand still gripping
the invisible truth serum.
But we both know very well: I have never played fair
with your heart.

A busker shifts into focus -
His surprisingly shiny, shiny shoes splashing softly
in a dirty oil rainbow. I shower him with a few paltry coins,
dregs of my gin-soaked shame.
We need a little background music for our demise, don't we?
A few warm-up strums and for a second I am sure
he will play our song. I'd grab you for a clumsy waltz
and we'd fall into each other, laughing.

He mis-chords - recklessly eyeballing the peacock parade
saunter past in the last ditch attempt
to snare two lonely miniskirts.
No. The endless supply of heady cocktails has not paid off
There will be no romance for you sirs.

Lost, I bumper-car through a stampeding herd of tottering heels.
You disappear into flickered seconds of black.
A half-hearted 'Goodnight' is offered,
Left to ricochet off the roral streets.

Corrina O'Beirne

JULIE'S TREE

. . . A pine, so straight and tall it stands,
Its crown of cones so large, I just can cup one in two hands;
Their geometric beauty so precise,
They surely, surely were created by some master craftsman
In some far-off mystic land.

It was so small, a twiglet stuck into a plastic pot,
Silvered, sprayed with white spurious snow,
A Christmas decoration, highly prized, beside my daughter's bed
And each New Year this annual symbol faded,
Till the day one sprouted green and Julie nurtured it upon its ways.

Just as I nurtured all my children every life-long day
And now they all have long outgrown their small, safe pot,
They stride the world in search of Camelot,
In the Italian garden, Jules and I had planted out her pine,
Into a space within a rose-red pillar,
Part of Owen Aisher's wall of Marley bricks
And tiles around the limpid pool.

And just as Julie grew, so did her pine,
Its roots too strong, like hers, to be confined,
Like her, it towers towards the sky,
Its pillar cracked
And I rejoice to see it so!

It has a place within my heart, has Julie's tree,
Which those who know not love will ever see
And if its strength declines, it fades and falls in future years,
Then I shall shed for it, a mother's foolish tears.

Sylvia Westley

WHAT PRICE PATRIOTISM?

Where lies the land for which we fought
And gave intensely of our youth,
Wherein were heroes, bearing fame, unsought
For whom we feel eternal ruth
Life was spent, without accounting cost
When into battle they were sorely tossed.

They thought that freedom lay upon the battlefield,
A prize to win, and share with comrades true.
A sword of fire, to wave and wield,
Believing victory from it would then ensue,
And there would be such glorious times to come
That they could beat the battle drum.

Those heroes found that war was hardly won.
Their mangled bodies death did not kindly look upon,
And hope receded with the quieted gun
For they found not freedom, but that it had gone.
The country in whose service they had been ensnared
Had left them with their circumstances much impaired.

With loudly babbling chorusing, the leaders they'd elect
Eulogised their conduct, and pronounced their worth
Yet in their actions were so very circumspect,
Denying they had promised them the Earth.

So, where the land, that cherished blessed plot
That said it would forget them not,
Yet in the aftermath of bloody war,
Found it needed them no more.

Florence Barnard

GORILLA

He fingered through the hay,
Picked some up to move it,
Slowly shuffling about his place
And when the floor was cleared,
Sat down and gazed about him.

He sat with arms down by his sides,
His fingers curled and resting on the floor,
His great domed head and deep set eyes
And powerful body in its natural pose,
Gave him a certain air and bearing.

For a while he sat, quite still,
His face without expression returned
My gaze, when suddenly, he moved
And with his arms upon his thighs
Squatted with his back towards me.

And there for sometime he remained,
Moving his head from side to side,
With at times, a backward glance
And then . . .
He fingered through the hay,
Picked some up to move it.

I watched him through the glass partition,
Crouched on the floor amid the hay scattered,
Confined by walls of brick and mortar,
Safe from poacher's snare in his captive
Environment, a far cry from the green forest.

Robert William Lockett

WHATEVER HAPPENED TO CHRISTMAS DAY?

Whatever happened to Christmas Day?
A roaring fire, children at play,
Cold and frosty fingers of ice,
Mum in the kitchen, cooking things nice,
Central heating was a thing for the wealthy,
But Dad said a brisk walk was very healthy.

We didn't have much, but what we had made us smile,
Christmas made us relax for a while.
Everyone came to Christmas dinner,
Pulling crackers, everyone a winner,
Eating, sharing, loving, caring,
Playing marbles with a little ball bearing.

Yes, Christmas was special, in days gone by,
We had little, but what we had we liked,
It wasn't for us to wonder why,
We took what was given, as was our right,
We fed the ducks on the frozen pond
Down at the farm, of this we were fond.

Whatever happened to Christmastide?
Walking by your mother's side,
Cheeks so rosy, nose of red,
You had dinner, you were well fed,
Then in the snow, you romped in play.
Whatever happened to Christmas Day?

Don Friar

A PRAYER FOR ANYBODY ELSE

My god sleeps on the streets and we still preach.
My god sells methadone like lollipops
For a one-time-only price of everything you ever had.
My god says the only thing we have to fear
Is fear itself, that and everything else.
My god is the god of bad choices,
Simple errors and colossal mistakes.
My god collects pennies and sleeps in doorways,
Reminding everyone, 'This was all once mine.'
My god is a cry for help in a darkened room,
Letting everybody know that time is fleeting,
That joy is worth more than money in your eyes.
My god set the Christ gods against the Muslim gods,
The Hebrew gods against the Hindu gods,
The atheists against the agnostics,
Just to watch it all go off.
My god sleeps on the streets, holding on for dear life,
Waiting for the night.
Some days I look for him,
On the corners, in the cathedrals,
In the hand-out lines and the obituary pages.
My god is a ghost on these streets,
A whisper in the wind, and we still preach,
'Just wait 'til he arrives.'
But I say this is all a lie
Because I want my answers gift-wrapped
And my hows and whys all signed for.

Jimmy Broomfield

UNTITLED

The endless night
That has no dawn
Is where you find me
Peaceful black,
Lonely fields.
Eternity I have,
Eternity I'll wait,
For the crescent moon to burst forth
From under me,
Wait for you to call me,
The song of my blood will follow.
Cracks underneath,
No paleness in the black.
An opening,
No you,
Alone, as always.
Habit of a lifetime.
Darker than dark,
The hole leads somewhere new.
Something different.
Unknown.
Dying to live,
Living to die,
Stay or leap,
Fall or fly.
I fall.
My wings guide me home.

Sarah Davies

FREEDOM

Like a wild bird streaked with oil
I wrestle madly in pain and fear
Tossed by turbulent emotions
In a sea of froth and foam
Huge waves threatening
Which way to go?
This way?
No, that
Turn here
Stop
Wait awhile
I writhe and squirm - my inward being
A mass of swirling agitation
Engulfed by darting messages, my brain struggles
In agony of spirit
I fall exhausted
To the ground
Asleep - fatigued
But even here my dreams do not allow escape
Where can I go?
What can I do?
The answer
The only answer is Jesus
He alone is my way forward
I must seek Him
Really seek Him
He will show me.

Richard Ford

HIS

Love, he said
Love.
What is that?
Is it reserved,
Is it free?
Heart radiant for all
Or an arrow defined
For one kind -
Only one mind,
Is that love?

Can I see -
Am I blind?
Could I learn what he meant,
And what his intent?
Love, human surrounds
In the family profound
Overcomes girl and boy,
Ignites feelings of joy -
So intense, unaware
That the world can all share
This emotion divine
Not yours only, or mine
But his.

Barbara Maskens

TO YOU, MICHAEL!

They say who misses friends, he gets dogs and cats
But you, Michael, you get millions of hearts.
Every one of your songs and melodies
Gets me drowned in my golden ages.
'Thriller', 'Black or White', 'Heartbreaker' and others!
You were always the best seller
With your long and rich artistic ways!
I've dreamed to know you personally,
And when you went away, I saw that lightness in my stars,
Showing with its true colours,
Smiling to me like blossom,
Heartily, making your acquaintance.

Hacene Rahmani

HOW BORING

Big fat crow
Sitting on a tree branch
Staring . . .
Staring . . .
Just
Staring at me.

Big fat me
Started staring at the crow,
Now
Both of us were staring -
Why?
I don't know.

Eyeball to eyeball
With nothing to say
Mesmerised by each other
For ages we did stay.

Fat crow got boring;
Crow thought I was boring too,
We both got very boring -

So

Off it flew!

Diana Mudd

DAD'S FIRST CAR - A TRUE STORY

The first family car,
Dad was the man,
After motorbike and sidecar,
Then a yellow and black van,
A camping holiday in Devon,
To the south west,
Along the way people pointed,
What was the best?
New OMO wash powder,
Washed everything bright,
Or OMO 97,
That already was all white?

Janet Mansi

ORION

Orion gazes from his celestial plane,
His icy glow illuminated by his Luna sister,
In deep shades of darkest blue hue he watches the Earth below,
Man scurries across the vast terrain,
His heart mindful of those higher than he,
What fates should befall so small and insignificant a creature?
The gods playing games with life by the roll of a dice,
Will they decide his destiny on such a foolish whim?
The hunter, strong and proud Orion, waits for his call,
His arm in anticipation drawn back, eager to strike.
Man casts a glance at the beauty of the heavens
In blissful ignorance of a deity's pleasure,
His eyes enthralled by a hunter's belt,
Should I hunt Man for his foolish pride?
Could there be a grace that will save him from his fate?
As his muscles tense for the inevitable blow,
Orion's eyes rest upon the sight that lessens his resolve,
For in Man there are few true gifts enlightening their dreams.
From time immemorial, Man has taken too long to see the truth.
It is love, hope, faith and joy that can save his own being,
For when Man's heart is on fire, his mind full of hope,
His body full of faith and his face filled with joy,
He lives truly the life of a god.

Kate Robinson

WEAVER OF WISHES

Weaver of wishes, weave me a dream,
Weave it with yellow, weave it with green,
Weave it with sunshine and weave it with rain,
Weave it with joy and weave it with pain,
Weave it with children going to school,
Weave it with men flying to the moon,
Weave it with people, joyous and bright,
Weave it with day and weave it with night,
Weave it with rivers, all flowing fast,
Weave it with flowers, peeping through the grass,
Weave it with mountains and free-growing trees,
Weave it with travel far across the seas.

Glenys M Bowell

FAREWELL TO THE CROCODILE PLASTER
(Written for pre-school leavers, read at the school nativity play)

The time has come to say goodbye
Both parents and children will leave with a sigh
We look down now on each smiling face
Reflecting the fun they have had in this place.

From finger painting and stick-a-brix
To drawing houses and making rocket ships
Our kitchens are adorned with these objects of art
Not really in vogue, but of us a part.

Our children report on the world that they see
The comforting words for the cut on the knee
The crocodile plaster to cover the harm
The teacher's smiling face to reduce the alarm.

The learning and sharing of lots of things new
Letters, numbers and computers too
Writing my name and counting to twenty
A great start to life, of which there is plenty.

So thanks to you teachers and Mrs Ellis, the head
In preparing our children for the challenge ahead
We'll remember these days with fondness hereafter
Farewell to St Peter's and the crocodile plaster.

Philip Eames

THE TAXPAYERS' COIN

The taxpayers' coin touched the hands of the poor,
Minted by the rich to open many doors.
The taxpayers' coin held heads of kings and queens,
Was lost to fields, to be found and risen again.
The taxpayers' coin made of copper, silver, iron and gold,
Was replaced by machines to be seldom seen,
But the taxpayers' coin was smart and hardy,
Hidden in chests, locked inside.
The taxpayers' coin in great ships sailed seven seas
But fell to great depths and surfaced again.
The taxpayers' coin will always return,
But in the end, what will we learn?

Geoffrey Louch

THE QUEST

The crowd in the vegetable shop
Were milling around,
All intent on buying the new vegetable
That was on show, and was on top
Of everyone's shopping list,
Of those who were able
To get near to get their share.
Young Jack was pushing between lots of legs,
He wanted to have a look too,
But Jenny was being pushed and shoved,
Only wanted an ice cream, also the loo.
Their mum tried to get near to the stack,
Which was getting smaller by the minute,
As those in front grabbed their loot from the rack
And made for the counter at the back.
Then out of the shop to look at their booty
And marvel at how it looked so fruity.
Was it a vegetable? It looked so good,
It stated on the wrapping, expounding on its virtues,
How to cook and enjoy it.
But what was its name? What was it called?
Even the adverts on TV and in the news
Had a question mark where its name should be.
We'll try to think of a name,
There may be a prize for who comes up with the best,
But we had better try it first before we start the quest.
Up till now we have bought . . . what is it?

Phyllis Wright

SOFT LIGHTING

As I'm not a creature of the night
From the sun I do not flee
But any sort of softer light
Has a greater charm for me.
See how candlelight tenderly
Brushes imperfect faces,
Revealing their beauty - but subtly
Hiding their disgraces.
At twilight everything grows dim
And is veiled in mystery
And it is just the most likely time
When a fairy you might see.
Moonlight and starlight have magical powers
Our everyday world to change,
Besilvering rooftops and blanching flowers
And extending fancy's range.
A family sits around the fire
In gathering evening gloom;
The leaping flames fill their hearts with cheer
And the warm comfort of home.
So not for me the garish delights of electricity
Though I still look forward to fairy lights
On the yearly Christmas tree,
But the softest most beautiful light of all
That you'd find in the world far or near
Is the love light that floods upon your soul
From the eyes of someone dear!

V M Archer

RACE WITH THE CLOUDS

Race with the clouds
Those chameleons of the sky
In their caves of light
Canyons of the deep unfolding gloom
Water - changed - to smoke and air
Drifting and thinning
Chambers rising, glancing in the sun
Their edges sun-tipped
The core dark fettered
The heart unreadable, dressed
In fine muslin, too high to touch

But always the high lands
A place to chase your dreams
To send your pain upwards
To seed those tunnels
As they drift and merge and multiply
To roar down valleys
Of puff-white and misty grey . . .

Until, laden with the heavy weight
Of thought, these new seeds plunge
Earthwards, torrents of words
To wash this nether land, the fields
The open leaves, the upturned soil
Drops of hope and fresh rivulets
Of fancy, pools of light and rain
From the centre of a cloudburst sky.

Pat MacKenzie

PUTTING FLOWERS ON MY FATHER'S GRAVE

A bleak Fen churchyard
Under a wide East Anglian sky
The only sounds, the sighing of the wind in the tall trees
The cawing of the rooks in the elms.
'A beloved husband - a beloved father'.

The countryside is awash with colour
With green leaves and bright flowers, that you no longer see.
There is blossom on the apple tree and shoots of wheat
Like tiny green spears, pushing through the rich brown soil
On the land that you worked and loved.

Your strong brown arms would lift me up
I would ride across your broad shoulders
Your old jacket smelt of tobacco, animals and the earth.
You were a sturdy oak, a giant, a god
You would be there forever.

My arms around your frail body
Feeling the sharp bones beneath the hospital gown
My face against your shrunken cheek
Yet your eyes still bright.
Country folk rarely speak them
But words of love flowed silently between us.

I touch the granite stone that bears your name
And I put bright flowers on my father's grave.

Joy Staley

MY UMBRELLA

As I was strolling to the shop
I saw some brolleys hanging up
What a beauty, the one I saw
Lovely cats printed - I did adore

I paid my pound and off I went
I really thought the pound well spent
I wondered why it was the only one
That was as lovely as that one

I saw then the handle quite worn
And sticky tape around its form
I wondered then - could it be new
Or had been forgotten by goodness knows who?

Well now it's mine, I've paid my pound
Off I go homeward bound
Oh good, it's raining, I give a sigh
I now go home holding brolley high

Vik said it wasn't new
Just hanging there whilst owner shopped
And then went off and quite forgot

Quite upset I said to him
Disguise it quick, re-wrap the stick
I don't want someone claiming it

The deed is done, the brolley's mine
Now I can use it all the time.

Shirley Katherine Monaco

UNTITLED

What do you do if you want to die,
But your body and mind refuse to comply?
What do you do if your heart is broken,
And cannot be healed by any word spoken?

Fall from a height and hope for no fight,
Jump in a river and hope they all quiver,
Put your head in a noose and hope it's not loose,
Swallow them quick and hope you're not sick.

Run in front of a bus and hope they don't brake,
Die in your sleep but you're always awake.
Jump from a cliff, aim for the sea,
Land on a boat, could only be me.

Cursed so healthy I don't even sneeze,
Why isn't life simply a breeze?
Never expected a lifetime of bliss,
But do I need to be punished like this?

Pray to a God that doesn't exist,
To take me away, I won't be missed.
I haven't enjoyed this life I've had,
Maybe that's why I feel so sad.

What do you do if you want to die?
Ignore the questions that ask you why.
Don't ask for help, put your head in the sand,
Sit and wait for the hammer to land.

Alan Orpe

MEMORIES

The stars fall like rain.
The flower petals lie on the ground.
The footsteps leave prints from the rain.
The bubbles in the champagne form sparkles in each and every eye.
The smiles of yesteryears and new tomorrows are forming
Into many days of glory, sadness and tears.
How many stars form a sparkle in one's eye like a diamond?
From opening and closing of doors.
Memories sustain in many different ways.
Like the sun coming up from Mars to the moon.
Dancing on water, from ice to the fire.
Windows letting the sun in, then closing the doors to that certain sparkle.
Picking cherries and plums under sunshine and blue skies,
Seeing smiles and happy days from eating cherry pie and drinking lemonade.
The heartaches and the lost, the cries and the sins.
The treasures of young and old.
River of flames will flow on.
The darkness stepping in with shadowy figures
Blighting pass with the cheesy light on the streets.
The world like a cog, the mirrors of uncertainty.
Of a working man's endeavours.
To pass the day in such haste.
Practical identity of the human race.
Like multicoloured lights moving throughout the world.

S Beatrice Ally

TEARS FOR HEROES

Silently they line the street,
Hankies in their hands,
Waiting oh so patiently
For the planes to land.

And as the vehicles pass,
Bringing their heroes home,
There's not a dry eye in the town,
As local people mourn their own.

Why are these fatalities happening?
People begin to ask,
Isn't it time we had a say
And took the government to task?

Why has no cabinet person come
To pay respect and mourn,
And meet the relatives of men
Who won't see tomorrow's dawn?

They stand condemned by the nation,
For all the fatalities and wounded,
For keeping the men short of equipment,
And cutting their compensation.

As the flags are slowly lowered,
And shots fired above the graves,
Please say a prayer for the families
Of these men, the bravest of the brave.

Cyril Maunders

THE POODLE PARLOUR

There's something not right in the Gornals;
there's a rumour the folk have gone soft.
That land of the cloth caps and the bulldog
transformed by yuppies and toffs.

Where once there were pugilist contests,
and bulldogs were bred for the fight,
the locals now go for a sauna
and frequent the bistros at night.

Now the dogs are still loved and admired,
but not for the strength of their grip,
pugilist prowess is forgotten
for something more stylish and hip.

Your dog can be pampered and spoiled,
its coat can be shampooed and cut,
the latest bouffant from the Paris today
can be worn by an ordinary mutt.

Whatever your canine requirements,
the makeover garments are here,
from pedigree perms to moggies with worms,
you really have nothing to fear.

So pamper your moggie today.
Give him that luxury treat.
From pedicured claws to tails and front paws
we'll turn him out stylish and neat.

Andrew Pardoe

IT MUST BE TRUE
(For Kayleigh)

It's in the paper - it must be true!
If it says - the sky is green
And the grass is blue -
You've read it in the paper
So it must be true!
They bully me (so says the head)
With his ginger hair - and face so red
I know - I'll tell the papers and TV
If it's in the papers, it must be true!
I'll wreck their futures
And then they will see
No one gets the better of me!
My friends - the governors
Will back me up - because they will see
It's been in the papers and on TV
So it must be true!
Three young people so eager to learn
Told they must leave and never return
To the school they love
And all their friends
But we will get justice for them in the end!
The sky will be blue
The grass will be green
When the truth is eventually seen.

Norma Spillett

LIFE SEASONS

Out from the reflective shadows,
Behind the so delicate screen,
With your back to the edge of sunrise,
And facing the opening scene.

Then into the springtime seeking,
Exultant 'neath clearing skies,
Walking barefoot in the garden,
Where from new life will arise.

So to the heat of summer,
Time proving its masquerade,
Shelter from shadowless noonday,
Under a fragrant tree's shade.

On into maturing autumn,
Seeds hardening and ready to yield,
The sunset mellowing vision,
In the view across harvest field.

Slowly then into winter,
Inner fires starting to glow,
Outlines blur at the edges,
Like particulars under snow.

So to twilight's shading,
Life shriven and clasped, hand-in-hand,
Stand with me in moonlight bathing,
Turned faces to the dreamt of land.

Ray Dite

AN EXERCISE IN FUTILITY

If the poets write the story,
Of the things in life I've done,
They may say to claim no glory,
Easy victory I've won.

They may ask what deeds of kindness,
Shown to those, this life we share,
Then a chapter goes unwritten,
For, in truth, I didn't care.

'Tell us then, some tales of friendship,'
Another silence there must be,
For good friends grew tired and weary,
Now there's none to speak for me.

'And did you love her?' they may ask me,
I'll answer honestly and true,
But in words there were unworthy,
I told everyone, but you.

They may shake their head in sorrow,
Rest their pen and softly sigh,
As my eyes wet with sadness,
I'll finally know the reason why.

They will leave me lost and crying,
As they slowly disappear from view,
On the wind, one final question,
'Just what kind of man were you?'

Stuart Wright

THE DEVIL BUILT A SHOPPING TROLLEY

I went down to the local supermarket,
Which is my weekly folly,
Put my pound coin in the slot
And pushed the devil's trolley.
I pushed it with all my might,
It promptly turned left, instead of right.
I tried cunning, using weave and weft,
The wheels appeared cross-eyed,
For no matter how I tried,
Going forward made it worse,
For it shot back in reverse.
I plodded on, determined to complete my shopping,
But this devil trolley would take no stopping.
It created some awful scenes,
Knocking over two senior citizens,
And a mountain of baked beans.
It had a life that was all its own,
It was the worst shopping trolley I had ever known.
Finally I reached the checkout, at the top,
Resolving in the future to use the corner shop,
Which would have suited me fine,
Keeping me happy as a lark,
Had I not remembered
Our local shop had been dismembered
And was now the supermarket shopping trolley park . . .

Gordon Bannister

BLIND DATE

I've taken the plunge and
Gone on 'Blind Date',
Between Cilla and I,
I should find a mate!

If I get the chance to
Go on the telly, I
Don't want a man like
A big blob of jelly.

I don't want a man with
A wart on his nose,
I don't want a man
With fluff in his toes.

I don't want a man
Who's like Mr Blobby,
I'd like to find a man
Who's like Cilla's Bobby.

I don't want a man
With knobbly knees,
I don't want a man
With bad breath like bad cheese.

But I would like a man who
Will be my best mate,
So I'm going to join Cilla
And go on 'Blind Date'!

Joan Beer

TO THE GOLDEN SEASON

The seasons of my sorrow
Led onto happy years,
Reaching to that far-off time
Was through a veil of tears.

The first springtime without you,
With dawns so fresh and new,
The fragrance of the morning,
Did each day help me through.

Across the meadows, deep and green,
Summer days were warm and sweet,
Whilst deep red roses' scent was blown,
White clouds on blue did meet.

The weary trees did drop their weight,
As autumn cracked into sight,
Sleeping leaves around my feet,
As swiftly died the night.

Carols on the air did flow,
Winter snow - Christmas was near,
The winds blew cold around the house,
But memories were warm and dear.

With heavy heart, yet full of hope,
Through each season - with a song,
Sang every dawning of each year,
Love - keeps we two as one.

Maureen Brudenell Masters

LOVE

These eyes of mine adore you,
They have from the start,
That day you took my heart,
Entwined, never to be free,
We are as one,
Our love has taken off into the unknown beauty
Of our souls which resigns deep.
Just look into my eyes,
You will feel love,
That needs you in every way.
Love is not to be understood,
Love is a thing only to grow, becoming eternally.
My dearest, I yearn to kiss you gently,
Our eyes meet, we see love.
We do not question love,
There are no answers.
Rest your weary head on my shoulder,
Let me take away your pain,
I am your love who will always be beside you,
Two hearts beating as one,
Our love has just begun,
Ripples of love take over our minds,
We share passion that has not been written about.
Wherever you are, my love,
I will always be at your side.

Shirley Cowper

THIS LOVE DID FIND US

If we had met when we were young,
And yet we lived and loved
Enjoyed the things we did
The friends we were among,

We could have held hands, touched
As we do now and warmed
To all the hidden thoughts
And tenderness that formed . . .

In such a short, sweet time. Not lost!
Though innocence has fled
And youth? Just disappeared,
But nothing did it cost

For now I am repaid
One hundredfold and blessed
With overwhelming joy,
By loving arms caressed.

No yearning now for years long spent
On other joys or bliss
That came and went with time.
For this love were we meant.

And age will just enhance
This pleasure which is ours.
Pray, may we dwell a while?
The wonder ever flowers.

Les D Pearce

BLOODSTAINS

First she wanted it,
Then she didn't,
Then she did.
Then she didn't.

Spiralling out of control,
Mind-numb,
Nowhere to turn,
But not at all dumb.

Over and over,
Why did she do it,
Get pregnant or the other,
God would surely spit.

She loved Him and her man too much,
Oh what a fool,
That one night stand,
Got to keep cool.

She wanted it with him,
Not another.
What was it with her?
The man wasn't her brother!

Now in a state,
Not knowing what to do,
He'll leave her now,
She thought she had a clue?

Jonathan Simms

ROSES FOR BARBARA

I gave Barbara roses
That summer's day
With grace, she accepted
Lovingly to say,
She placed those roses
In sweet array
Those roses I gave Barbara
That summer's day.

With memories so dear
Ne'er to fade
'Neath shady bower
As oft we would lay,
Radiantly they bloom
Fain do I say
Those roses I gave Barbara
That summer's day.

Where life has its calling
From whence you may stray
From dawn to their evenings
Come sunshine or rain,
'Tis with love, joy and happiness
I lovingly gave
Those roses for Barbara
That summer's day.

Terrence St John

SILENCE

I waken in the silence,
Aware of calm and stillness,
I feel a sense of wonder,
That You are sharing in my illness.

Because it's night, I cannot see,
Yet I know I'm not alone,
I feel Your very presence, Lord,
As I walk through paths unknown.

You talk to me, I listen,
The silence has no end,
You tell me not to be afraid,
But this is hard to comprehend.

'Put your trust in Me,' You say,
'I promise I will guide
And whatever pain you suffer,
I'll be there by your side.'

Slowly the days and weeks go by,
I'm carried through my pain,
You give me strength to face each day,
You bear my stress and strain.

You promised not to leave me
And these words gave me hope,
I thank You for the power of love,
Your promise helped me cope.

Anne Smith

UNTITLED

With stunning looks and very clever
Diana searched for love forever
met a prince and soon was married
during which two sons she carried

Years went by and soon was clear
that lasting love was not so near
Her gallant efforts all in vain
the British people felt her pain

Continuing her royal duty
the press admired her stunning beauty
she travelled far to meet the sick
her caring touch did just the trick

The royal prince was not impressed
about her roles and caring quests
Diana's estimation grows
and earnt the nickname England's rose

A fateful night and in a dash
herself and partner had a crash
The doctors fought to save her life
of a princess, mum and former wife

The day the people's princess died
the British public wept and cried
Diana, girl, we all regret
your tragic loss we won't forget.

Steve Selwood

INFINITY

Infinity, most difficult,
Of all things to define.
Long, long way off and spreading,
Out still further into time.
Infinity it travels back,
It also travels forth.
How can a mortal ever make,
Someone such mysteries disgorge.

Men's lives are so well measured,
With limits well defined.
How could there ever be,
An answer he could find?
Man, I fear, will have to be,
The one who has to wait and see.
Oblivion may be the path,
That all men have to tread.

Or maybe when, Man's had his day,
Has travelled on to pastures new.
It's possible, there may be one,
Who can show him the way.
Explain the workings of the universe
And how it did espew.
Tell Man how infinity should fit,
Into a mortal's view.

Jack Blades

Autumn

Whirling and dancing, borne by the wind,
Chasing happily down the street,
Piling themselves up in shop doorways,
Or swirling around, by your feet.

Out in the country, along the lanes,
An ever growing carpet I see,
Russet and gold, cascading out,
And such beauty is wholly free.

Naked branches lay their witness,
As the wind strips them bare,
With the heralding of the winter,
There's a beauty cold but rare.

Autumn is a pause in nature's cycle,
To regain our breath, to prepare,
For the hard realities of winter,
When we know not how we shall fare.

A watery sun filters through branches,
The little rill is swollen with rain,
The barn in the nearby farmyard
Is stacked high with summer grain.

Autumn's colour is unsurpassed,
Bronze, red, gold and evergreens,
Of all seasons, this one for me
Has the most wonderful, magical scenes.

Robert Quin

BEAUTIFUL GIRL

People supposes that under her clotheses
This beautiful girl has a body like Venus
What no one knows is that under her clotheses
This beautiful girl has a very large penis

They look at her from top of head down to toeses
They see this great swell of two bosoms like roses
They note her fine boneses and feminine poses
And think, what a beautiful girl

But if she don't shave for a month then her nose is
Choked up with hairs, she is bearded like Moses
And if she uncloses her legs then her hose is
Proof, she's no beautiful girl

But people supposes on clotheses and poses
Their ideas are based on our outer regalia
What the girl knows but will never expose is
The fact that down there she has male genitalia

On external looks people make diagnosis
Their eyes see some things and their mind then imposes
An idea on which it then somehow closes
And which it will never unfurl

And if this is true, men, then what I propose is
Don't feel obliged to wear doublets and hoses
If you want to oppose this, wear the right clotheses
You can be a beautiful girl.

Mab Jones

FOR THE SICK

As I lay in this bed today,
For all in pain I wish to pray.
Though I've had to suffer too,
Mine's nothing to what others do.
I watch them take it with a grin,
Knowing how they feel within.
They miss their homes and friends each day,
So help them to get well, I pray.
Most of all I ask You, Lord,
To be with those in the children's ward,
For they suffer more in there,
For children it's more hard to bear.
Lord, help them all and ease their pain,
That they may soon go home again,
But give a special blessing too
For all that nurses must go through.
They have to work through all the hours,
To do what is beyond our powers.
We thank You for the doctors too,
It's sometimes miracles they do.
You help them with their jobs all through,
And show their hands just what to do.
To all who suffer in our land,
Please, Lord, give them Your helping hand.

Nita Garlinge

MY DREAM

A dream of me or a dream of you,
nothing feels better than a dream come true!

A smile without cost, happiness that's never lost,
all the world's hate washed . . . cleaned
and every box of love
ticked not crossed!

Let's stop fighting wars with no purpose,
stop hurting the innocent before they curse us,
let's stop harming things that would never hurt us!

Imagine a world filled with love and serenity,
the air filled with the smell of peace and tranquillity,
everyone becoming friends not enemies,
being there for each other, offering a helping hand,
being united, taking a stand!

People not judging by colour or religion,
picking up a book on peace and doing some revision!

I dream of a world where my family could blossom and grow,
a world where a smile and some Love, could make it glow!

So if I fall asleep let me dream,
for only in my dreams will I get to see,
the world changing for the better erasing its horrible history!

A dream of me or a dream of you,
nothing feels better than a dream come true!

Sageer Khan

FLEETING VIEWS

Windows are moments where people meet
Sometimes they're broken
Sometimes they're complete
Windows are moments
Often too brief
Windows are moments
Sometimes in grief
Windows are moments where people meet
Windows are moments
Paired or alone
Windows are moments where people meet
Windows are moments
Passing through
Windows are moments
Just going to
Windows are moments were people meet
Windows are moments
Captured in time
Windows are moments
Some of them mine
Windows are moments where people meet
Windows are moments
On many paths
Windows are moments
Old photographs
Windows are moments where we meet.

Peter Payne

HOW LUCKY WE ARE

How lucky we are
To have been born so free
In a country so calm and so green.
A country so strong
We are proud to belong
And feel joy with each changing scene.

A winter that's mild
Like the touch of a child
And a spring that brings joy to us all.
A summer so bright
A moon clear at night
And soft colours when autumn leaves fall.

How lucky we feel
With friends that are real
When neighbours are there by our side.
When the church's foundation
Is there for the nation
To help us, to lead and to guide.

There are so many places
With so many traces
Of Man's inhumanity.
That when we wake up each morn
Let's give thanks we were born
In a pleasant green land that is free.

Helen Langstone

CANCER

Cancer has affected many of us in our life
When you lose someone to it, it's like getting stabbed with a knife
You wouldn't wish it upon anyone, that's for sure
Especially when news rings true that they can't find the cure
If God created the world, why'd He create hurt and pain?
No positives can be taken from losing anyone, there's nothing to gain
You just have to try and stay positive through it all
Keep your chin up, just try and stand tall
Nobody ever said life's meant to be easy
But when you hear the news, you start to feel all queasy
Your stomach sinks and your heart starts to race
People can sense something's wrong, they see it in your face
Pain written all over you, no words to describe it
Opening up to people can help you if only a little bit
Bottling up emotions only makes it harder in the long run
What's happened has happened, there's nothing that can be done
You stand there staring straight up to the sky
Asking the Lord what have you done to deserve this? Just asking, why?
Then the clouds seem to open and rain starts to pour
And you start thinking you can't take this anymore
But don't give up on life, not just yet
Because with time, you'll find the easier it'll get
As they say, time heals everything
Things can only get better, you never know what life will bring
So my message to you is simple, just hold your head high
Don't go knocking on Death's door, as you won't get a reply.

James Williams

A FRIEND IN NEED

I saw him watching me from across the street,
He would raise his hand as if to greet
Then his head would go down and he'd walk away
And leave me wondering what he wanted to say.
He looked so careworn, lonely and sad
I was sure something had happened - something bad.
The days passed by, each the same,
I did not even know his name.
If there was to be change it was down to me
So I thought I would go and ask him to tea.
I plucked up my courage and knocked on his door
And soon I heard his feet on the floor.
I said, 'I'm Jan and I've come to see
If you would like to come to tea?'
He shook his head and away he went
And I went home, my courage spent.
A short while later at his door he stood,
I called, 'Do come. It would do you good.'
He came and told me he had lost his wife
And did not know how to move on in life.
They had no family to help him there,
His neighbours really did not care.
So we became friends, him and me.
I go for coffee and he comes to tea.
Two lonely people who now have a friend,
Goodness knows where it might end.

Janette M Coverdale

CARRICK-A-REDE ROPE BRIDGE

The name carraig a rede means
The rock in the road as it is known,
Situated near Ballintoy coast ground
With water surround.

Seventy feet in length
One hundred feet in breadth
It leads to Carrick Island
Water below for salmon fishing by hand.

The bridge is erected in spring
When the birds breed and sing
Flowers on show, colours aglow.

Taken down in autumn
Fishing net brought in to see
What is caught in.

It has a rope handrail
With wooden slats
To the island trail.

It leads to Larrybane, steep hill
This will give you a thrill,
Where you can find old quarry.
Take time, do not hurry.
Old caves and limestone
History is knowing.

Marie Coyles

EYJAF-JAKALLJOKULL - A NAME TO REMEMBER

As volcanoes go, it's not very big
It usually wears cloud - just like a wig
One day in April this hill lost the plot
By baring its head and opening the slot
Smoke and lava and steam issued out
The beast was angry - of this there was no doubt
Prevailing winds carried emissions quite wide
Aircraft were grounded - all parked side by side
People queued and their plans were all thwarted
The gods had spoken, so flying was aborted
Volcanic ash contains glass so it's said
Engines don't like it and will often go dead
For days the ash cloud affected air travel
Ferries and trains the crowds did unravel
Humans it seems with nature do clash
(Be it bird droppings or volcanic ash)
The volcano above has a partner close by
'Katla' is its name and, it too, may let fly
For down the years this pair have erupted
Almost together the environment they've disrupted
So if the reaction continues between this violent pair
More flights may be grounded because of ash in the air
To look on the bright side of nature's own rage
I'd rather write 'Katla' at the top of this page!

Alan R Coughlin

THE SUPREME END OF HISTORY

Where's the space within my head
That I can lay my mind to rest?
It is as hidden as the sea breeze in a storm,
The oasis in torrential rain.
It is deep, deep down,
In a crevice, laying next to my smile.
Not the everyday stick-it-on-and-think-of-better-things smile,
But the smile that leaves the lips
And reaches down, down into your gut and lingers.

That's what we strive for,
Live, let and die for
In the pouring rain
Where we struggle and strain
Yet we relish the pains
The God-given grains
That feed the lines around the eyes
And let us shine right through the lies.

Alas! I am as far from The Beginning
As The End - my mind's singing.
Lost is the path that leads to the crevice,
Or so it seems so, but hey, what do I know?
In the pouring rain, there is no horizon,
The infinite number just carries on rising.
This far-sighted searching may not ever lead
Deep, deep to the space, where all is agreed.

Hannah Cowan

OUT OF DARKNESS

In a dark place
With angst and despair
A broken heart
In a state of repair

Confidence lost, no aim, nor no goal
No life, no spirit, an empty soul

Wishes, dreams and promises broken
Those telling words still left unspoken
Happiness however is just within grasp
The darkness surely cannot last

Awaken the mind, and use the brain
To bring back life, and make sane once again
Knowing that feeling of a well-balanced mind
Can be sometimes lost, but never hard to find

Darkness to light is not far away
It is within reach as it's coming your way
When it arrives, grasp with all thy might
And rapture yourself in its light

The darkness will then fade away
To form a new beginning
A new you
A new way.

The End

Adele Hodgkiss

THE GIRL AND THE LAKE

She reflects upon the surface
as the cold wet arms of the lake
take her in their deadly embrace.
She feels the cold tendrils curl
around her calves, her thighs, her waist.

The water pales her skin
it darkens her lips
It shadows her clear, serene eyes
ecstatic in its aqueous grip.

The darkness envelops her
the currents caress her
as the lake takes her under;
binds her in a fatal matrimony.

A cold, waxen and bloated wife,
torn from her former life.
The lake is a jealous lover,
needy and clasping and hungry.
It pulls and it tugs; an insistent caress.

The flow of the undertow
balloons her white dress
as the life finally flows from her eyes
and bubbles rise from her throat
carrying the last of her sighs.
The lake is a jealous lover.

Steven Kenny

PICKPOCKETS

shouts! sparkly shiny stones?
catch us if you dare:
over the bridge
jump the ridge
hide, quick! they won't find us here
bloodshot eyes dart right and left
searching . . . hold your breath . . .
look! look!
-headrush-
run!
past drummers and singers
dancing and turning
snakes and fires
prancing and burning
no time to rest dodge the puddle slip on the steps
over the bridge jump the ridge past the guard dog
that snaps at your heels
no, don't let them reel you in! we're almost there
so close now, we're almost free
be careful my brother just one more corner
just one more stone just one more step don't trip don't

fall!

next time my brother
next time I'll hold your hand

Cezanne Jardine

THE LOVE

It's hard work, but it's a natural progression,

To make the transition from a low to high,
But when you get it you will know the reason why,

So take the chance and nurture it like a flower,
Use it and control the amazing power,

It's so precious never take it for granted,
It's what you have always wanted,

Some you may leave with a push or shove,
But you will know it's genuine and it's called true love,

It can be easy or sometimes hard,
But the feeling's unique when Cupid's dealt you that card,

From your eyes to the tips of your toes,
There is nothing quite like 'the love' that grows,

But the hurt you feel when that love goes,

So keep it safe and secure,
That love you have for evermore,

In the end remember the start,
The seeds of love began in your heart,

So make your heart the thing you follow,
Because losing 'the love' makes it bitter to swallow.

Lee Blunt

THE SPONGE AND THE BUBBLE

The sponge and the bubble
met on a sunny day,
said Bubble to the sponge,
'Would you like to play
a game of cat and mouse,
in a cardboard box?'
Said Sponge to the bubble,
'First get rid of Fox.'
The fox pricked up his ears,
and went to go away.
Bubble said to Sponge,
'Now let's start to play.'
The game went on and on,
Sponge he was the cat,
he pounced on Bubble fast
and ate her and was fat.
Sponge he licked his lips,
then spat poor Bubble out,
then Fox returned to home
and he began to shout!
Poor Bubble was in tears
and Sponge stormed out the door
and Bubble was a mouse,
alone again once more.

KJ Lee-Evans

TO MY NIECE SHARON

Little girl with eyes so brown
And so very dark your hair
You are yet so very young
Not a worry, not a care
And your cheeks are so rosy
Your skin is so soft to touch
You are not so very tall
And you don't talk very much
When we meet in the garden
The smile on your face will tell
All that you would like to say
Your eyes will do it as well
As you run about and play
With your doll's pram by your side
Cuddly toys are rarely seen
These are usually left inside
In the summer when it's hot
And you want to keep quite cool
We all know where to find you
You are in the swimming pool
As each day you grow bigger
We shall hold close in our heart
The pleasures you have given us
In whose life you've played a part.

Joan Herniman

TIME

Time
      Is
           The
                  Essence
                        Of
                              Life
                                    Captured
                                          In
                                                One
                                                        Second.

Carol Bradford

NEVER WANTING TO LET YOU GO

White clouds above, taunt me.
Laughing out loud, 'Shapes, figures.'
From the wilderness, beauty meets beast.
Captured in a heartbeat,
Under your spell, mesmerise.
Yearning unconditional love,
As one together, on land.
Stamping hooves, flared nostrils,
Roam wild and free.
Darkness then light.
Seasons come and go,
Longing, tireless waiting,
On the warm glittering sand.
Screaming, deranged quarrelling,
Reckless damage said.
Hear your words, your voice.
Now, only silence and the sight
Of leaping waves
Like disfigured, outstretched, bony arms and hands,
Recoiling again and again.
Search and search, hope fades.
Kneeling, weeping sorrow.
Under starlit morning, shine vast and far,
Forever captured is 'my soul'.

Sharron Hollingsworth

THE TRACTOR

The tractor's in the field
Reaping a golden yield
It's the tattie harvest
There's no time for rest
The sun's beating down
Get the tatties ready for town
There will be time for play
At the end of the day
The yield is a good grade
Time the sacks are weighed
Now they're rolling down the road
The lorry has taken away the load.

Frank Tonner

PHOENIX

Whenever we fall
Like a great waterfall
We flow so fast
Past all our life's effort
The toils of the past
Just like the rapids
That sweep all in its way
But the beauty
Of this life that seems so crazy
Is the ability to rise again
Just like a phoenix
There is a way to begin
And a life to rebuild
For hope is not blind
And strength lies within
The depths of every human
When we rise we learn
We don't repeat the same mistakes
And no matter the work it takes
Do not give up to defeat
There is no obstacle we can't beat
No mountain we can't climb
Everest is shamed
By the beauty of the human spirit.

Debra Ayis

GRAND DESIGN

The spiderwebs
Twinkle by dawn
Mystifyingly
Like a model suspending
In a toddler's eye

But growing beyond
Home and universe

Field after field
Of little galaxies . . .
I stick to the path
And my head is spinning -

Lee McLaughlin

STONES

Jagged and smooth
Rough-hewn from quarry
Broken from wall
Smooth-washed by the sea
Formed in a river bed.
Sometimes I feel jagged
Rough, sharp-edged
Hurting others and myself.
Often I feel smooth
Healing and gentle to touch.
The smooth stone I held today
Has holes
Two deep ones
What is hidden there?
Even in my gentleness
In my kindness
Danger lurks.
Is there a serpent lurking
Do the holes contain some demon
Are they just empty
Reminder of sins past?

Rev Shirley Ludlow

AGE

Getting old is not a crime
Though we are besieged
By the thief of time.
Sight goes dim, joints become stiff
We feel we have reached
The edge of the cliff.
Time with us all is getting short
We do not use it like we ought.
Every day should now be a bonus
Not be made to feel like an onus.
Enjoy sunrise, air that is fresh
Tomorrow is another day
And is something which is far away.

Carl Kemper

SOCCER WORLD CUP 2010-2018

England for the Cup 2010
Winning easy? Winning well?
England for the Cup 2018
Hosting easy, hosting well
The tenties are good for English sport
London Olympics 2010
Rugby League World Cup 2013
Glasgow Commonwealth Games 2014
Rugby Union World Cup 2015
Soccer World Cup 2018?
All hosted in the UK
But of all these
Only the Olympics
And the soccer World Cup
Are worth hosting and winning
This century England have won
Rugby Union World Cup 2003
Cricket 20/20 World Cup 2010-06-29
But soccer World Cup 2010 or 2014, or both!
Is bigger than these other two
Melted together!

H G Griffiths

FAMILY

I said to my friend the other night
Have you ever wondered what the fuss is all about?
'Families!' he said,
'Some are good and some are bad,
Some are happy and some are sad,
Some are close and some are apart,
Some are friendly and some are not.
Some are better than others,
And others are better than most.
Some are there for each other
And some are forever lost.
So . . .' my friend said to me,
'Have you ever wondered about your family?'

Ana-Marie McKeever

JUST ONE DAY

If I was granted just one wish
a wish that might come true
I'd put a spell on all the world including me and you
I'd wish for just a single day
there could be no blood or tears
let all the world be happy
and forget their pride and fears
let every race of children
know only fun and games
be happy and contented
without the calling of bad names
no bloodshed on our conscience
no blood spilled on the ground
only green grass growing
with flowers all around
if only just to stop the wars
to let the mad be sane
to let the needy never want
and the starved be fed again
let all the world be happy
and hope that day might stay
the longest, happiest in the world
if only, for just one day.

Chrissy Baynes

YOUR LOVE

I wish I didn't love you, but I do;
I don't have the strength to pick myself up again;
I wish I didn't love you, but the love I feel is real and natural;
I wish I didn't love you, but I do;
I don't have the strength to pick myself up,
When you pick me up and spit me out again;
I wish I didn't love you, but I do;
This is the power you have over me;
The way you touched my heart by looking into my eyes;
I wish I didn't love you, but I do;
My heart calls out to you with everything it has;
My heart will not let go or let me move on;
I wish I didn't love you, but I do . . .

St Catherine Henville

AUTUMN GLORY

The beautiful colours of autumn
Can make our hearts pound with delight.
The colours all blend in their splendour -
The yellow and orange so bright.
As nature portrays her true beauty
We value the seasonal glow -
And watch as the leaves tumble downwards
When strong autumn winds start to blow.
They make such a wonderful carpet -
A marvellous pattern - quite rare
That rustles and glows in its beauty -
And leaves the grey trees in despair.
A season so full of enjoyment
Can stir up the artist within -
And bring it to life on a canvas
In style that much pleasure can bring.
All seasons can give us great pleasure,
They vary in colours untold,
But autumn stands out as the grandest
And thrills us with colours so bold.
The colours of autumn enchant us,
They're there for the whole world to share,
When days of dark sadness surround us,
The memories lift our despair.

Glenys B Moses

MIRACLES DO HAPPEN IN LOVE!

In a placid lake of existence,
I saw you from a safe distance.
You were standing tall on a pinnacle,
I was lying low, waiting for a miracle.

Could this happen?
Can our relationship deepen?

Meandering questions arise in my mind's sphere,
With a thousand earthly phantoms to fear.
I was waiting for a Messiah or a Cupid,
To redeem me from feelings timid.

Traditions shut my mouth,
I moved to the north and you to the south.
Fate had something in store,
Crossed paths cast us ashore.
You came into my life again,
My heart was beating your name in refrain.

Suddenly the storm of your love hit my shore,
And at last you occupied my inner core.
You held my hand with an enduring promise,
Of love, affection, companionship and great bliss.
I was thrilled to the summits of wild joy,
Beholding you as a bride, happy and coy!

Supriya Choudary

SALVATION ROAD

Rising up from the pit of Hell,
Let's just see who's got a soul to sell.
Someone for whom
Redemption means least
And bring them down
For a pagan feast
Give them a chalice
To sup of his blood
To help cleanse their soul
Of whatever was good
Their eyes look out
With a meaningless stare
No feelings remain
For what do they care
In a nothingless void
A-twix time and space
Do we no longer fit
A 'refined' human race
The living dead
Forever to roam
The 'road to salvation'
The one that will never
Ever lead home.

James Curwen

THE SKETCH

Henry Moore stood there sketching
In the field of statue and pool
He had seen two lovers entwined
Moments in time
Frozen
It's cold, it's cruel
That they will not be
Forever borne on a plinth
On the Embankment
But will separate, disintegrate
Through fear of love and that is all.

Vernon Ballisat

CARAVAN SITE

The autumn days hail
An end to the season
The friendly caravans
Travelling homeward
To face a redundant winter.
The golden summer
Of 'Punch and Judy'
Carefree days are over
The 'fun bus' beats a hasty retreat
With the freak downpour
Causing fresh laughter!
We will miss the sight
Of the residential caravans
Their pleasing colours
Glimpsed through the trees
The children's swings
Shall be removed
With the telephone box
'Out Of Order'
Till we meet again
To reminisce
With many a laugh
Come again next year.

Irene Grant

A LITTLE OLD WOMAN SITTING ALONE

A little old woman sitting alone
Waiting for a friend to phone
In her little rocking chair
With a bun in her hair
Small and little, she is sitting
Darning her socks and doing her knitting
A black cat sitting on the window sill
Coal fire burning in the grate
Ten o'clock and it is late
To her bed, warm and cosy
Dreaming of the husband she once had
Memories make her very glad
She was the mama I once knew
God bless me and also you.

Susan Westphal

THANK YOU!

I look out of my window,
once a beautiful land
but now it all shattered
by the adult's hand.

I don't want to grow up,
don't want to become like them,
enjoying every moment
and leaving us with the rest.

I never saw ice or snow,
I want to when I grow up, you see,
I bet I won't be able to though,
'cause the grown-ups wouldn't leave it be!

My kids will never hear,
the growl of a lion or
see cute panda babies
because of some nasty set of species
not looking at anyone in *particular!*

Yes, mess the world up adults,
get all the pleasure from Earth
and leave all the filthy mess
to us, the next *generation!*

Yagnaseni Bhattacharya

REFUGEE

Do you know me? Don't you see?
I'm calling you to set me free
Like the stars up in the sky
Set me free so I can fly
Like the water in the ocean
Set the action into motion
It's so dark, so isolated
I am alone, I'm not related
My roots are gone, my branches weak
I want to go, I want to seek
Do you know me? Don't you see?
I'm calling you to set me free
I have had enough, I have to go
If I'm not free I cannot grow.

Celia Smith

A BUSY DAY

Not so much rivalry, but just a chance to take part,
As soon as I take up pen and paper, I find my mind goes blank,
To fit the bill maybe a romantic verse with matters of the heart,
But ideas come fast and furious, I don't know whom to thank.

I have lived a long and fruitful life, I think without contradiction
And now the days just race on by,
But can claim of no particular distinction,
Just hang on in there, not so fast! you hear me cry.

It's down by eight, the schedule is tight,
The house needs going over,
I vacuum through, using all my might,
A flick of the duster, I'm afraid the new pin won't last forever.

Then weed the garden, that's a must,
The lawns, all three, now need a manicure,
The watering can during the drought is in what I trust,
If I'm on my feet much longer, I shall need a pedicure.

So on and on jobs still need doing,
No chance for one to put one's feet up,
Ah! A cup of tea that will keep me going,
Drat it! I've fallen to sleep and see the broken cup.

John Waby

TOO LATE

How dare you love my children?
How dare you take them in?
How could you be so kind?
Is love so blind?

You gave them love
You gave them shelter
But I turned your love into my hate
But I said sorry
Was I
Too late?

David Bakal

GROWING UP

River Usk, you River Usk
Spring from the Brecons deep
Within that mountain's ancient rock
Your lifeblood's waters seep.

Downward, ever downward
Throughout the heart of Gwent
In mystic, mad, meandering
Your childhood miles are spent

Playing with the rapids
Your waters mischief white
Sending flapping, stilted herons
Aloft in awkward flight

Your youth does not prepare you
For adult future shocks
The magic muse deserts you
As you surge through sordid docks

Your sparkle will be extinguished
When you end your journey south
And you taste the waiting kiss of salt
From the Severn's silted mouth.

Hugh Rose

AGE, TIME, LIFE

Age?
What is age
compared with
the spirit of life within?

Time?
What is time
compared with
the force of contentment
in everyday life?

Life is a strange flower
which is able to grow
beyond age and time.

Genio Halvdan Kittil Engen

JESUS, MY SAVIOUR

Living in another world
Not so far from here,
Is Jesus Christ, our saviour
A friend who is most dear.

His home is above in Heaven,
A place He wants us to share,
He wants to make us welcome
And to show us that He does care.

So we must follow Him
And He will show us the way,
To tread the right path
To keep us from going astray.

Jennifer Bell

BIG BANG

I be a mouse crying the night away
Shameful is Man
Gnawing my toothpick
The silent driver of time

Man be an ape
Bananas be his staple
Throwing skins
Plastic lies

Aid a bandage
Heals the needy
Thrown aside
Morals and thoughts

Ships at sea
Raising a flag
Needles sharp
Pain endures

Penguins perish
Waves lick oil
All is black
Big bang.

Anton Nicholas

SIMPLE WORDS

Simple words can mean so much
Each and every day
Like a kind and gentle loving touch
Worth more than words can say

So when sleep beckons me
When the day is through
I shall always be
Forever in love with you.

John Mangan

A BLACKBIRD'S LAMENT

My feathers are dusty,
My poor throat is dry,
My wings are so heavy,
It's an effort to fly!

But where is my bowl,
Full of water so clear?
And where is the lady,
That I loved so dear?

The patio's empty,
My table is bare,
No crumbs and no currants,
My lady's not there.

The house is all closed now,
The garden so still,
As I huddle alone,
On her window sill.

Every day I return
And hope, but in vain,
For my bowl and my lady,
Will not come again.

Sonja Mills

SUMMERTIME

Summertime is here once more,
As we see our plants sprouting up from the ground,
And as they are coming alive,
With such glorious colour of different shape and size,
We wonder how beautiful the flowers are,
With different colour of petal.
They just sit there waiting for the sun to come out,
To make our garden a wonderful place.

D Hallford

SUSPENDED IN TIME

My eyes are overwhelmed by the sudden onslaught of tears,
Which overflow and slowly make their journey,
Down each cheek, until they hit the bottom and stop,
Dangling as if suspended by time.

My fists tighten and clench,
As I hold onto my side, to stop myself from falling,
My head is spinning out of control,
An involuntary gasp escapes my lips.

My lips start to quiver
And my hands start to shake,
I am trying desperately not to lose control,
However, control is slipping out of my grasp.

All thoughts and reason escape me,
My inhibitions run wild and I give in,
My stomach is shaking violently,
As my gasp turns into a thunderous laugh.

My stomach is starting to hurt,
My vision is blurred beyond all recognition,
My laughter is loud and boisterous,
My legs buckle and I am on the floor in uncontrollable fits of laughter.

Kimberly Davidson

DANCING

Dressed in black,
Hand on back.
Then your chest
Meets my breast.

We start to dance,
A sidewards glance.
We flow,
Fast and slow.

We feel so proud
Floating on a cloud.
We're in a world
Waiting to be unfurled.

We have no fear.
As gallantly you steer,
Gracefully guiding me,
Making emotions run free.

The music ends,
We now descend
Back to our seat.
Ecstasy, complete.

Sandra Moran

FEAR

I do not fear death,
Only forgetting about you.
I do not think of my bones in the ground,
Only missing looking after you.
I do not fear the fiery furnace
Or the darkness at the end.
My only fear is leaving you here,
My heart, my lover, my friend.

Peter Butterworth

GRAVEYARD SPEED DATING

The cold and misty air contains a deathly musk
A stench that hovers over the graves
Stirring from the ground of depth
Lost souls looking upwards to be saved

Bony hands clutch their invitation
Tight to their skeletal chest
They hope to attract a new dead mate
One they can touch and maybe caress

Darkness is their family friend
As they sit beside their first date
Beauty is in the socket of the beholder
As a speciality, their head rotates

Stripped of flesh and brains
They now judge on spirit alone
They talk about previous lives
And reminisce about earthly homes

The church bell sounds its tune
It's time to swap around
The truth is they will never find new love
While they all sleep six feet underground.

Chris Meredith

I TRIED

I tried to tell you I wasn't coping,
But no one could hear me.

I tried to show you I was breaking,
But no one could see.

Please forgive me if you're hurting,
It was never meant to be.

Despair was slowly winning,
I was no longer me.

Rachel Sutcliffe

'FALLING STARS'

Many stars have gently slipped
From out the darkened sky,
Sometimes you see them glitter
Within a baby's eyes.

How many stars have kissed the trees
With diamond-sparkled dust?
As they fall in graceful flight
As all the stars must!

It makes me wonder when I wander there
Through forests, still and deep,
Am I walking unaware
Upon the dreams of stars that sleep?

If I found a fallen star
Upon the forest floor,
I would be so happy,
I couldn't ask for more!

I would give this special star
To make the world a better place,
And say God sent it to us
To save the human race!

Maureen Thornton

THREE HAIKUS

Doe crosses the lawn
Forest backdrop surrounded
Rose petal driven

Throaty tree frog choir
Perched on surrounding branches
Falling rain cascade

Early summer rain
Lively monarch butterfly
Fluttering away.

Diana Kwiatkowski Rubin

POETRY RIVALS' COLLECTION 2010 - THE PASSIONS OF THE POET

A LITTLE THING CALLED LOVE

I still recall when we first met,
The smiles we gave, I can't forget.
My spirit soared with lark and dove,
A little thing called love.

And when we wed, became as one,
Our lives entwined and just begun,
How close we came, so hand in glove,
A little thing called love.

Our family proud but never vain,
And days of passion without pain,
Did not concede to push or shove,
A little thing called love.

Yes, you and me, those halcyon days,
We wandered through life's twisting maze.
Together always, still hand in glove,
A little thing called love.

The autumn leaves now turn to flame,
There's no return from whence we came.
Our lives were sanctioned from above,
A little thing called love.

David Jones

HEBRIDES

Where the blue of the sky meets the blue of the sea
Where seagulls cry and the wind's always high
White sands and marram dunes
Flag irises gilding loch shores
The June machair, a painter's palette
Of multicoloured wild flowers
Evocative scent of peat reek
That hangs in the clearest of air
Harsh cries of the grey-garbed heron
Seal song from the midnight rocks
Clinking of rigging on fishing boats
And from the sombre Sabbath kirk
The haunting sound of Gaelic psalms.

Pam Russell

OASIS IN THE CITY

Walking along a deserted street
A solitary policeman on his beat
Dead-eyed windows everywhere
From empty buildings seem to stare.

Nothing here to catch the eye
Except a stray cat slinking by
When, round a bend, to my surprise
A sight most pleasing to my eyes.

A grand old house from yesteryear
From time when there was land to spare
A plot left here, forgotten by Man
Where time and nature had made their plan.

By old stone walls wild roses grew
Honeysuckle, honesty and feverfew
Convolvulus and Russian vine
Climbed high above wild columbine.

So here was a garden not fashioned by Man
But a moment of pleasure for everyone
A tiny oasis suspended in time
Away from city noise and grime.

Doreen Gardner

I LOVED THE 80S

Apart from big mobile phones, fashion that wasn't very hot,
and unfortunately sad, when John Lennon got shot!
The 'Iron Lady' thought she was the best . . .
but the general public wasn't that impressed!

However, my lovely girlfriend, in 1980 was born,
probably Tanya came out and gave a big yawn!
She is the second best thing in my life . . .
maybe one day, hopefully, be my second wife!

In 1981, I learnt to drive with BSM . . .
I bought my first car (Austin 1100), which I always wanted, then!
I moved departments and worked at HCC's Arts . . .
Peter Symonds College, started 'PHAB', where girls played darts!

Holidays in Europe we had, my dad, Gillian and I.
We went to most places, passed the Alps, which were very high!
Ask me where we haven't been
And I would love to go and watch the lovely scene!

As I said to you, so many times before . . .
I wish I had the courage to ask girls out more!
Royal weddings, Jackie from work, music and my 'Paying Mate' . . .
plus a 'TV reporter!' - the 80s to me were very great!

Barry Ryan

TURKEY FOR CHRISTMAS

A chick turkey comes our way,
Just right, we thought, for Christmas Day.
We fed him well, to grow and get fat,
Chick turkey never thought like that.

Chick turkey sort of read our minds
And did not think us very kind.
He proposed to run away,
To find somewhere more kind to stay.

He turned up at local pub,
Where he found, he was the hub.
He showed punters where to park cars,
In restaurant, big table by the bar.

He was so good for the trade,
His future life was really made.
No thought now for Christmas time,
Have to settle now for beef with lemon and lime.

Now to keep feathers in his skin,
Now to pray for kith and kin.
There was not same luck,
For neck was stretched and feathers plucked.

Reginald Gent

GENTLEMEN FORWARD, LADIES BEHIND

When I first met the club I was really impressed
With the sensible way everybody was dressed
In good boots and parkas they all looked so right
And packs on their backs, not a handbag in sight

The leader led off, he has recce'd the route
The rest all step forward in merry pursuit
We're all so looked after, as we wind our way
And counted like sheep just in case we should stray

There's plenty of help if we come to a stile
It slows down our progress for just a wee while
But like the Paul Jones that we have at a dance
To get a new partner it gives us a chance

The backpacks we carry contain our packed lunch
In a chosen location we sit down to munch
The calling of nature has brought us all out
The marvellous scenery is what it's about

Another call of nature is bound to occur
And toilets int' country are exceedingly rare
I beg you imagine the view you would find
On the call, 'Gents go forward and ladies behind!'

Mary Williams

A'CALLING

There are whispers within the mist, my sweet
For my soul they do but chase
Cutting through an icy dawn
I'm wrapped in a chilled embrace

And as I hear these whispers sing
As I dance to melodic tunes
I sway amidst their privileged sounds
For they grasp a life that's strewn

Unto the heavens I tilt my chin
Seeing treetops of oak and lime
With morning dew beneath bare feet
This moment shall but decline

So take the time to listen, I beg
To a silence of an auric art
For you'll catch the faintest whispers
That shall bind a fractured heart

Now, as this summer's sun has set
And an autumn moon is nigh
It's time to feel their fire
And let, a contented sigh.

Carly Burns

SLIMMING

Slimming seems such fun
Until we reach a point;
Where fat reduction comes
Off in subjective joints.

Slimming is a doddle -
So some say in trying.
But how we seem to struggle
When we are food buying.

Slimming is another hobby
For some whose fads gather;
Where slipping into slim from tubby
Becomes a rule - no fatter!

Susannah Woodland

THE WONDERMENT OF LIFE

From the very first day when we are born
Life brings to all so many challenges
The baby found to have a rare disease
To the young soldier maimed in war.

The sunshine that excels new life
The feelings and emotions that bring joy
Enables so many to overcome many obstacles
That at first glance showed no future.

Nature always trying to give the clues
To aid life itself to be creative
So whatever the problems
We can wonder at what can be achieved.

The bees and the sweet taste of honey
The plumpness of the harvest fruits
The aroma of blossoms and flowers
A new life born, a life for the future.

Giving to all that we can find the strength
That can build hope and understanding
So that the needy as well as the meek
May themselves also find this wonderment of life.

Barry Scott Crisp

IS THIS THE BEST TIME?

I looked at snowdrops
And they made me smile
Daffodils and tulips
Then bloomed for a while
The pear tree blossomed
Like a bride dressed in white
And songbirds were nesting
From dawn until night
There's a spring in my step
When I walk down the road
As the power of nature
Seems near overload
The north wind that blew
At last went away
And a warm summer breeze
Cools the heat of the day.

Peter Cullen

SELECTION BOX

Sit thee down my dear
at teatime, switch on the telly
look at all those adverts
describing happenings in one's belly

Adverts for incontinence pads
some gunk to cure diarrhoea
not to mention Pampers
still enjoying your tea, my dear?

A delicious plate of stew
then they tell you what goes plop
you lose your remote control
and are begging them to stop

A local cat enjoys the stew
those advertisements make you cough
your imagination ran amok
potty-training finished you off

Afore ye have your tea
change channels to the BBC
you can be fully nourished
having eaten all of your tea.

Trevor Vincent

MY GRANDSON

G is for the greatest gift the Lord has sent me from above
R is for a reason that he sent me someone else to love
A is always knowing that my life could not stay sad
N is to feel needed for this beautiful little lad
D is for a dream I wished for, now at last come true
S is for Sarah, my daughter, through her life and love
   she got me through
O is the overwhelming love she will give to this little one
N is now I am happy at last, to see my daughter with her own son.

Thelma Barton

POETRY RIVALS' COLLECTION 2010 - THE PASSIONS OF THE POET

THE PICTURE

She lies dreaming, laid back, at ease
Ample, young and fair, in the breeze
Her skimpy robes streaming
Glide around, not hiding her comely body.
The goatherd blows his flute
The babies fly around holding hands
Wings of gold.
Some hide in the tree above her,
Some creep up and touch her hair softly
And love her.
Cupid's bow is drawn and straining
No arrow to shoot yet.
No man in sight, for he is in her mind
And the babies are waiting to be born.
Only Cupid knows where his arrow is.
As a love life dawns -
She is ripe and so near this stage.
Ample, young and fair.
Beneath the tree of life, she's nearly there,
She lies dreaming.

Hazel Yates

LOVE LOST

Yet now I am old.
When I close my eyes,
Remember his breathing,
His sighs,
His heart beating.
Yet still, I will
Now I am old.
Yet now I am lost,
When I close my eyes,
Remember the cost.
His heart, yet still and never will
To beat again,
Oh love lost!

Maggie Kitson

CHANGES

Life is a cycle of perpetual changes,
As a currency of human existence it ranges,
From the minute we appear on this island so small,
Continuous challenges and changes face us all.
Development of growth, body and mind,
Struggling to survive, searching to find
Who am I, and why am I here . . . ?
From childhood, adulthood, marriage or career,
Daily we are confronted, new challenges appear.
We accept and learn, eventually all becomes clear.
Our hearts lead us, where our talents lay,
Awakening, fulfilling our needs day by day,
Learning from life's problems, overcoming dismay,
Becoming stronger, helping others on their way.
As master of your ship, be in command as she sails,
Be aware, be prepared for the storms and the gales.
Natural changes in life there have to be . . .
In this cycle of life, and through all eternity
Travelling through life - wherever you are -
High above, shining down, is your guiding star!

Stella Bush-Payne

WHAT I SAW

I did not see what I saw
I didn't even see it
But if I saw what I'd seen
I'd tell you, but would you believe it?

If you saw what I'd seen
Would you tell me that you saw it?
Then you'd know that what I saw
Was both what we saw, cos we had seen it.

Niall McManus

DEAR DOGLOVER

Your friend wants to go walkies,
He has brought you his lead.
Can you keep up with him,
If he walks at his speed?

You must let him sniff;
At the base of each tree.
He just seeks out the scent,
Of the friends he can't see.

You may need his help,
When you say, 'Let us roam.'
Cos he'll show you the way,
By your scent to get home.

It is not you that smells,
I think you'll agree.
But I may catch you sniffing,
When under a tree.

The scent you may smell,
Is not badger or possum.
But the aroma of nectar,
From a tree that's in blossom.

Snikpohd

GOODBYE GORDON

Goodbye Gordon, you have left us
Though it broke your heart to go
Could it be that you are going
To a cottage in Glencoe?

David Cameron has beat you
And he has put on your crown
Now the division bell is ringing
So it's goodbye Gordon Brown.

Terence Iceton

SOMEWHERE BEYOND

Somewhere beyond these golden sands
There is a valley of seclusion
Where we strolled together
When summer days were warm and long

Beneath the green and yellow sunlit trees
Swaying in the breeze of nearby sea
There we walked by shaded lanes
Nowhere was there such tranquillity

Somewhere beyond these golden sands
There is engraved a heart-shaped crest
Where our names lie deep entwined
At the place where wanderers rest

If we should return one day
To walk again where flowers appear
Just to relive those happy days
Would bring more than a tear

Better now just to remember
What joy those fleeting hours were
Than try to capture youth so tender
At this time of late September.

Pauline Kavanagh

MAN

No one to hold your hand,
To love or make you cry.
So how much do they cost,
And where do you go, to buy?

Men and women go together,
Just like bread and jam.
On your own wonder which one,
Guess the bread, a bit bland!

Because you are on your own,
People tend to follow you around.
With all the aggravation and nastiness,
Like in the jungle, hunted by Man!

The people that call from the distance,
They are trapped and want to be free.
A quick smile and eye contact,
And you know, best let it be!

Guess we are not 'yes' men or women,
For we are the bread and jam.
The reason we are on our own,
Is that we are the man!

Ann Beard

MY SUMMER GARDEN

Tall, scarlet poppies, best of May and June,
stand out supreme among the waving grass,
crown jewels of the borders, lovely, bright,
towering above the cranesbills as I pass.

These latter glories, sweet and mauvey-blue,
grow next to white moon daisies, tall and true,
which I have left in clumps upon the lawn
to cheer me when I look out at the dawn.

Forget-me-nots, no sweeter pure sky-blue,
remind me of my childhood home and you,
dear Mother, who could tell me all the names
of flowers and trees, and share my youthful games.

Tall Granny-bonnets, fragile pink and cream,
near blue and white campanulas - summer's dream,
the flowers of last year's planting, food for bees,
and happy in the shade 'neath apple trees.

Gold honeysuckle scrambles up through shrubs,
while sweet peas offer fragrance in their tubs.
Tiny green pears and apples, damsons and plums,
foreshadow autumn's ripeness when it comes.

Joan L Carter

SUMMER VISITOR

Sir Hummingbird Hawkmoth has come to our shores
To visit the English bowers
He's darting around like a young dragonfly
To sample the best of our flowers.

Is he a hummingbird? Is he a moth?
His fluttering dazzled the eye -
He entered our garden one bright, sunny day
Right out of a cloudless, blue sky.

His wings were a blur, as he hovered above
Extending a tube from his head
To hoover the nectar from beautiful blooms -
For that is the way that he fed.

He flitted around by the buddleia bush
Like a moth that encircles a light
Then he revved up his wings and ascended on high
And just disappeared from our sight.

He may have returned to an African land
Or even the south coast of France
But we'll never forget his charisma and charm
And his flitting and fluttering dance.

Jonathan Bryant

THE SURFACE CLOWN

I may be a clown
At least that's what you see,
But underneath it all
I'm longing to be free.

For inside I'm crying
Longing for the day,
When you will save the love I hold
Cos in my heart you'll stay.

Why can't the people who know me
See beyond my smile?
They only glance in a passing blink
Believing I'm a circus-like child.

Why will no one listen
To a soul so full of tears?
When the day of emotions arrives
Alone I'll face the fears.

Continue I will to hide it deep
And live my life each day,
For as long as all think it so
Just a clown I'll stay.

Nicola Scott

WEATHERWISE

Where would we be without the weather
Nothing to bespeak or blether
And if suppose it were not raining
Would we then be uncomplaining?

Where would be the crops and flowers
If it were not for the showers?
Remembering the leafy trees
Swaying gently in the breeze.

When we think of Ethiopia
Are we not in our Utopia?
And when it comes to climes extreme
We're in a land of pleasant green.

I shall arise and get me dressed
Instead of lying in depressed
For there is nothing wrong with fashion
When it comes to pride and passion.

God never let you hear me moaning
Never grumbling, never groaning
When they're on about the weather
Please grant that I may keep my tether.

Norma Anne MacArthur

YOU COULDN'T STOP ME BEING WHO I WANTED TO BE

You. Tried. I. Can. Grant. You. That.
With. Mockery. Put. Downs. And. Vicious. Chat

You. Thought. You. Could. Force. Me. Into. A. Little. Shell
Except. You. Forgot. That. Time. Could. Tell

Me. How. To. Grow. While. I. Was. There
It. All. Allowed. Me. To. Prepare

Who. Am. I
Who. I. Am
Now. I. Prosper
I. Always. Did

I. Guess. I. Owe. You
A. Thanks. Or. Two

Because. If. You. Couldn't. Stop. Me
Being. Who. I. Want. To. Be

Then. That. Begs. The. Question

Who could?

Naomi Smallwood

POWER

Everything falls from the hills to the seas
Dead beasts, dead birds and dead branches from trees
And even the rocks over eons of time
Are lured and seduced by the call of the brine

The power of the seas which we cannot defeat
Albeit with a heart when it gives what we eat
In this many thousands drowned far from the land
In a quiet ocean bed of soft cushioned sand

The ultimate victor
The one which remains
Terra firma all gone
No one left to explain!

Cyril Joyce

CHANGING TIMES

Bob Dylan singing, 'The times they are a-changing'
I am fourteen, fifteen years old,
'The sixties'
I am in the backyard of my home in Ballyfermot, Dublin
My parents? Around somewhere,
Joseph, Eugene, Edmund,
Somewhere in the house,
I listened.
The sun was warm
The singer sang out,
'The times they are a-changing'
Words that spoke to me.
Forty-six years later
In West Wales,
Bob Dylan is again singing about 'Changing Times'
My fourteen, fifteen-year-old son listens!
He hears something?
He asks, where is Bob Dylan from?
I remember where I am from,
My parents, my brothers, who have gone!
'The times they have changed'.

Christine White

I KNOW MY PLACE SONNET

I haven't got a gammy leg
Didn't roger fags at school
Never made the House of Lords
You've noticed! Poetry hasn't metre rule
Took no grand tour to catch the clap
Swimming! Can hardly keep afloat
Couldn't compete with that Byron chap
(Mind fancy giving Bysshe an open boat)
Sisters have never been my bag
Never had a wet nurse play with me
And cuckolding sounds a painful drag
So no blue mercury going in my tea
If now my offering hasn't rung your bell
Well you lot and Byron can all go to H***.

Charles Keeble

GOD'S WORLD

I thank God for the beauty of this day,
He has watched over me, and helped me along the way.
I try to fill each day, with wisdom and love,
Silently in my room, I say a prayer to God above.
When evening falls and shadows loom at night,
I know the Lord will stay beside me, until the morning light.
For God knows what is on my mind and helps me each day.
When I feel sad, He enlightens my heart,
The sun shines with a beautiful ray.
God gives me peace and joy, in simple things,
Birds in flight, with outstretched wings.
I have mornings in which I feel life anew,
Then I can cope with tasks I cannot usually do.
With God's help, I in return, will give Him prayer and love,
Then feel His loving power, flowing from above.
I see a beautiful rainbow, often a summer rain,
Colours reflect through my windowpane.
The sky changes colours, from pink to red and then a heavenly blue,
These are miracles to behold, the grass sparkles with morning dew.
All these wonders, are life's pleasures not silver or gold,
For all these pleasures, are miracles to behold.

Joyce Willis

GREEN WITH ENVY

Such beauty surrounds us
But we so often take it for granted!
Such beauty surrounds us
But we sometimes fail to acknowledge it!
For me, being caked in green gives me . . .
A sense of reflection
A sense of connection
A momentum of effortless timelessness
A moment to appreciate such beauty that embraces me.

Tracey Celestin

MANKIND

This is our land, sky, sea and air,
We are mankind from planet Earth,
A mixture of countries and languages
And shades of skin,
Loving our families deep within,
Each changing season rekindles the earth,
Babies bring love from the moment of birth,
Men yearn for adventure, whatever their race,
Eager to discover outer space,
We are Man, but are we kind?
Our duty to leave a better world behind,
Now we are warned of global warming,
We must listen and take warning,
Nations talk together,
Working for peace,
Wars never seem to cease,
Hunger and poverty, suffering great,
All countries help with great haste,
This is our world, sisters and brothers,
We must help to give aid to each other,
A better world living on Earth together.

Eileen Gallagher

THE GIRL WITH THE ROLLING EYES

I fell in love today! It was on the train
I couldn't help myself - I was lost
She sat opposite me, smiled, often rolling those eyes -
Whatever was her name?
Hair set tight against her head as though embossed

My secret glance caught her looking straight at me
She winked! And I winked next
Her faultless skin so clear and black - as ebony
Oh, those rolling eyes and flashing smile - they had me hexed

Buttoned-up shoes, gold on her ears
Untainted - but surely you derive
Life hasn't caught her yet - nor the years
For she was, no more than five.

Anthony Michael Doubler

UNTITLED

The rickshaw, full of fireworks -
Jasmine and Rose.
Gypsies traverse the Mongol steppes,
Out of work trapeze, harlequins -
Muscles now of clay and stiff terracotta.

Coconut milk and caramel,
Concertos in the courtyards of fable,
Kites, now neon in dream.

The patchwork fabric of the caravan roof,
Rain-washed gold under a mountain mist.

Two,

Jesters, paint long ago stripped away,
Are never to rise out of the shale.

They, and a jade hatchet, unrisen bread -
Crypt-treasures lifted from an opium bunk -
Wearily wave for miles.

Arabian slippers, gnawed from their feet,
Stabbed into the falling rock.

Thomas E Dixon

ANOTHER'S SON, ANOTHER'S DAUGHTER

Another's son, another's daughter,
Today they live and work amongst gunfire and mortars,
To undertake a task that many others would not accept,
To assist other nations and their peoples protect,
To heal those who are injured, to safeguard their homes,
So they may live, work and; in their homeland each day freely roam,
Not persecuted for their birth; creed, religion, or race,
Not forced to seek refuge in another far-off place,
So in time their precious mountains and fertile farmlands,
Will be governed by virtuous, and democratic hands,
So in time the text written in the archived history books,
Is that our nations did not stand by and just merely look.

Lorraine England

CHILDHOOD

Spinning, spinning, spinning
Faster and faster
Dizzier and dizzier
My eyes crinkled against the wind
Clammy hand holding
Clammy hand
Losing grip
And we're laughing
Stumbling, tripping
Still spinning
Break away
Fall, squeal, bump!
Giggling in a heap
My leg or your leg?
Gasping for breath
Stumbling to our feet
We look at each other
Our eyes speak and
We grin
We hold hands again and
We're spinning!

Zoe Jacobs

I COULD BE

I could be a famous racing driver
Going fast around the track
I could be a famous ice skater
And end up on my back

I could be a famous jockey
Riding at Epsom on a horse
I could be teeing off,
A famous golfer on a famous course

I could jump out of an aeroplane
In my tunic of red
Everything is a dream
When you're asleep in bed.

Terry Knight

LAUGHING

I'm laughing at your funny face,
I'm laughing at this funny place,
I'm laughing in my space,
I'm laughing at a fast pace.

I'm laughing and cannot stop,
I'm laughing, feeling the bop,
I'm laughing at your top,
I'm laughing with a cop.

My stomach hurts, my cheeks are sore,
Yet I want to laugh some more.
Just want to laugh day and night,
Want to laugh 'cause it feels alright.

I'm laughing with Pat,
I'm laughing at the cat,
I'm laughing at the mat,
I'm laughing as the cat sat.

Giggle, giggle, giggle,
Giggle, giggle, giggle,
Giggle, giggle.

Rachel Willmington

LADYBIRD

Ladybird upon the floral frock,
Red and dotted with black spot.
Fairy glides and wings
To distant rock,
Beneath the rainbow's golden pot.
Where willows billow above the grazing flock,
Ladybird across
The meadow green
Does light foot, daintily trot.

Keith Newing

KISMIT'S KISSES .

Let me once more breathe you in with my eyes
Feel your gentle touch on my tempestuous soul
Hear the hallowed tunes of your sweet voice on the ether
Know the light in which you reside
Enter again our utopian world
No more will bitter tears flow
Or rage's darkness descend
Our dice have been thrown
Fickle fates will decide

Kismit kisses our karma
As if tripping over something unseen
We stumbled upon ourselves in light of each other
Building a trust on the spot at our understanding,
Our surrendering
We discover a sweetness and boldness surprising ourselves
Doubt may arise here and there only due to fears that are untrue
But we fill the hollowness that dwells within
Excitement builds as I hear your softer voice from afar,
a divine siren
How you tempt my loneliness to give up its self-indulgent cocoon.

Audrey Williams

MY FUNERAL POEM

Don't cry for me, don't be sad
You shared my life, for that be glad
Don't cry for me, sing and be cheerful
I don't want to look down and see you all tearful
Don't cry for me, think of the memories you've got
The laughter we shared, it was quite a lot
Don't cry for me, I've enjoyed my life
The ups and downs, being a mum and a wife
Don't cry for me, I love you all so
You can't get rid of me that easy, you know
Don't cry for me, I want you to shout
'She knew what enjoying life was all about!'
Don't cry for me, no more tears
Raise your glasses to me and say, 'Cheers!'

Shirley Jaggard

THE YEAR

January, cold with snow and icy winds
February, life returns the promise of spring
March, the hares that box with pride on the fields
April, gardens come alive, flowers start to appear
May has sunshine and showers, waiting for summer
June's dawn mist and the odd warm days
July is beach and BBQ weather with golden tans
that match golden sands
August, balmy nights, nature's colours changing
September's autumn shades with longer nights pending
October sees children in costume, Halloween pumpkins alight
November bonfires, nearly Christmas, the shortest day
December, log fires, mulled wine, cosy nights spent in
I cannot wait for the new year to be rung in.

Jane Cooter

SUMMERTIME

In the bright sunshine
The artist sat
Painting.

While children paddled their boats
In the bright blue stream.

Grandparents and babies fed the ducks
And made them squeak with delight.

The leaves on the trees
Swayed gently on the
Bright summer day.

Young lovers
Stole secret kisses
As they sat on the bench.

The scent of the summer
Flower roses, gardenia, azalea
Setting on a green velvet lawn
Makes the perfect
Summer day.

Mary Porter

A SILENCE TO REMEMBER

Hearing silence and feeling so in tune
A beautiful and tranquil silence
A silence to remember.

A sound so pleasurable
Hearing water trickling down
And birds fluttering about.

Lying in the soft, green grass
Watching the sun dimming down
And smelling fresh country air.

Sunlight reflecting onto my skin
A blend of memorable colours
Delightful to gaze at.

Dizzying beauty surrounding me
Colours of every persuasion
To persuade me to stay here forever!

A mixture of beauty and silence
Enduring in my heart and mind
What more can a man ask for?

Tawfeeq Elahi Samad

A TASTE OF SUMMER

The planets and the universe have been around so long
But do we really know where they all came from
And are we the only planet in the solar system
To have lots of kinds of living things like you and me upon them?

We have been told by our parents, and we know that they never lie
That there is the 'Man in the Moon' up there in the night-time sky
He must be getting on a bit, and so must be 'Old Father Time'
Though he only works at night and not out in the warm sunshine.

He also brings 'Tomorrow' and makes 'Yesteryear' appear
He does this 365 times and then 366 each leap year
He then gives us one of his finest, that's known by us as 'Today'
He knows that each one will be like a fine, full-bodied Beaujolais.

Philip Anthony Amphlett

INDIA

India - where camels roam across wild deserts
Or elephants do, majestically for maharajahs
Where one can visit the Holy Ganga
In order to study astangas of yoga!
Where one can taste bang! Lassi in Varanassi;
Where the Holy Devali and Shivarati festivals are held each year;
Bangra and Carnattican dancing provide great entertainment
and cheer!
They're held in praise of enlightenment and the hearts of the gods
Who happened to be called Brahma, Geneshi, Hanuman and Shiva,
It certainly makes a difference to being a disco diva!
Discover the magnificence of the days of the Raj,
Visit the superior Taj,
Sing to Hari Rama, chant with the Dalai Lama,
Or simply relax and enjoy a sweet cup of chai,
In-between watching the rickshaw drivers and wallas pass by;
Whilst enjoying the silks that one can buy!
Read about the Sangha and Samsara;
Learn about yantras and mantras;
You might even want to try a little tantra!

Colette Breeze

END OF THE MEAL

Windows, lights, reflection in the balloon
Of a round, empty glass, lipstick printed.
A pale blue, fluted sorbet dish, empty
Save for smears of cream and a silver spoon.

Another glass, thin-stemmed, still full of deep
Ruby wine, fading to bronze; a squat carafe,
Thick-rimmed, narrow-necked, holds iced water;
Clear, sharp-cut sides have a turquoise sheen.

A pure white cloth, creased now, shows pools of light
From a chromed basket holding French bread
Crumpled napkins, whose careless shapes conceal
Spots and dabs; we sit at ease, stare into the night.

Josie Earnshaw

SUMMER DELIGHTS

The days are long aglow with sun
It's high summer, time for fun
Beaches beckon from far and near
We swim in waters blue and clear.
Perhaps a paddle with shoes in hand
Or leisurely stroll along the sand.
Those who are younger than I will handle
Surfboards leaning at perilous angles.
I watch from my deckchair in stripes of blue
Children with buckets and spades, how cute,
Each with their own ideas of a castle,
A flag blowing proudly on each finished model.
It's surprising how tiring the sun can be
We must leave this scene and head home for tea.
The season is short, enjoy every moment,
Then reminisce through winter's dark days.
The soft summer evenings seem never to end,
Barbecues spent with family and friends.
Yes, summer is a delightful season,
Making us smile for no apparent reason.

Freda Symonds

YOUR LOVE

Your love makes the rain fall
Your love makes the sun shine
Your love makes all the rainbows
Now sitting high in the cloudless sky

For your love is the love of an angel
So tender, warm and strong
Your love is the love of an angel
I long to hold and love my whole life long

So please, my sweet angel, let me hold you in my arms
So I can feel your warm love and tender charms
Please let me love you beneath the starlit skies
And not only at night when I close my eyes.

Donald Tye

DUNKIRK, REMEMBER 26TH MAY 1940

Seventy years ago this week,
Little boats sailed from the creeks,
Through canals and down the rivers,
To brave the Channel's mighty rollers.
Engines chugging, spluttering, straining,
Across to France, the lads are waiting.
Soldiers lying in the sand dunes,
Hiding from the enemy fighters.
Crouching as they scream towards them,
Machine guns rattling, spewing bedlam.
Patiently the men are waiting,
Praying for a miracle to happen.
Little boats of every size,
Bringing hope to the army's eyes.
Yachts, launches, ferry boats,
Barges, ketches, anything that floats,
Gathers up the ragged army
And turns defeat to a glorious victory.
Our little ships, a heroic fleet,
Seventy years ago this week.

Joann Littlehales

KEEPING MUM

Backwards motion, dissolving to crowds, for one moment's escape
When I super concentrated,
became diluted to taste
Became passive, to passing of time
Owned by what I borrow, steady my hand to draw a line
Beneath ill-fitting dialogue, awkward, clashing rhyme
And there's no room at the inn-crowd, a muse: or plain amusing?
Like letters to God, burnt with incense, destroyed, and rising
Rise, too early, with children whose souls incubate in my warmth
Might I melt away to a puddle, splashed by the feet I taught to walk?

Meriel Malone

UNTITLED

I am now in my twilight
Sitting under the skylight
Dreaming dreams, and thoughts ever changing
Some ideas discarded and others retained
Diving deep into my memory, before it is drained
And more of my thoughts rearranging
Yes! I find it inviting this poetry writing
I started at around age of twelve
Things come to my mind in varying kind
When into my thinking I delve
I do it mainly for pleasure
And now I have much more leisure
I've been retired now, for 22 years
Yes I'm now 82, and have many a view
And see things from many an angle
Of course, I am much the wiser
I don't need an advisor
Yes, with most things I am able to cope
And it isn't a rumour, I've a great sense of humour
I just do not give up hope

Peter J Sutton

THIS LIFE

This life is full of ups and downs
Many smiles, but often frowns
The good and bad days come and go
The pendulum swings to and fro.

Sometimes we find a way to cope
At others - we just sit and mope
But please, believe the black days end
There is light just round the bend.

Though often like looks bleak and drear
It will change - so do not fear
Time and tide, they know no bounds
Yet tranquillity will still be found.

Mavis Johnson

UNTITLED

Just try and keep up to date
Don't get yourself in a state
Try and think hard about what you do
And make everybody think of you

Just try and keep up to date
Bills will come and bills will go
In and out of your house like no one will ever know
For we all need money, don't you know?

Just try and keep up to date
With a lifestyle others hate
Working, just working is all you do
No one will ever help you.

Keith Powell

TO MY GODCHILD

I would not bless you, little one
As godmothers are wont to do -
With fervent wishes that the sun
May shine perpetually on you.
For sorrow is but part of gladness,
As hill of dale, as day of night.
And lives that are untouched by sadness
Can measure neither dark nor light.
This then, I wish for you - the peace
That follows pain. The ecstasy
Of love fulfilled and the heart's ease
Of healing grief. The power to see,
To know, to be, to feel all things;
To shed compassionate tears; to soar
Up to the sky on gilded wings,
To mourn for some, rejoice in more.
For you, the ready heart that fears
No hurt; that glory's in the giving
Of love and laughter, warmth and tears.
For this, my little one, is living!

Anne Hetherton

THE FUNFAIR

We had a picnic in the sun,
Then we went to the fair to have some fun.
There were rides galore,
Some we had not seen before.
Big rides, small rides, some in-between,
Some rides to make you scream.
Hot dogs, toffee apples,
Candyfloss with which to grapple.
Dodgem cars, 'No Banging',
But you can still hear clanging.
Pirate ship goes so high,
You feel you can touch the sky.
Waltzers going round and round,
When you get off, you might fall to the ground.
When it's dark, there's lots of lights,
Lots of colours shining bright.
It's time for bed, I hate to say,
But we'll come another day.
But for now the day is done,
I must say we had loads of fun.

E Riggott

THE DRAGONFLY

Darting back and forth along the streams
The dragonfly hunts, on rainbow wings.
Resting on a bulrush stem, it dreams
Of ancient forests where no bird sings.

Where stately fern trees silently grow,
And no flowers bloom to please the eye.
Where creeping creatures cannot yet know
The joy of ascending to the sky.

The wind sways the rushes to and fro
And the dreaming dragonfly awakes
To hunt, like ancestors long ago,
Along woodland paths, ponds, streams and lakes.

Diana H Adams

DON'T BE A CHANCER

When you go for a smoke, a laugh and a joke,
Read the label then laugh if you can,
But you won't see the joke, for the curse of the smoke,
If the doc admits you for a scan.

If smoke causes cancer, there's only one answer,
Quit when you know you're ahead,
For better to crave, than to go to your grave,
Ridden with cancer and dead.

Please put an end, to your smoking my friend,
Hesitate now and you're lost,
Don't be a chancer, beware of the cancer,
And thus, be aware of the cost.

James Baxter

THE LIGHTHOUSE KEEPER

I was floating on an endless tide
Across the lonely sea
Through storms and tempests I survived
And still it remained just me

Then one day a light I spied
Shining brightly in the dark
From the rocks it guided me
I could feel a certain spark

Landing on this friendly shore
The lighthouse standing there
I knocked upon the oaken door
And you stood there oh so fair.

The vision of you took my breath
As sweet as ice cream
You were golden-haired and bare of breast
Simply heaven in dungarees

You are the prettiest lighthouse keeper
I've ever seen . . .

Russ Pratt

ALEXANDER THE GREAT

Son of the gods, your future looked bright
Your finely-chiselled features radiated a powerful light.
You were a world apart from mere mortal man
Upon the wind, you and your stallion, Bucephallus ran.

Great nations were subjected to your rule and power
With your warriors you shared many a victorious hour.
After many a tough battle, Persia was won -
For King Darius the sun no longer shone.

Your words were like honey, good and sweet,
Your spurred them on bravely on the battlefield.

Suddenly, the God of the heavens struck you down,
He took away your illustrious crown.
In sweet, golden youth, you were taken away,
You breathed your last, one fateful day.

You had no warning,
The entire Greek world was mourning . . .
Great warrior and brave knight
Gone was your legacy and gone was your might!

Iris Ina Glatz

THE MYSTERY OF THINGS

To be conceived, to be born
To be alive, alive, O.
The three great to be's.
Is there a greater thrust to life?
No greater thrust than the many rainbows
In your life, some vanish early, like
The morning mist, some, discovered late,
Bring happiness to a dreary life. The time
Strips our illusions and our rainbows of
Their hues and, as the bard said,
Fortune never comes with both hands full,
Gives to one a stomach but no food,
To another, food but no stomach.
Such is the mystery of things like,
The many serve the few, and the
Many will sing, tell tall tales
And the band plays on.

Gerard Kenny

LOVE'S LABEL

Love, the very best tonic in all the world,
The most powerful drug ever made.
Also one of the very best feelings
And will never ever fade.
Jealousy, love's ugly cousin
Does sometimes try to stay,
But in actual fact, it brings us closer
So that 'thing' can go straight away.
Love can happen to anyone
It'll hit you like a brick.
So try and fight it if you want
Or accept it, take your pick!

John Stewart

WAR AND PEACE

There's a snarling and jarring
When men go a-warring -
There's a drench and a stench
In the mud-filled trench
Where soldiers are trying to aim -
Some are wounded and crying
Some are screaming and dying
And calling their loved ones by name.

There's flame and there's flare
There's blood, blast and blare -
And the pain -
What *is* Man doing to Man?
Is it for glory and power or greed
That war is raging again?

And now we are wearing our poppies
Reminders that strife has to cease -
Each poppy represents
A young man's life
Nobly given for peace.

Jane Finlayson

DREAM FOREVER

If dreams could be bound within the pages of a book,
I'd dream forever,
The happy times we spent together,
Reflections in the mirror,
I stare and see many shadows passing,
Just beyond my grasp,
Loves and passions of yesterday float by,
Hidden in the clouds on high.

Without the past, there'd be no present,
Time to reflect and pray,
Thankful for memories parcelled within forever,
A tapestry of love and care in my heart to settle.

A gift beyond belief, to recall,
Bringing strength as I remember . . .
You were part of me and I part of you,
To cherish whether today or tomorrow,
My heart is full of joy and feels no sorrow,
For it is you, that is so special
So let me dream some more - forever.

Liz Dicken

UNTITLED

I will write a song
and I will sing it to you,
I will dream you a dream
and hope it comes true.
I hold your heart in my hands
and feel its bright glow.
I will dance to the music
with you by my side.
I'll return your heart now to you,
if you will love me as I will always love you.

Ann Warner

EVENING

Rind of a moon,
Fields with folded wings,
Sleeping, twilit
Under a fading dome.

Slow wisps of silence,
Streams dissolve;
Insects, suspended, dart -
Erratic particles
Testing edges of the dark.

Evening settles like a dust,
Levelling the landscape,
And sighing hills subside,
Relinquishing their thrust
To safely hide
Where slow light lingers,
And only stiffened fingers
Of the rushes write,
Pencilling in charcoal
Long fringes of the night.

Michael Cotton

THE FAMILY DOG

The dog is known as Man's best friend, provided you're the master!
But if your dog controls your house, you're heading for disaster!
He'll tear up shoes, he'll rush around, an awful household pest,
So please take time to train him well, he'll become a loving pet.

He'll love to go out walking, he'll always come to heel.
He won't go rushing on the road, making car wheels squeal.
He'll give you endless fun and games, while playing with his new ball,
He'll always give you comfort, if you're not feeling well!

If you start to talk to him, he'll smile and wag his tail.
He'll never snap or growl at you, his love will never fail.
He'll never scold or nag you, he's always out for fun.
He'll bring your shoes when you are tired, when the day is done!!

Robert Neill

FEATHERS THAT HAVE FALLEN

(I dedicate this poem to my aunt Rita. Thank you for looking after me so well. Thank you for being a great godmother)

When my aunt died,
For ages, I cried,
Watching my family weep
And lose sleep.

When out walking around,
A feather fell to the ground,
Knowing she was near,
Watching me here.

Sending a special message,
At a wanted stage,
Thanks for minding me
And my family.

Thanks for watching,
Minding and caring,
Thanks for being there
And showing you care.

Darran Ganter

THE STORM OF LIFE

The storm of life won't let me be
Pain and suffering is all that I can see
People struggling to survive
Mothers and babies losing their lives
We have seen many people suffering in our lives
Some have lost husbands and some have lost wives
The storm of life has covered me
It has rocked me and swayed me like the wind blowing in the trees
The storm of life has come once again
And the struggle goes on and we don't know when it will end
So many people have given in
For they feel that they just cannot win
But the storm of life will always be
That's why we should live in love, hope and harmony.

Roy Gunter

MOMENT OF MADNESS, A LIFETIME OF REGRET

My life flashed before my eyes as my hands gripped the wheel
The lurch of the car from side to side and the deafening tyre squeal
What made me go fast and take that risk, God will only know
My life is full of deep regrets and an awful lot of sorrow

The things I was taught when starting out simply left my mind
I am the man behind the wheel who might as well be driving blind
The cars were wrecked and damaged beyond all recognition
All I could hear was the gentle sway of the keys in the ignition
I opened my eyes and looked around at the total devastation
Glass, blood and smashed up lives beyond all comprehension

I look back after all these years still full of regret
A tragic time in my life that I will never ever forget
A mother, a daughter, a waste of young life
She never had the chance to become someone's loved wife

There's one thing in life I don't want you to forget
A moment of madness, a lifetime of regret.

Andrew Cain

BEFORE THE ROOSTER CROWS

Before the rooster crows, I should admit
To knowing you, at least a little bit,
For you have known me before earth's crust
Was seen and carefully planned me, from life's dust.

Before the rooster crows, I must decide
To love You more than self, from deep inside,
For You have loved me unto sacrifice,
Pure agony and blood, sin's shameful price.

Before the rooster crows, I will proclaim
Your name, in word and deed, accept men's blame.
How could I hesitate, or worse, deny
My Lord, if love for me, should make You die?

Ingrid Rankin

POLLUTION

What are we doing?
What have we done?
We have murdered the birds,
With the black, oily scum.

What are we doing?
What have we done?
Killing the fish and the coral,
As if there is no tomorrow.

What are we doing?
What have as done?
Polluting the beaches
And the fresh air
And nobody seems to care.

What are we doing?
What have we done?
With this black, oily scum,
Crude by name and crude by nature,
Let's control this enemy of the Creator.

David Hamey

UNROOTED

An empty sting, such hollow wince
The worth was brief, yet stand alone
I'd hurt once more and thousands since
A single beat was mine to own

Your loving movement wrecked me deeper
Now always changed, now always burnt
The sweetest burn a soul should keep here
Most brutal changing, lesson learnt

That brush which broke my heart's perception
Cleared my mind, my eyes see new
Ruined all, beyond deception
I'll ache each day, wonderful you.

Carlene Dandy

ACTUAL SIZE

Tiny used words like autumn and snowflake;
Full-size words like tools and paper, like Blake,
Tiny was self-obsessed, a little depressed;
Full-size stood head and shoulders above the rest.

Tiny couldn't remember the ends of the jokes,
Especially the one about these two blokes.
Full-size rolled out rows of brilliant one-liners;
Tiny was on the bill but Full-size was the headliner.

Tiny thought of himself as an intellectual
And did not feel the need to grow. Tiny felt substantial.
Full-size recognised genius, he touched it;
Full-size knew it was possible to take-off and orbit.

Ian Davey

REMEMBRANCE

Ridiculed by an unnatural nature
being criticised close to extinction
this is what our world has become

Our minds are forming to recognise the bloodthirsty knowledge
to perfection not knowing in how a simple task
to many cannot be completed without exterminating one's nature

Bah! What nonsense we behold
if perfection is what we want
then why are so many heroic people out on the battlefield
stepping out onto no-man's-land
while the perfectionist are quivering in the trenches?

It is an impossible task
that we have destroyed the young's minds
or is it because we can't accept who we are
We are not perfect that is all natural a nature of the human being
oh how stubborn we are to see what is in front of our eyes
instead we send those to the battlefields
and send them to their deaths.

Imogen Brand

I WILL NOT BE CAST DOWN!

I will not be cast down!
Oppressed or overwhelmed
by all this tragedy.
I will not lose my light
in this cold, cold wind:
I need my light to see by.

I'll not be screwed by fear
into a knuckle,
hard and dense with doubt.
I will not lose my heart
in this sea of swirl and trouble,
I need my heart to love with.

I will not an unbeliever be,
amid these spirals of divinity.
Nor fear the heart of darkness.
I will not lose my sense of Self
at these gates of transformation.
I need my Self to live in.

Tony Dougan

IN THE NAME

In the name of eyes, mirrors of change,
In the name of bodies broken by rage,
In the name of smiles, laughter and tears
At home in streets and in fields,
In the name of fruit budding in blossom,
Of trees and their thrusting roots
And branches stretching towards the light,
In the name of the mentally ill, of drug addicts,
The homeless, refugees, of the unborn,
In the name of us all
In spite of shared humanity
Crawling in single lanes,
I pray: Lord, save us from any fall,
Open our hearts to share
The meaning of vision, hope and prayer.

Angela Matheson Cutrale

WRONG

What did I do wrong?
Only cared,
Only shared.
Things said
Cannot be undone,
Said in private,
All along.
How could I be betrayed,
And what for?
I am now alone,
Scared and prone,
Do I trust again?
On my own in pain,
My life on hold,
I hope they are proud.
When I die,
Will they cry?
Too late then,
Never forgiven.

Garry Bedford

UNTITLED

The softness of his gaze,
the subdued murmurs of uncertain affliction.
Rationality left behind and forgotten,
blind ambition traversing the wings of my mind.
My heart flickering like a dying lantern,
and my eyes dazed with sweet seduction.
The moon's cantillations and her plucking at my heart.
Embellish my visions with your desire and your passion,
love me with your body as if it were imperishable,
and with your mind as if it were as intricate and entangled as the world's design.
Love me with every element of your mortality.

S Jean Brenner

THE HOPES OF A STREET CHILD

Take a leap, with no path ahead, no road to the side,
No sky above your head,
Memorise when there was a bed, a ceiling above
And a mouth that was fed.
There's no limit, no desire, no thirst,
But there's belief, belief of being first.
This is laughter; there is sadness,
But there is no regret, even in all this mess.
Life is beautiful when I look around me,
Fresh, wet mud covering my foot till knee.
The smell of my body soaked in days and months of sun,
Eating parched grass with the baby calf; now that's my type of fun!
And the yellow colour on my nails, that I see the wealthy people trying to paint,
Apparently it's the reason I sometimes faint,
If a wish were granted,
It would be for all the dying greenery to be replanted,
For, if they die, so would I . . .
There is hope that one day God will convey
And when He does, it will all be okay!

Jainisha Patel

MUSIC OF THE SPHERES

It's time to consider a mystery,
multicoloured, not virgin white.

As long as minds can remember,
the universe has been waiting
for its themes to unravel.

It's not unreasonable to expect
a prophecy here . . .

'Every age will end on a bright silver note -
try an 'E': the sound of the longest symphony.
It will end, then the music will begin again,
this time in a different galaxy.'

Daniel Crowley

THE MELODY OF LOVE

True love is an emotion - a feeling deep within
A longing, a desire attracting her or him
A drum beating out the rhythm so perfectly in time
Bringing out the harmony melodious and sublime
The heart throbs to the music - emotions soar and rise
Reaching a crescendo which vibrates across the skies
True love is like a melody perfectly in tune
Filling the air with music, morning, night and noon
Though sometimes it may fluctuate, ebbing high or low
It never ever ceases and the evidence will show
A sweet and melodious harmony, so perfectly in tune
No matter what the day or year, December, March or June.

Dorothy Durrant

MIRACLE ON THE MOUNTAIN

Move man, move
So the mountain moved
Be still and know that I am God
Move the mountain, be still I say
Let the problems dissolve, send them away
How can a mountain move my Lord?
Be still and know that I am God
A seed so small all faith be known
How the planets move on their own
The gentle breeze into a gusty storm
Quell your fears, never feel alone
For the mighty hand of Christ our Lord
Will still the storm be it on His own
He gives us all a job to do
From the tiniest skill to the greatest mountain moves
And yesterday has gone, yes gone
This moment in time will move on, move on
Each day that cometh in a speck of time
Seize the day before it moves on, moves on.

Christine Renee Parker

CUTTING CAULIFLOWER

And the chopping and the chatter
Almost meaning pares apart;
Tapping knife blade on the counter
Mutes the screaming of the heart.
'This appointment with the doctor . . .'
Losing force amongst the leaves,
As sharp steel squeals through cauliflower.
As we smile when we should grieve.

And the notches on the worktop
In our psyche etch as stone;
Fingers tracing jagged engrave
Fearing cancer crops our own.
Witness florets cold in hard chalk
Scalpelled off, to hail the bowl,
Thudding rhythmic under our talk,
Mocking heartbeats, bruising soul.

But we chatter and we slice,
Denying all our ill-providence.

Anthony Webster

SEASIDE HOLIDAY ENDS

Gone the cloudless, windswept sky, gone the ever restless sea
Gone the golden, sandy beach, now just a memory
Gone the children's peals of joy, their splashing in the waves
Now heard in seabirds' cries alone, faint echoes in sea caves
Gone the Punch and Judy show, gone the ice cream van
Gone the mobile oyster bar and hurdy-gurdy man
Gone the magic roundabout, gone the children's slides
Gone the gypsy palmist, gone the donkey rides
Gone the music of the band, gone the minstrel show
Gone the theatre on the pier, farewell to Pierrot
Gone the fairground dart stall, gone the soft-toy prize
Gone, the carefree days of childhood, and blue remembered skies.

Nicholas G Charnley

I CAN'T REACH YOU

I didn't get to tell you how great you were
I feel I didn't make good use of our time
Were you so unhappy? Were you so sad?
Did you just get too curious?
Could anyone have helped you?
All my curiosities go unanswered, I just can't not know

Can't you hear me? I don't understand why you went
Why wasn't it another prank, why couldn't it just be a joke?
It's not, it's as real as I am here writing
I miss our random chats, I miss your laugh, your smile
I can't get you back, I can't get you back

I can't bring myself to clear your details
I still don't want to believe you're really gone
What happened to Plymouth, your dreams, your plans?
You've gone somewhere much further,
Somewhere we can't visit
No phone calls, no emails, we can't reach you,
I can't reach you there!

Ann Dempsey

LIVING IN TUNE!

My mind is like a slender thread, thin as a gossamer wing,
vibrating to the sound of God who causes it to sing.

The fine retuning of its strings, joyous worship brings
and harmony and peace result, when I acknowledge and exult.

But if I go another way and cherish not, my God, this day
the thread becomes a thicker chord, sleeved around with dusty word.

Though I don't notice how I've changed, my life has strayed a different range,
and then I fall and look again, to find the Saviour who heals pain.

But He's already seeking me, and only needed bended knee.
He raises me to stand once more, the God I live for and adore!

Gill Mainwaring

FOOD FOR THOUGHT

We all need food to eat - that is true
Special treats, which are good, for me and you;
In this busy world we all rush around,
Our feet sometimes hardly touch the ground.
People feel the pressure of today's world
As into it all, we are harshly hurled.
But no matter what we do,
Let's not be too busy, or we will rue,
To feed the heart!
What food does the heart need?
On compassion and understanding, it will feed.
Kind words, loving deeds, it appreciates.
Sarcasm and cruelty, it truly hates.
Let's not be too busy to say, 'I care.'
Let's not be too busy, gifts to share.
Life can give us lots of food for thought,
Some gifts are priceless, cannot be bought,
But it's so important from life's start
To feed the heart!

Ann Margaret Holden (Rowell)

COMING HOME

Hear the west wind fall,
Hear how the mighty call,
As the green leaves hush me coming home.

Their embrace is wet and sweet,
In their dark shadows our eyes meet,
I am welcome here,
Where those have passed,
Through melodies and lightning fast,
Sighing in the waters' pool,
This is home and not forgotten,
Memories brought like seeds of night.

Natalie Williams

LUTHER

A lovely ginger cat came wandering here one day,
But he must have been quite frightened as on seeing me, ran away.
I set myself a challenge as I wished that he would stay,
And become my special cat pet to be cared for every day.
Next day I put out food and milk near the trees and by the fence,
I saw him taking both these things and he seemed a lot less tense.
This went on for many weeks but near him I could not get,
So I persevered and called to him till at last he became my pet.
I named him Luther and put food near the door,
Quite quickly after eating this he jumped onto my floor.
He comes now at once when I call his name
And at last with love, he is quite tame.
He let me then caress his head and stroke his soft smooth back
Oh what bliss, he seemed to say, these things I did really lack.
Now on my bed he'll purr and sleep,
So can forget the time when he had no keep.
Friends who come now say he's a gorgeous cat,
He lets them give him a gentle pat when indoors and on my lap.

Mary Rose

WHEN ONE CHAPTER ENDS . . .

It's time to say goodbye to the house where I was born.
I've put my books away,
Cinderella married her prince,
All the fairy tales I've read have now come true;
I've played my last game with many snakes on the way,
Then I climbed the ladder to the top, to gain the prize waiting there.
My dolls just sit and watch as I quickly pack my case,
Ready to ride in a silver coach,
They call a limousine, that will carry me,
To the fairy tale of my dreams.
So now with trembling hands,
I must take down that misty cloud of white hanging there,
And slip it over my head,
Ready to take that magic journey to the church
And meet Tom, my prince!
Waiting there to turn the page, as we move together hand in hand
Into the next chapter of life.
Like a fairy tale, may it be, they lived happy ever after.

Audrey Allen

CRETE

White stucco walls reflecting the sun
Long, lazy days, holiday fun
Spectacular sunsets, lovingly shared
Passionate moments, uncompared
St Catherine's beach, turtles at night
Laying their eggs, a wondrous sight
Fishing boat landing outside our hotel
Filling the air with a pungent smell
Black cloths spread under olive trees
White sails billowing in the morning breeze
Glasses clinking, birthday surprise
Champagne sipped under inky skies
Black-clad mourners winding up the hill
Stark reality, time stood still
White knuckle ride in the mountain path
Gorges dug by nature's wrath
A perfect jewel in nature's scheme
Magical Crete, or was it a dream?

Catherine Hislop

OPEN HEART

None will ever see that look,
The one that you gave me.
No one will ever think the thought
Or feel the heat that went through me.
If melting ice could resist the flame
And stand forever always the same,
Just a singular virgin heart,
Never to be part of a part,
And always to resist the risk of a broken heart.
Like a childless family's regret
Who waited too long for a stronger bond
Or a bigger fund, but fell apart just the same,
Saying 'one day' or the tomorrow that never came.
Don't know why I was open to change
And answered questions again and again,
But I feel it was worth maybe being sometimes a fool,
Even though the heat, sometimes intense,
Has now created a rippled pool.

Rod Pilkington

TO THE TAX MAN

Dear Mr Tax Man,
I heard from you before May,
A message on my pay slip,
A large portion of my wages taken away.
A letter I did post you,
But you didn't seem to read,
Pointing out my situation, in my hour of need.
I tried to telephone you, but no one at home, it seems,
Oh Mr Tax Man, you can be so mean.
I used to claim my over sixty-six allowance
But it seems you've just forgot,
And I claimed my spouse's portion,
But now it seems it's not.
So how, Mr Tax Man, can I reach to you
And make you see it my way?
I have a point of view.
Oh, and by the way, I had no answer both times I rang,
So is it part-time for you Sir, you and your gang?

Rosemary Whatling

TRAMONTANE

Tramontane excites me, dares me,
Blows me free, and clean, and carefree.
Seems so hostile, violent, vicious,
Yet coquettish, now capricious.
Set out cold, but walking warms me;
Set my stride and rhythm calms me.
Blues of sea and sky delight me;
Heaps of plane leaves, crisp, invite me.
Autumn vines in elegant splendour,
Gold and ruby, melt me tender;
Pounds my heart with wordless passion,
Lifts my head, my face, my vision.
Tree and mountain merge with me
And I with them, yet consciously.
Beyond this beauty, thoughts of you
Surround me, fill me, hold me true
Till you are with me, here, today,
And I am truly blown away.

Nesta Nicholson

THE ONLY WAY IS UP

We both have a mountain to climb,
But we have each other,
To reach the very top,
Our friendship is strong,
And whatever happens,
We will climb on.

Life is like a challenge,
With a mountain of hurdles
That get in the way.
We will knock them down
And fight our way through.

Then climb towards the top,
Reaching our goal,
Feeling like new.
The only way is up now,
With a great future
And plenty more adventures too.

Andrea Ratter

THE NUN'S VALLEY

In Madeira you will tread
Volcanoes that are long since dead -
      A mild, entrancing vale;
         Right in the crater's open heart
Where fire and brimstone once took part,
You'll find there dale and trail.

Light shadows move upon the ground,
Where turféd hills with sun are crowned
      And trees majestic wait,
And little birds with trilling song,
The branches in the treetops throng,
From dawning time till late.

Below the ridge there is surprise -
A bright, enchanting paradise,
   In which you'll like to stay,
Where velvet slopes of brightest green
Drift us far away.

Nola Small

NANNY STATE

All units to the megastore for nice tubes of your food,
Beef, lamb or pork, open your mouth, then wipe it,
here's some fruit for a good mood.

You came out from your cubicle in time for twelve hours' work,
Afterwards we have sun rooms where future wives may lurk.

A sports room full of everything your heart could ever need,
some machines you can play on just before another feed.

The bedtime music that we play when you are in your shower,
will lull you off to sleep in under half an hour.

Everything is done for you until your work days end,
remember that the government will always be your friend.

Then when you breathe your last breath, the lights will all go dim, those minutes on the vision service will not be too grim.

Your relatives will get the diamond in a white gold ring,
thank you for a lifetime's work, it was a real nice thing.

Jean Paisley

LIVE LIFE TO THE FULL
(Advice from mother to daughter)

Make life a cornucopia of delights
Embrace it, take every opportunity,
Don't let the grass grow,
Under your feet, dear.
Be sure to give yourself
Lots of delicious treats.
Be loyal, be true,
To families and friends.

Try and get on with your colleagues,
You don't have to like them.
I know it's a bore, darling,
But it's the only way to keep in the swim
And of course, continue with the gym,
Keep yourself really trim,
Don't be too serious,
Live, laugh and have fun.

Elizabeth Jenks

MR JACK FROST

In the night
Jack Frost came.
His fingers stroked
My windowpane.
The air was crisp
And sparkling clean,
There were trails
Where he had been.

By noon the sun
Was shining bright,
The air was warm
The wind was light.
By eventide the clouds
Were tipped with gold,
The sun went down
The wind was turning cold.
And Jack Frost came . . .

Doris Mary Miller

POEM

Do I still have the words
Now that I'm old
Has the passion of youth
Become still and old?

I read many books
To feed my mind's hunger
Tales of heroes and villains
Of pillage and plunder

How to gather sweet words
That will please one who reads
And create an impression of
Joy and good deeds

Not an easy exertion
But worth making a try
So this is my effort
My last soliloquy.

Mavis Downey

COCOON

Take my hand openly
break through the seal
Judge not what you can see
but what you can feel

An error of sight
is of human design
We're blinded by needs
so we openly lie

Again to you I call
as my soul passes on
Forever in tether
my heart screams for one

Exit the comfort
enter the open
Watch with new eyes
as your cocoon's broken

Adrian Horton

CHATS WITH A TEENAGER

'Where have you been to tonight, my son?'
'Ah, nowhere again.'
'That place really must have something
You go there so often.'

'And, what did you do there?'
'Ah, nothing.'
'You really must enjoy doing that.
You do it all the time.'

'And, who did you go there with?'
'Ah, no one.'
'Well, it saves you getting bored
With the same old faces.'

The experts all say that it's good
To chat with your teenagers
And take an interest in their lives,
It brings you closer together.

Margaret Dilloway

THE STRING

Blowing in the wind
Wishing to make my mark.
Dreaming to be of value
Waiting, just waiting.

A long process it had to be
Cutting, washing, dyeing, weaving, spinning.
It was hard going through the mill.
At last I am free.

Brown, slim, not too long to tie or hold in a bow or trim
Travelling over land and sea even in the air I go
Keeping parcels safe
Bringing cheer to someone dear.

When shoelaces break I stretch out and through the holes I go.
This I undertake best of all,
Make a ring of me, circling your little finger I will be
Then we will both remember.

Hazel Wilson

EASTER 2010

In the silence of Good Friday
I heard the sounds of Calvary
Nails knocking in the mind
That never sleeps

Echoes of eternity
Deep glimpses of a dream
Caught unconscious
As they seeped into today

Tomorrow comes unbidden
How to greet you
With a heart that
Like the tomb is open?

Will we ever know?
Uncertainty skins us hollow
As the bells that peel
For resurrection's hope.

Paul Thompson

HOLD MY HAND!

I was born into a world of darkness
My eyes had been left behind,
So afraid, alone and bewildered
Until the touch of a hand, so kind.

Each time my fears enveloped me
One touch and I felt so secure,
This gentle touch of communication
I wasn't alone or afraid, anymore.

No words could help me to understand
But the touch of this hand and I knew,
Everything was going to be alright
As long as I could hold on, to you?

After two long years the light came through
The end of my darkness had come,
At last I could see as I held that hand
The tears in the eyes of my mum!

Christopher Thomas

THE RUGGED SILHOUETTE

The dark and rugged silhouette stood out against the sky
Of tangerine and crimson, as the wispy clouds sailed by
This figure seemed so human; I wondered who it may be
And had to investigate more, for all of us, you see

The amazing vivid sunset cast shadows where I walked
And soon the birds that I'd disturbed flew by me as they squawked
'Leave him be,' they seemed to say, in their special kind of way
And still in mind, I had to find, an answer on that day

To my surprise, as I advanced, the figure did not move
But I could see that it was worn, with many types of groove
My silhouette, a blackened tree, contorted, weathered form
A friend to many creatures, was a shelter from the storm

So now I know why all the birds, created such a din
This weathered mass of timber, was a home to all within
And when I spy the silhouette, upon the distant hill
I know the birds are comforted, from winter's bitter pill.

Nigel Lloyd Maltby

SECOND HAND HEROES

They were for sale in the market
Eight discs of silver and gold
A shame for the men that had earned them
Their story will never be told

How grateful our wonderful nation
Felt at the end of the strife
To the men who had fought so bravely
And to those who had given their life

They wrought those medals for valour
They were given with pomp and acclaim
The men had a 'Pass By' and dinner
To acknowledge their right to some fame

The world then promptly forgot them
They were left to struggle and strive
They had to sell their medals
In order to stay alive.

Pat Adams

HURTING

Hurting, hurting, feelings that float
Sailing alone again in my love boat
Holding back the tears with a lump in my throat
She didn't even tell me, not even a note

Hurting, hurting, feelings are low
Lost in the woods, don't know where to go
Keeping so quiet so no one will know
My feelings had blossomed and started to grow

Hurting, hurting, feeling the stun
Eyes that were blinded by her bright sun
I was a kid having such fun
Believing that I had landed the one

Hurting, hurting, feelings had shone
It looked the best, but was really a con
I love that girl, but now she has gone
Please pick up my pieces and help me move on

Aidan Martin

THE POND

Just by the pond where fish did jump
The air was pure and balmy,
Such peace surrounds this lovely place
That helps you think more calmly.

The daily cares and worries
Are left by the kitchen sink,
While you can lean against a tree
And indulge yourself and think.

If worries overtake you
Just let them flow away,
There is some way to solve them
You just need to find the way.

I hope I'm not the only one
Who knows this magic place,
That helps you feel that you have won
Your special share of peace.

Mary Cole

THE SEA AND THE SKY

They are locked in eternal union
The sea and the sky compete
Like two spoilt children
If only they could speak!

The sky is jealous of the waves
And of the surf's soft sigh
The sea is envious of the clouds
That adorn her sister, sky.

The clouds are reflected in the sea
And are seen there just as plain
The water's sucked into the clouds
To fall again like rain.

And so the two spoilt children
Each share an equal space
And kiss on the horizon
In a sisterly embrace.

Sandie Miles

A VISIT TO THE DOCTOR'S

I said, 'I've not got an appointment,'
As I stepped in the surgery door,
I didn't know that I'd wake up feeling sick,
And know to phone up the day before.

The receptionist gave me a long, sideways look,
And said this would simply not do,
It was clear that she viewed me like something
She had just wiped from the sole of her shoe.

I had to wait over an hour,
Cos the doc had so many to see,
He went to the loo, made six phone calls and then,
He finally got round to me.

I'm not going back to the doctor's,
No matter how rotten I feel,
If I can't let him know several weeks in advance,
And book up my time to be ill!

Mick Nash

NIGHT OF MADNESS

He sat watching over the cars below
And ruffled his wings in the summer rain.
He stretched his tired, stiff, achy legs and flew
For it was time for the gargoyles to reign.

The skies above the sacred church grew dark,
As down the hill the evil beasts did fly.
Not a patch of blue was soon to be seen,
Now nowhere to escape to should you try.

A great thundering sound came from below;
The cold hard ground was starting to vibrate.
Steam could be seen rising from subway vents,
How could Man survive this new fragile state?

I knelt down, hiding my face in my hands,
I could not let them see me cry and shake!
I was not the hero to save this tale,
But you were next to me shouting, 'Awake!'

Barbara Pearce

JACK'S POT

Blink, think and focus, it takes just over a second,
Don't listen to their lies and don't be beckoned,
Don't part with your money or your information,
A fool's downfall doesn't take much preparation.

Blink, focus and think, it takes a second and no more,
Turn away from bright lights they will make you poor,
You cannot win a fortune with one simple question,
When the answer is in front of you as a suggestion.

Focus, blink and think, it takes a second or so,
You can itch and scratch for a pound a go,
Pound after pound you itch and scratch,
How hard can it be just to make it match?

Blink, blink a tear, because your pockets are hollow,
Think, think a thought, there is money you can borrow,
Focus, focus the cards and quiz line numbers are a joke,
Blink, think and focus, it's all the gambles that make us broke.

David Marland

NIGHT FROST

There is tapping on the windowpane
The hour is late and chilling,
Out there in the dark of night, the moon
Is full, the stars bright, like diamonds.

In the twilight the frost is sparkling
And thick, covering all in sight,
The snowdrops hang their heads
And daffodils hide below the soil.

The earth frozen and hard, bulbs
Waiting for the warmth of the sun,
To chase away this cold layer of
White iciness now far spread.

Seen in this morning's first light
Bushes red with berries frozen and still,
While lacy patterns form on the windowpane
Night frost was tapping, waiting to come in.

Beryl Smyter

A TRANQUIL TIME

Ripples on the ocean,
Rippling far, rippling wide.
Flowing emotion,
Ebbing, with the tide.

Hills rolling eastward,
Rolling into one.
The meander of the river,
Follows the setting sun.

Twilight is fading,
Darkness takes its place.
Shadows are forming,
Across your gentle face.

The starlit sky above,
Casting moonbeams on the sea,
Here, with you, beside the water . . .
Is where I want to be.

Hazel Hudson

CHRISTOPHER

'Is there anybody there?' said the visitor
Stroking the patient's head,
Tears falling silent at the bedside
As she leant over the bed.

'Nobody there,' said the staff nurse
'Not since this time last week,
There's no one there to hear you,'
So I bent and kissed his cheek.

I spoke again to my brother,
'Is there anyone in there at all?'
No answer came and the red-hot tears
Again began to fall.

'Tell him I came and he wasn't home,
That I kept my words as I wept,
That I didn't let him die alone.
Then I kissed him again - and I left.'

Lilian Fulker

OCTOBER 31ST 2005

A little girl was born today
Her name is Ashleigh May
She has made my son a grandad
At forty years of age

So that's made me a great grandma
And my husband a great grandad
All the more the merrier
I'm sure that can't be bad

She is as pretty as a picture
And as bonny as can be
Another photo for the album
Another leaf for the family tree

Born on my father's birthday
That's another added joy
Happy birthday, darling Ashleigh May
And many more may you enjoy.

Decima Watkins

FEBRUARY SNOW

February snow, so light, fell sporadically
against a sky of aquamarine.
A sparrow pirouetted a distant aerial,
its frosty antennae glistening in the bright sun.
Overhead, seagulls flew out of sight over rooftops so near.
Pinioned perfection in flight, whilst carrying
a cargo of plumage to bear.
Cumulous clouds then appeared from over
a cuneiformed horizon of granite skyline.
A sight to behold as the sun rose on this frosty morn!
The birth of a new day, with the promise of spring
carried in the chilled air.
Snowdrops now growing where absence had been.
Nature's alarm now alerting their growth as a new year rolls by.
New buds now forming on branches captured the eye.
All this and more gave banquet of hope, and a reasoned goodbye
To a garden of growth, with a view of the sky!

Christine Flowers

SUMMER'S BUTTERFLY

The spotlight is on you, summer's butterfly,
The birds love to sing their sweet song to you, as they fly,
They can't believe how beautiful you are,
You're summer's shining star,
You flutter with ease,
In the gentle breeze,
You flutter as high as the treetops,
You flutter in the woodlands,
Where once grew the snowdrops,
You flutter in summer your destination,
In Nature's height of pollination,
You flutter in the valleys low,
Where a river runs through
And in the gardens where there's sweet honeysuckle,
Foxglove and lavender blue,
You rest on a flower as the warm sun shines,
Remembering summer's happy times.

Joanna Maria John

BEWARE, MY FRIENDS, OF MISCHIEF AND MAYHEM ON ALL HALLOW'S EVE

Beware, my friends, of mischief and mayhem
On All Hallow's Eve
Be careful on Halloween night
As pixies come out to play their tricks on us humans
When you least expect it, they might take it upon themselves
To create mischief and mayhem with magic
Causing cats to howl, owls to hoot
Bats to screech and flutter against the inky-black sky
Dogs might bark, trees might even seem life-like
Just for a lark,
And then for the final trick
A witch flying across the moon, cackling as she goes
Or is that just your imagination playing tricks on you again?
Beware, my friends, of mischief and mayhem
On All Hallow's Eve.

Jessica Powell

DEAR GRANDDAUGHTER

Dear Granddaughter,
Terminally ill I await my God.
Look up to the universe this night
I am that star that shimmers bright
My footsteps in the sand will soon take flight.
I will be that blackbird in morning song
That awakes you to help you carry on.
I will be spring's downpour of rain
That will wash away your bereaved pain.
Do not grieve like a funeral wreath
I will have only been a fallen leaf
My God has come, He is with me here
I see His aura brightly lit
Yours is this world with me always in it
By your side and never far
Your one and only
          Grandma.

Diane Full

TIME WILL TELL

I've reached my allotted three score and ten,
So it's not a matter of if, but when.
I made a will some time ago,
Will they be happy when they know?
I've sorted my clothes as best I can,
And I've even sent my shoes to Oxfam!
So I'll just sit down and have a rest,
(But I want to watch 'Flog It', I confess.)
Now how come I got to be so old?
The Queen is pushing eighty-four,
So perhaps I should expect much more.
I'll dye my hair and buy new clothes,
I'll go to the gym and then who knows!
I think I've got my second chance,
I'm going to sing, I'm going to dance!
I'm going to chase the blues away
And learn to live just for the day!

Judy Hopkin

SOMETHING FAINT AND FAR AWAY

Something faint and far away
Something I loved.

'Did you - do you exist in reality?'
I ask the fleeting dream or long past memory
'I did - I do.'
A recent dream is so like something in the past
- The long past.

The struggle to remember is the same
Sometimes, something stands out, but this one is
So faint and far away
And yet so poignant
Is it from my childhood home?
Or longer past?
Or Heaven?
Something faint and far away
Something I loved.

Jacqueline Ives-Ward

CIRCUS

She swirls like a ballerina
clasping onto fame
as she smiles through the air
angels in waiting for her fall

Smoking gypsies wait to dance
happy clowns sit on saddened wooden seats
fading into the crowd

The ringmaster fixing his moustache
into a figure of eight
Lions roar fire that splitter into darkness

Crowds neighing and the rattle and roll
of popcorn girls selling cinder toffee en mass
People gather
monumental voices whisper and speak

The circus is upon us every day and week.

Leah Rouse

WINDOWS

Do you ever wonder
about the people
behind the windows
of the houses that you pass
What their lives are like
how they live
and would they tell you
if you asked

Do you wonder if
they're good or bad
if they live in fear
do they need a helping hand
those people who live there
behind those windows
of the houses
that you pass.

Daphne Cornell

THE MAN WITH THE BLUE EYE

The man with the blue eye
looked at me with anguish and despair.
He was desperate,
with a rugged look to him.
Worn out and tired, he tried to say something
but no words came out.
There was only one feature of his face
that caught my attention,
the blue eye glaring at me with power
at first looked like a sapphire marble,
but then as the sun beamed down
on the sides of his face
it was like the night sky had browned the pupil
with a sudden burst of determination.

The man with the blue eye asked questions,
But I wasn't the one to provide the answers.

Neelam Shah

IT'S NEVER TOO LATE

There must be other people
And creatures in the universe,
But we must be very careful
When we reverse,
We don't know who they are
Or what they are like,
Or where they're from,
But we may wonder if they will survive
If and when we are all gone,
There must be other planets,
Places to explore,
But we must be very careful,
We don't want to cause a war,
We have to find a way to communicate and translate,
To find out who they are and what they are,
It's never too late.

John Walker

CONFLICTING COLOURS

White, bland, unthinking vacant soul, open to stories told
Grim, hateful new ideas sprouting, harbour jealousy
Blue, numb brainwashed mind, cloudy lingering icy cold
Purple, insane thoughts arise, turn raging ebony
Red, angry, vengeful, seething, hatred makes a convert bold
Black, vile, destructive evil, breeds inhumanity

From purple raging hatred, projectile vomit spews
Black, sullen, threatening vitriol burns within a mind
Red, fiery energy, volatile with insane views
Purple clouds with violent shades their thoughts to murder wind
A homemade bomb, blood splatters forth red's most deadly hues
You are black, you are red, all dark colours you will find

Ninety-nine percent embrace Amber's loving clutch
In black moods of fiery anger we cannot agree
Earthy brown some sombre souls, yet they don't hate that much
Creed nor colour of our skin, but our humanity
Will dye our world bright yellow, bring sunshine when we touch
We are rainbows, we can be gentle colours, you and me.

Elizabeth Scharer

AN OLD TEDDY BEAR

Just an old, discarded teddy bear
Lying on the bed.
Worn out and tattered by the years,
Pillowing my head.
Once, when I was young and firm,
You kissed me with your lips,
And against your silken body press,
While in tease, my fur you did caress.
Alas, no longer soft and cuddly,
I hide my very need.
Soon, I will be replaced by a teddy
Oh, so neat and new.
Then, I'll be thrown out to the floor,
Or cast, forgotten, behind some cupboard door.
My colour faded and my squeaker gone,
Waiting there lonely and all forlorn.
My love crying out silently for you.
Crying out . . . crying out silently for you . . .

Maurice Colclough

JERUSALEM PILGRIMAGE

I've been on a pilgrimage to Jerusalem,
I've seen where Jesus was born;
I sailed on the Sea of Galilee,
Where miracles He performed:
I travelled the Judean Desert,
Paddled my feet in the Dead Sea,
I went on a cable car up the mountain
And had lunch, cooked by nuns, in a monastery:
I was splashed by water from the River Jordan,
I had lunch in a kibbutz in Israel:
I visited magnificent churches,
Built to celebrate the birth of our Lord:
I walked the Stations of the Cross,
I've seen the place where He died:
I've looked inside His empty tomb,
I know He is still alive!

Hetty Launchbury

POETRY RIVALS' COLLECTION 2010 - THE PASSIONS OF THE POET

MY FRIEND'S FLAT

I've lived in my flat for years,
The neighbours upstairs are driving me to tears.
One lot moved out, others moved in,
Just my luck they're the worst family there's been.
I stay at my sister's most days,
To get away from the craze.
I wish I had a cat or dog for a pet,
The neighbours' pets I wished I'd never met.
They bark, they miaow,
Causing them to have a row.
One day I'll move,
Then get into the groove.
The neighbours from hell
Can ring my bell,
But to their surprise I'll be gone far away,
So I can get some peace, hey! Hey! Hey!

Jayne Manning

ANOTHER YOU

Creeping darkness across the land
Innocence lost
Immortality found
My life it takes on
Twists and turns
A spectator as
The embers burn
Down to a cinder
Blackened ash
I hide my tears
From the sun
Keep in shadow
Moving on
Searching for life anew
Another town
Another you.

Samantha Williams

MY WALKING HOLIDAY

I have always fancied hiking across dale and moors
Striding through sun and rain, always out of doors,
So I got the book and thought, this looks good.
I bought plastic trousers and a coat with a hood.
Then I paid my money and got into the car
Drove to Devon - it seemed rather far.
We got kitted up and collected our grub
After a mile or so my shoes started to rub.
The reality of it all came as rather a shock
As with dripping hair and soggy sock
We tramped around in the mist and rain.
By the end of the day, my leg had a pain.
So I have now decided, if I want to explore
I will go by car, not tramp the moor.
Though my companions made the holiday fun
It was my first and very last one.

Lynne Walden

OUR DANCING YEARS

We have waltzed in old Vienna, you and I,
Where the lovely notes of Strauss caress the sky.
We have tangoed in Paris, to the tune of Jealousy
And our foxtrot was a beautiful thing to see.
In Russia with the Cossacks we've flung our feet out wide
And in Greece we did our version of our English Palais Glide.
In Spain we danced Flamenco, though we lacked a lot of rhythm,
And our rumba in Brazil caused a lot of criticism.
With friends we stripped the willow to the beat of Jimmy Shand
And we quickstepped to Glen Miller and his trumpeting big band.
We've danced towards the sunrise with oak leaves in our hair
And we joined the summer solstice and the druids dancing there.
We've danced the world together since we were joined as one,
But our knees are now arthritic and our dancing days are done,
But one last dance, my darling, one dance for you and me,
We shall dance the dance macabre to our local cemetery.

Dorothy Beaumont

STEADFAST SUITOR

Compass needle, you are faithful
To the north, your ancient lover.
Other devotees may be deflected
But not you, a constant suitor.
Here, in this boiling weather,
Sun-torturing, you keep troth
With your far, frozen north,
Point inexorably to your darling.
But does he care for you,
Blue compass needle? Remain true
To your steadfastness? Wind
And snow scurry mercilessly
In that white, unfeeling Arctic circle,
Caring little, poor compass needle,
For though you are always true,
The Pole has quite forgotten you.

P B Norris

WINTER BLUES

I'm beginning to get the winter blues,
I'd like to go on a ten days cruise,
I'll get the brochure, have a browse,
To see what options they arouse.
I like Egypt, but maybe too hot,
I'd better find a cooler spot,
I would have loved to have seen the Nile,
But will postpone it for a while.
Greece is the place that beckons me,
Sailing on the Ionian Sea,
Lovely coves and tranquil bays,
To drop anchor and temporarily stay.
Then to watch the sky at night,
With thousands of stars shining so bright,
It's a wonder for all to see,
Reflecting their jewels in the shimmering sea.

Dulcie Beatrice Gillman

YOU WALKED AWAY

You walked away and stole my very heart.
You captured it right from the very start.
The moment that you glanced your eyes my way,
Those darkened pools that held me in their sway
Enfolded me. Of them I was a part.

That very moment, pierced by Cupid's dart,
I saw a masterpiece of finest art,
And as you turned your hair danced, as at play.
You walked away.

I stood and watched you with my love, depart.
The tears flowed freely and my eyes did smart.
I begged in silent words that you might stay,
Not leave me broken-hearted, in dismay.
Though you held the key to my life's start,
You walked away.

J G Ryder

REUNION

We met as student nurses a long time ago.
Our hearts were young and full of fun in spite of tears and work.
Three years did pass and soon the nurses called us Staff.
Our ways in life a long way went to be a nun in Africa called this friend.
A midwife I did strive to be and then my love he found me.

A half century and five have passed
And thoughts of times of old.
What became of old friend since was it nineteen fifty-five or four?
The power of the Internet, what joy for young and old.
My friend it seems after five long years did think to UK would go.

We two old widow women in Birmingham did meet.
Fifty-five years we shed as up and down escalators went.
Remembering and recall brought our happenings up to date.
We lucky, happy oldies our memories live on.
The friendship knot was tied for which we give our thanks.

Eluned Ellis

FAST FOOD MUMS

Fast food mums, standing at the fast food counter,
animal carcasses in a burger bun box.

Fast food mums, fast food mums, fast food mums
feeding their kids fast food,
can't cook, won't cook,
fast food, fast food, fast food mums.

Fast food mums, they want it now,
fast food mums, they need it now,
can't wait, won't wait,
fast food, fast food, fast food mums.

Fast food mums, fast food mums grow fatter on fast food,
fast food mums grow sicker on fast food,
fast food, fast food mums, end up on a hospital bed.

Fast food, fast food, fast food mums.

Alex Cyril

LEAVES

The wind blew the leaves to her front porch door,
And the sycamore leaves she picks up from the floor,
She'll paste them in a scrapbook,
For her lover to take a look,
The lover who has gone across the sea
To fight in a war of liberty,
He never came back,
The telegraph came,
Said he died in the first attack,
No one was to blame,
She gave a bitter laugh
And tore it in half,
And scattered it amongst the leaves,
The leaves the wind blew to her front porch door,
For this sad young lady with the scent of sycamore.

Alan Pow

THE WIND

It comes in like thunder
Goes out like a lamb
Tossing and turning the corn
Making horses in the seas
Boats that rock
Corn that blows
Trees that rustle
Leaves that crackle
When walking with your feet
How they blow and swoop
As you try to catch a leaf
As it goes by your side
When walking with your dog
Then it's peace and quiet
The anger now has gone.

Elaine Day

MUSINGS

Where has the 'agile dash about me' gone?
The person who could bend 'easily'
To put socks on?
The one who never needed a stick,
The one who always did things quick?
Hard to say but, it's not nice - feels wrong.
Simple tasks now take me twice as long!
I've developed an arthritic hip
That's the culprit - giving me gyp!
An operation will be done,
After care could be fun -
Then, maybe months hence of here,
That 'agile person' will suddenly appear!
Then dash, bend, stretch and hurry (will be normal)
Without this pain and worry!

Barbara Buckley

NEED

Sometimes I am forgetful
Maybe my heart is so full
Of the world and all of its trouble
Wars and killing make it double
Double the strife, the pain to life
Laughter is rare, despair is rife.

Despondency shows in certain faces
In shanty towns and other such places
Too many in this day and age
Maybe it is now we turn the page
To bring about true changes permanently
For their world needs it desperately.

Affluent classes open your eyes and hearts
To obliterate their need and bad parts.

Ellen Spiring

LOVE IS

Love is feeling butterflies when you look into my eye,
Love is how you make me feel, I'm on a natural high,
Look is our beating hearts entwined into one,
Love is our hearts as we connect as one,
Love like ours is rare to find and feel,
Our love is breathtaking and our love is so real.

Love is the spring flowers as they flourish with our heart,
Love is not bearing a second we are apart,
Love is feeling you and knowing how much you care,
Love is knowing we share something so beautiful and rare.

Our love has the deepest, purest meaning,
Our love leaves us with the most incredible feeling,
You are my beautiful love and my love for you is true,
My love so deep and passionate and it's all for you.

Hayley Huttlestone

THE ROBIN

A robin chirps on a vein-like branch
Causing pink blossom to flutter and descend
As if snow had defied the seasons.
Its breast is grey not rusty,
Watched intently by the local cat.
Oh, I have sent the robin many times
But of course this is a fallacy.

For the robins of yesteryear
Have long since fallen from the trees.
But on such a day in warm spring air
I can dream of immortality
And free myself from the stress of life,
Watching nature under an azure sky
As innocuous clouds pass gently by.

Guy Fletcher

THE VOICE

Of the trees woods and forests
Of the planet
I am the voice
Of the lakes streams and rivers
Of the oceans
I am the voice
Of the myriad coral reefs
Dying in silent anguish
I am the voice
Of the ceaseless pain
Of invaded rainforests
I am the voice
So the Earth may live
In splendour once more

Neil Ommanney Roper

INDEX

Name	Page
Abhilasha Tyagi	136
Adele Hodgkiss	255
Adele Rawle	164
Adele Simone Pierce	25
Adrian Horton	334
Aidan Martin	337
Alan Orpe	227
Alan Pow	353
Alan R Coughlin	253
Alexandra Martin	92
Alex Cyril	353
Alison Williams	202
Alma Sewell	147
Alvin Culzac	46
Ana-Marie McKeever	264
Andrea Ratter	331
Andrew Cain	318
Andrew Pardoe	230
Angela Matheson Cutrale	321
Anna Greaves	77
Ann Beard	291
Ann Dempsey	326
Anne Furley	59
Anne Hetherton	310
Anne Leeson	207
Anne Smith	241
Anne Szczepanski	205
Ann Margaret Holden (Rowell)	327
Ann Voaden	118
Ann Warner	315
Anthony Michael Doubler	299
Anthony Webster	325
Anton Nicholas	273
Arthur	165
Arthur May	53
Audrey Allen	328
Audrey Williams	303
Barbara Buckley	354
Barbara Dunning	151
Barbara Lambie	86
Barbara Maskens	218
Barbara Pearce	339
Barry Dillon	103
Barry Ryan	281
Barry Scott Crisp	285
Beryl Mapperley	61
Beryl Smyter	340
Brian Fisher	139
Brian Grace	193
Brian Morton	131
Bryn Strudwick	130
Carlene Dandy	319
Carl Kemper	263
Carly Burns	284
Carol Bradford	260
Carol Paxton	71
Carrieann Hammond	40
Catherine Hislop	329
Catrin Thomas	68
Celia Smith	270
Cezanne Jardine	257
Charles Keeble	297
Chris Meredith	277
Chrissy Baynes	265
Christine Flowers	342
Christine Renee Parker	324
Christine White	297
Christopher Thomas	336
Ciara Duggan	173
Claire Rogers	67
Colette Breeze	306
Colin Burnell	199
Colleen Biggins	145
Coralee Harrison	65
Corrina O'Beirne	210
Cyril Joyce	296
Cyril Maunders	229
Daniel Crowley	323
Daphne Cornell	346
Darran Ganter	317
Dave Slater	172
David Adamson	52
David Anderson	74
David Bakal	271
David Blakemore	142
David Gasking	12
David Hamey	319
David J C Wheeler	209
David Jones	279
David Marland	340

Name	Page
David Ord	162
David Watkins	166
D Carr	198
Dea Costelloe	177
Dean Cooper Elston	78
Debra Ayis	262
Decima Watkins	342
Derek Haskett-Jones	154
D Hallford	275
Diana H Adams	311
Diana Kwiatkowski Rubin	278
Diana Mudd	219
Diana Robertson	159
Diane Full	344
D M Griffiths	158
Donald Tye	307
Don Friar	214
Don Woods	111
Doreen Gardner	280
Doris E Pullen	105
Doris Mary Miller	333
Doris Townsend	115
Dorothy Beaumont	350
Dorothy Durrant	324
Dorreen Young	163
Dulcie Beatrice Gillman	351
Eddie Byrne	48
Edna Sparkes	47
Edwin David Bowen	128
Eileen Gallagher	299
Elaine Day	354
Elaine Harris	97
Elizabeth Bevans	205
Elizabeth Jenks	332
Elizabeth M Procter	50
Elizabeth Scharer	347
Ellen Spiring	355
Eluned Ellis	352
Emma Thacker	76
Eric Savage	94
E Riggott	311
Evelyn Eagle	149
Farah Ali	89
Fergus McAteer	99
Florence Barnard	212
Fran Hunnisett	101
Frank Sutton	106
Frank Tonner	261
Freda Symonds	307
Fredrick West	135
Gail Charles	141
Garry Bedford	322
Genio Halvdan Kittil Engen	272
Geoffrey Louch	221
Geoffrey Speechly	156
George Edward Bage	116
Georgie Ramsey	187
Gerard Kenny	313
G F Pash	46
Gillian Humphries	171
Gill Mainwaring	326
Gladys Burgess	54
Glenys B Moses	266
Glenys M Bowell	220
Glynnis Morgan	175
Gordon Bannister	234
Graham Peter Metson	90
Grant Meaby	95
Greta Robinson	195
Guy Fletcher	356
Gwendoline Douglas	170
Hacene Rahmani	218
Hannah Cowan	254
Hayley Huttlestone	355
Hazel Hudson	341
Hazel Wilson	335
Hazel Yates	287
Helen Langstone	249
Herdis Churchill	72
Hetty Launchbury	348
H G Griffiths	264
H J Clark	80
Hugh Rose	272
Ian Davey	320
Imogen Brand	320
Ingrid Rankin	318
Irene Grant	269
Iris Crew	161
Iris Ina Glatz	313
Jack Blades	243
Jacqueline Ives-Ward	345
Jacqueline McLaughlin	75
Jainisha Patel	323
James Baxter	312
James Curwen	268
James Williams	250
Jane Cooter	304
Jane Finlayson	314
Janet Hewitt	181
Janet Mansi	219
Janette M Coverdale	251
Jason Pointing	188

Name	Page
Jayne Manning	349
Jeanette Gaffney	208
Jean Paisley	332
Jennifer Bell	273
Jennifer Hooper	180
Jennifer Parker	206
Jessica Powell	343
Jessie Shields	25
J G Ryder	352
Jimmy Broomfield	215
Jim Wilson	185
Jo Allen	186
Joan Beer	235
Joan Fowler	110
Joan Herniman	260
Joan L Carter	292
Joan May Wills	119
Joanna Maria John	343
Joann Littlehales	308
John Beals	39
John D'Arcy	112
John Hickman	93
John Mangan	274
John Murdoch	196
John Stewart	314
John Waby	271
John Walker	347
Jonathan Bryant	293
Jonathan Simms	239
Josephine Foreman	150
Joséphine Kant	191
Josie Earnshaw	306
Joyce Hefti-Whitney	134
Joyce Willis	298
Joy Staley	225
Judy Hopkin	344
Julia Pegg	192
Julie Paton	200
Julie Preston	123
Kate Robinson	220
Katey Russell	70
Kathleen McBurney	121
Keith Newing	302
Keith Powell	310
Keith Tissington	206
Kenneth Jackson	57
Kimberly Davidson	275
KJ Lee-Evans	259
Kriss Simone	84
Laila Lacey	143
Laura Cheshire	174
Lavinia Bousfield	34
Leah Rouse	345
Leah Vernon	52
Lee Blunt	258
Lee McLaughlin	262
Len Peach	183
Les D Pearce	238
Lilian Fulker	341
Lisa Livingstone	100
Lisa Mills	127
Lisa Pease	107
Liz Davies	133
Liz Dicken	315
Lorraine England	300
Louis Cecile	124
Lucy Green	16
Lynne Walden	350
Lynn Martindale	17
Lynn Noone	62
Mab Jones	245
Maggie Kitson	287
Margaret Day	30
Margaret Dilloway	334
Margaret Hickman	108
Maria Howson	204
Mariana Zavati Gardner	179
Maria Sheikh	29
Marie Coyles	252
Mark Anthony Love	120
Mark Boardman	197
Mark Tough	64
Martin Harris Parry	178
Martin Norman	11
Martin Selwood	117
Mary Cole	338
Mary Porter	304
Mary Rose	328
Mary Williams	283
Maureen Brudenell Masters	236
Maureen Thornton	278
Maurice Colclough	348
Mavis Downey	333
Mavis Johnson	309
Melissa Brabanski	63
Meriel Malone	308
Michael Cotton	316
Mick Nash	339
Morag Grierson	114
Naomi Smallwood	296
Natalie Williams	327
Neelam Shah	346

Name	Page
Neil Ommanney Roper	356
Nell Thompson	184
Nesta Nicholson	330
Niall McManus	288
Nichola Keel	79
Nicholas G Charnley	325
Nicola Scott	294
Nigel Lloyd Maltby	336
Nita Garlinge	246
Nola Small	331
Norma Anne MacArthur	295
Norma Spillett	231
Nsikak Ukpong	24
Olive Willingale	73
Omer Ahmad	169
Pam Lutwyche	155
Pam Russell	279
Paramita Chakraborty	122
Pat Adams	337
Pat MacKenzie	224
Patricia Stone	26
Pauline Anderson	38
Pauline Kavanagh	290
Paull Hammond-Davies	146
Paul R Denton	138
Paul Thompson	335
P B Norris	351
Peggy Howe	113
Peggy Morrill	160
Penelope Kirby	125
Peter Butterworth	276
Peter Cullen	285
Peter J Morey	46
Peter J Sutton	309
Peter Payne	248
Peter Ridgway	102
Philip Anthony Amphlett	305
Philip Eames	221
Philip J Loudon	168
Philip Mee	20
Phyllis Wright	222
Rachel Connor	60
Rachel Keers	21
Rachel Sutcliffe	277
Rachel Willmington	302
Ray Dite	232
Reginald Gent	282
Rev Shirley Ludlow	263
Richard Ford	217
Richard Mahoney	202
Rob Barratt	58
Robert Brooks	195
Robert Collins	109
Robert Keith Bowhill	85
Robert Neill	316
Robert Quin	244
Robert William Lockett	213
Rob Wheeldon	22
Rod Pilkington	329
Ronald Rodger Caseby	203
Ron Constant	66
Rosa Johnson	140
Rosemary Whatling	330
Roy Gunter	317
Roy Hobbs	176
Roy Mottram-Smale	132
Royston E Herbert	53
Russ Pratt	312
Sageer Khan	247
Sally Elizabeth Taylor	15
Samantha Williams	349
Sammy Wells	148
Sandie Miles	338
Sandra Leach	204
Sandra Moran	276
Sandy Phillips	83
Sarah Davies	216
Sarah Penrice	91
Sarah Sidibeh	98
S Beatrice Ally	228
Shane Jordan	201
Sharon Lambley	18
Sharron Hollingsworth	261
Sheila Bruce	157
Shirley Atkinson	56
Shirley Clayden	191
Shirley Cowper	237
Shirley Jaggard	303
Shirley Katherine Monaco	226
S Jean Brenner	322
Snikpohd	289
Sonia Richards	129
Sonja Mills	274
Sophie Mason	42
St Catherine Henville	265
Stella Bush-Payne	288
Stephanie Foster	182
Stephen Guy Craggs	104
Stephen Shimmans	152
Stephen Timothy	81
Steven Jackson	2
Steven Kenny	256

Name	Page
Steve Selwood	242
Stuart Wright	233
Sudakshina Mukherjee	190
Sue Gerrard	167
Sullivan The Poet	32
Supriya Choudary	267
Susannah Woodland	284
Susan Westphal	269
Susie Field	88
Sylvia Olliver	44
Sylvia Westley	211
Tawfeeq Elahi Samad	305
Ted Medler	1
Terence Iceton	289
Terrence St John	240
Terry Knight	301
Tessa Paul	137
T G Bloodworth	39
Thelma Barton	286
Thelma Jean Cossham Everett	189
Theresa Hartley-Mace	28
Thomas Baxter	203
Thomas E Dixon	300
Tony Dougan	321
Tony Douglass	82
Tracey Celestin	298
Trayce Hamilton	39
Trevor Leah	144
Trevor Vincent	286
T Stuart	153
Tyrone Dalby	36
Usmaa Umer	194
Valerie Hall	29
Vernon Ballisat	268
V M Archer	223
Wendie Hayes	126
W H Stevens	96
Winifred Curran	194
Yagnaseni Bhattacharya	270
Zoe Jacobs	301

FORWARD PRESS INFORMATION

We hope you have enjoyed reading this book - and that you will continue to enjoy it in the coming years.

If you like reading and writing poetry drop us a line, or give us a call, and we'll send you a free information pack.

Alternatively if you would like to order further copies of this book or any of our other titles, then please give us a call or log onto our website at www.forwardpress.co.uk.

Forward Press Information
Remus House
Coltsfoot Drive
Peterborough
PE2 9JX
(01733) 890099